9/5/85

To Denise + Steve

May you continue to have love + peace in your family —

Joe

P.L.U.S. PARENTING

Other books by Dr. Joseph Procaccini and Mark W. Kiefaber:

Parent Burnout

P.L.U.S. PARENTING

By Dr. Joseph Procaccini
and Mark W. Kiefaber

DOUBLEDAY & COMPANY, INC.
GARDEN CITY, NEW YORK
1985

Library of Congress Cataloging in Publication Data

Procaccini, Joseph, 1942–
    P.L.U.S. parenting.

    Includes index.
    1. Parenting.   2. Leadership.   I. Kiefaber, Mark,
1949– . II. Title.   III. Title: PLUS parenting.
HQ755.8.P76   1985   646.7′8
ISBN 0-385-18984-2
Library of Congress Catalog Card Number 84–18844

To our parents,
Kay and Al Procaccini
Mary Jane and Otts Kiefaber

Who gave us an understanding
of guidance and leadership and
who teach us even today

Contents

Introduction

"Parenthood is one of the easiest jobs to get, but one of the most difficult to perform," a father at one of our workshops in Phoenix recently pointed out to us and his fellow parents. "We rarely get any training. Everybody just expects you to know what to do instinctively. Of course, very few of us do." These comments are not atypical and we hear them frequently as we train and counsel mothers and fathers. During the past several decades there has been much concern for improving parenting techniques. There have been all kinds of guides and "gurus" espousing one approach or another. Some have been excellent and others not so good. Most of the interest has centered on parenting philosophies and/or skills, parent-child relationships, or occasionally on the mental and emotional development of fathers and mothers. However, one of the most important facts has been systematically forgotten: parents are leaders. In fact, they manage the world's oldest organization, the family. We have found that the lack of recognition of this role and the consequent failure to treat and develop mothers and fathers as leaders has led to many of the current parenting difficulties.

During the past several years we have counseled hundreds of parents and lectured before and trained in workshops thousands of parents throughout the United States and in Canada. Likewise, we have participated in scores of radio and television interviews and question-and-answer sessions from coast to coast, in Canada, and in Australia. During this period we have found the need over and over again to apply what we know about leadership to the parenting role. In our own parenting we found ourselves more successful as we utilized our knowledge of sound management and leadership principles and practices.

There has been much research and development in the area of leadership during the past several decades, much of it most useful for parents. We gradually developed a body of leadership knowledge that was most pertinent to successful motherhood and fatherhood. We coined the term and created the concept of "parentship" (a fusion of parenting and leadership) to describe and convey this notion. It is based on the recognition that families are organizations and follow the same dynamics as all others: they go through periods of birth, growth, decay, renewal, and sometimes death. Parentship is founded on the principle that families will be successful and increase their strength, longevity, and capabilities if they are managed well. Good intentions are not enough. Most parents have them. Leadership is what counts and makes all the difference. P.L.U.S. (*P*arent *L*eadership *U*sing a *S*ystem) is a program for training mothers and fathers to be competent parents.

HOW P.L.U.S. PARENTING AND THIS BOOK WORK

P.L.U.S. Parenting has been designed primarily as a leadership development program. It is built on some major premises: (1) parent leaders are not born, but made; (2) parenting is a science as well as an art; there are rules to follow, but individual style can make all the difference; and (3) parenting ability is increased through mental development, skills, and knowledge of the needs of both self and children. P.L.U.S. Parenting is comprehensive in scope and includes discussions of the specific components of effective and efficient family leadership: planning, decision making, communicating, motivating, problem solving, budgeting, evaluating, etc. These functions, vital to leadership, are applied to tasks that are integral to the management of a family.

We continue to offer P.L.U.S. Parenting workshops for those who wish to develop their skills in parentship. The material included in this book has served as the course of study for these programs. Now it is being presented here as a self-help guide.

This book can be used several ways. Parents can read it by themselves. They can read it and discuss the material on a regular basis with their spouses. Another use would be for a group of parents who come together for mutual support to use it as a discussion guide. The book could also be the resource guide for a full-blown parentship program sponsored by a school, church, neighborhood center, hospital, social agency, etc. If it is used for this purpose, the recommended P.L.U.S. Parenting workshop plans included in Appendix II may be useful. The book also may be utilized as a parentship guide for professionals who help mothers and fathers having difficulties in their family leadership roles (e.g., family physicians, psychologists, counselors, social workers, educators, or clergymen).

No matter how this book is used, the reader must keep one thing in mind: as in all leadership development, excellence in parentship takes time. The material presented here will be most beneficial if it is read, thought about, discussed, and practiced in a systematic way over a period of time. It cannot be learned overnight or over a weekend. Rather it may take weeks and even months to truly absorb and incorporate the parentship concepts, insights, and suggested behaviors. It will not be easy to change patterns that parents have been following to lead their families. Whole thought processes, emotional makeups, and value systems are geared to support those entrenched ways. However, with patience, self-discipline, self-confidence, and perseverance, parents can learn to be more skilled. The key aspects of contemporary parenting are described and illustrated here. The reader will have the opportunity to develop and practice parentship through self-assessment exercises. Successful parentship development, whether accomplished through private counseling, public workshops, or self-help reading must always include a planned system of learning, reflection, practice, and evaluation. The material presented here is organized in a manner that will allow and encourage this kind of growth.

Our research and development in the area of "parentship" has included a conceptual analysis of leadership theory and practice, a systematic reflection of our own experiences as professionals as well as parents, and extensive interviews with mothers and fathers and professional practitioners who work closely with parents. The anecdotes used throughout the book are drawn from our counseling, workshops, presentations, and interviews. All the names and some locations have been modified to honor and protect confidentiality.

No book can be written without the assistance of others. We are especially grateful to all those parents who enthusiastically shared their insights with us so that others might learn from their experiences. Meeting and interacting with such wonderful people has truly been the high point of our professional lives. Likewise, we appreciate the help provided to us by professional colleagues. We would like to acknowledge Chris Hipple for her research and insights on communication; Katherine Phillip for recommendations on home management and financial planning; and Linda Mosher for her consultation on the use of computers. We also thank Linda Birney for her suggestions concerning the organization of material; Geraldine Gray for her help as a reference librarian; and Charlette Hinchliffe, Nancy Marshall, and Dorothy Scharpf for typing and organizing materials. Much appreciation is expressed to Peggy Nolan for all her support. Special thanks go to Nick Ellison, our agent, and Adrian Zackheim, our editor, for all their keen advice, help, and encouragement.

JOSEPH PROCACCINI, Ph.D.
MARK W. KIEFABER
Baltimore, Maryland

P.L.U.S. PARENTING

Prologue

"I don't know where the time has gone! In two years he will be applying to college, and frankly I don't think that I can afford it. He does well in school—almost all A's and talks about going to Yale. They have some scholarship money but not enough to really help us. With the kinds of salaries I have made, I should not be in this predicament," a father in Darien, Connecticut, recently lamented as he shook his head with a helpless, frustrated, and quasi-guilty expression. "Is it my fault? How did I know that tuition was going to be so high? Then again, maybe I should have done better planning."

"We were supposed to go to the World's Fair in New Orleans this summer, but my oldest son has to work at the gas station in order to keep his job and my youngest boy can't get anyone to do his paper route. Both of them were supposed to take care of this and get replacements for themselves, but they kept putting it off until it was too late. Now, my husband and I probably won't get a real vacation this year. I feel bad for him especially because he only gets two weeks a year. We were really looking forward to this trip. It's unfair to our little seven-year-old daughter, too." A Georgia mother shared her family's plight with us and her friends in Atlanta recently.

"I don't know. It seems that no one can make a decision around there. When you call them up for the simplest thing—like a visit or an invitation to a party or a day at the ball park, there is total confusion. It takes forever for them to let you know if, when, or how they will participate. He checks with her. She checks with him. They pause, delay, and procrastinate. It got unbearable and I stopped dealing with them and so have a lot of their other friends. It's too bad because actually they are nice people." A Pittsburgh housewife described her and her husband's foundering relationship with some close friends in this way.

In each of the incidents described we can see both the symptoms and the consequences of the unmanaged family. The Connecticut father's lack of financial planning will most probably preclude a top-rate college education for a very capable son. The Georgia family's much desired vacation has been preempted by a lack of follow-through by the boys. The Pittsburgh family that could not make decisions is quickly becoming socially detached even though it wants to remain connected.

The key to successful management in the family is to develop a system whereby order can be established with the least amount of energy. Left to their own devices families will become chaotic. What happens if children are allowed to play with toys whenever they want to and in whatever fashion? Chaos. What happens when there is no system to assign chores or a schedule for household care? Chaos. What happens when there is no family schedule to follow for meals, study, work, and recreation? Chaos. What happens when one does not regularly groom the yard? Chaos. What happens when there is no financial planning? Chaos.

Unmanaged families are characterized by the occurrence of many "crises," schedule conflicts, poor planning, continuous budgetary problems, and confusion—in short, symptoms of chaos. There are many of them—and it is small wonder, because so few family leaders use a management system, that is, a concerted effort to put order into chaos.

But parents are, in fact, executives. They administer the most important and one of the most complex human organizations: the family. Like leaders of other kinds of organizations, they can perform their roles effectively or they can perform them poorly. While there are some "born" leaders of families, most have to develop leadership skills through training and practice. Of course, there are some who are neither born nor trained family leaders; and generally their families suffer. If you are a mother or father and are reading this for self-help, begin by completing the Parent Leadership Index to determine the areas of parenting which are the most and least developed in you.

PARENT LEADERSHIP INDEX

Instructions: Read each statement and indicate the level at which it describes your family.

1	2	3	4	5	6	7	

Inappropriate description   Appropriate description

_____ 1. My family has an overall stated purpose and each of us in the family has a set of personal goals.

_____ 2. My family is structured enough so that day-to-day family life is predictable.

_____ 3. In my family it rarely happens that some really important piece of family news is not acted upon because not all of us knew about it.

_____ 4. In my family we constantly encourage each other to think positively.

_____ 5. My family gathers together and discusses things when important problems need to be solved.

_____ 6. In my family we delegate things because it is important to get help when you need it.

_____ 7. In my family we use discipline to teach children how to correct errors.

_____ 8. In my family it is easy to assess one's success because we all know what is expected of us.

_____ 9. Most things seem to get done on time in my family.

_____10. There are very few arguments about money in my family.

_____11. In my family we seldom have to re-do things because we do them correctly the first time.

_____12. There are established procedures for most of my family's activities.

_____13. In my family listening is just as important as telling.

_____14. Different approaches are used to motivate different members of my family.

_____15. In my family everyone is encouraged to "put in their two cents worth" when we are trying to solve a problem.

_____16. In my family we believe that "if you need help, don't be afraid to ask for it."

_____17. In my family the rules and respective punishments for breaking them are understood by everyone.

_____18. In my family we regularly sit down to discuss if the family is meeting its goals.

_____19. In my family we work hard and accomplish much.

_____20. In my family we usually have the money we need when we need it.

_____21. In my family we do things together but we also encourage each other to do our own thing.

_____22. In my family tasks usually get done when they should.

_____23. We have regular family meetings where important things are discussed.

_____24. When somebody does a task well in my family, he or she receives positive recognition.

_____25. When problems arise in our family, we seldom point the finger of blame.

_____26. In my family if we do delegate something, we do not stand over the person doing the task to make sure it is done right.

_____27. In my family we usually make the degree of punishment fit the seriousness of the offense.

_____28. In my family evaluation is perceived as helpful to growth.

_____29. In my family the priorities and the order of what gets done are clearly understood by everyone.

_____30. My children understand the value of money.

_____31. My family generally plans things well in advance.

_____32. In my family we divide up the tasks according to what needs to be done and who does it best.

_____33. In my family those who speak up do not get put down for it.

_____34. When my children handle responsibility well, they are given more.

_____35. In my family we know when to look outside the family for advice on possible solutions to problems.

_____36. We are not afraid to ask others for help in my family.

_____37. In my family special privileges and responsibilities are given to those who have "gone beyond the call of duty."

_____38. In my family all of us are encouraged to continually help to improve each other.

_____39. In my family we keep a large calendar on the wall where all family members can note events important to them.

_____40. We generally stay within the family budget.

_____41. My family generally handles crises without panic.

_____42. In my family most of what needs doing gets done.

_____43. In my family we are open to various points of view on an issue.

_____44. In my family we really believe that "If a job's worth doing, it's worth doing right."

_____45. Problems are generally resolved as promptly as they can be.

_____46. In my family if we delegate, we choose either the person who is best able to do a task or one who could benefit from learning.

_____47. In my family it is not always considered wrong for children to express anger verbally.

_____48. When a family member performs poorly in some area, there is a tendency to focus on the behavior, not on the person.

_____49. In my family everybody appreciates the importance of another person's time.

_____50. Family members understand the importance of saving some money for the future.

Scoring: This index is divided into ten sub-areas, each assessing key parental leadership factors. For each leadership factor add up the ratings for the signified numbered items.

Factor	Item numbers	Total
Planning	1, 11, 21, 31, 41	_____
Organization	2, 12, 22, 32, 42	_____
Communication	3, 13, 23, 33, 43	_____
Motivation	4, 14, 24, 34, 44	_____
Decision-making/Problem-solving	5, 15, 25, 35, 45	_____
Delegating	6, 16, 26, 36, 46	_____
Disciplining	7, 17, 27, 37, 47	_____
Evaluating	8, 18, 28, 38, 48	_____
Home management	9, 19, 29, 39, 49	_____
Budgeting and accounting	10, 20, 30, 40, 50	_____

Interpretation: For each sub-area, scores will range from 5 through 35. Determine the presence of each leadership skill by using the following scale:

28–35	strongly present
21–27	moderately present
13–20	minimally present
5–12	hardly present

The scoring will allow you to determine to what degree each leadership skill is utilized in your family. This information will be helpful in setting the priorities of your own parentship development program. You will most probably have to expend more time and effort in the areas that are not developed and focus less attention on the areas that seem to be in place. In attempting to determine why the specific deficiencies exist, you should consider several possible causes: inexperience, lack of training, fear, emotional blocks, etc. Many difficulties in parenting involve several factors and they almost always involve one's mind, body, and feelings.

Effective leadership in the family is a three-part development. It involves *thoughts* (understanding of the family as an organization); *feelings* (developing the emotional ability to survive in the complex and ambiguous setting of family life); and *specific skills* (knowing how to do what has to be done to maintain high-quality family life and to reach family goals).

Like all leaders, parents have a fundamental dilemma: on the one hand they have to influence the behavior of the members of the family so that goals are reached and life runs smoothly; on the other hand, in order to have a strong family, they have to encourage each member to grow. Because of this contradictory set of parental obligations, conflict in family relationships is *inevitable*. You are pulled in two directions by this double set of responsibilities flowing from your leadership role. You become a "human wishbone" that could snap if pulled too strongly in one direction or the other. How you handle this dilemma can be the key to your success as family leaders. When everything is said and done, failures in parenting almost always stem from a lack of recognition of or a simplistic solution to this dilemma.

Not knowing the correct formula for the parenting ingredients of control and growth often carries with it much internal anguish. Am I controlling too much? Not enough? Am I allowing too much freedom? Not enough? This kind of pondering can last a lifetime. These questions cannot be resolved by a mathematical equation.

This pain that is felt by parents stems from their lack of certitude and the resulting shaken confidence. Anne, an Arizona mother of three elementary school children, recently shared this feeling with others at a workshop: "I often think that I am too pushy with my kids, especially when it comes to their school work. However, as soon as I let up, their academic achievement drops off. I have the feeling that they really are beginning to resent the pressure that I am putting on them. I worry about this because I don't want them reaching a point of frustration and just giving up . . . or when they get older looking back at this period of their lives with a lot of bad memories."

Another mother at the same workshop pointed out that she had similar doubts and anxieties when it came to her teenage children's friends: "I want them to learn to associate with all kinds of people and ultimately to select their own friends. I can't be by their side every minute. However, I really feel obliged to forbid them from seeing certain kids and I exercise that responsibility. My kids hate me for it at times and tell me that I'm ruining their lives! Whenever they tell me this it hurts deeply and I wonder if perhaps I am overreacting and judging their friends too harshly. I feel that I have to go with my instincts, but don't really know if I am doing more harm than good."

Furthermore, the amount of control and growth needed by one child may not be appropriate for another child in the same family, nor might it be suitable for the same son or daughter at another age or stage of his or her development. The search for the correct balance is a never-ending struggle for mothers and fathers because of the dynamic nature of the parenting process.

Some parents, because the ache of this internal conflict is too unbearable or because they hope to escape the pain altogether, are seduced into avoiding the dilemma by ignoring one side or the other. Some opt for control and cancel out growth: "I don't have to worry about any conflicts. In my house I'm the boss. As long as the children live under my roof, they'll do as I say. If they don't like it, then they can live elsewhere after they're eighteen years old. More parents should have a philosophy like mine. Ninety percent of the family problems would be avoided." These words were spoken publicly by a participant in one of our parents' workshops in Rhode Island recently. At least half the audience applauded enthusiastically on hearing these words. They can be attractive to the ears of parents who are weary from the constant internal state of bewilderment that often accompanies the leadership process in the family. While this approach to parenting, no doubt, will bring about order and maintain it in the household, it will also suppress the need to grow which is present in every healthy child. This systematic and ongoing restraint will lead to nothing good. Eventually the children will either act out their frustration in a dramatic eruption of antisocial behavior or turn to other people, drugs, alcohol, even cults, to help them cope with their long-imposed suppression. The suffering that the parent would have experienced in dealing with the dilemma in the first place will most likely be magnified tenfold as children desperately attempt to put a balance back in their lives, often too quickly.

Other parents choose the growth side of the formula and abdicate control responsibility. They often do not have the know-how, the desire, or the energy to implement and operate a system of rules and policies for the household. Stan, a father of two sons, ages twelve and ten, put it this way: "I'm present in my home, but I'm kind of emotionally divorced from my children. I certainly will support my boys, protect them, and pay the bills. But I just can't get into the day-to-day tug-of-war with them. In fact, I usually hang around my office into the early evening so they will be either studying or in bed when I get home. I let them do their own thing and sort of watch them from a distance. I'm sure that they'll turn out to be fine. After all, I do love them and they know that." This well-meaning federal government supervisor in Washington, D.C., is most likely going to be in for a rude awakening. No doubt, his children are already beginning to feel the insecurity of impending chaos. They see their mother struggling to keep order while their father's lack of involvement in the process fuels their unsatisfied need to be controlled and their fear of abandonment. More than likely their crying out for some form of father-imposed restraint will begin with verbal or behavioral flirtations with defiance of the established household order. If these transgressions are ignored or the response on the part of the father is of low intensity, the violations will continue to increase in severity, often in a graduated step-by-step process. First, it might be sarcastic comments directed toward mother or father, then it might be "roughnecking" in the living room, followed by staying out at night past curfew; then a neglect of studies or homework may ensue. If the controls are not implemented, the father may witness school truancy, joyriding in automobiles, and even drug taking and selling. Each act is a statement of disobedience and rejection of the family values and principles as well as a plea for the security that comes through an ordered household. Even those children who may be headed toward eventual self-destruction will generally give parents the opportunity to intervene and impose restraints at each step of the way.

An understanding of the nature of this control/growth dilemma and what it means emotionally for mothers and fathers is necessary for successful parent leadership. Success or failure in parenting can often be traced back to how this dilemma was handled. We hope that the material that follows will help parents see this dilemma as an opportunity for family growth and not as a problem to be avoided.

1

Primitive Principles of Parentship

While every family is indeed unique, each is also very similar not only to other families but also to most other small organizations. We have acquired much knowledge about organizations and much of it is useful for the managerial role of the parent. The foundation of successful leadership in the family, as elsewhere, is to know the *nature* and *dynamics* of the organization which is being managed: What is the nature of the beast? By knowing one will be able to "conquer" it. On the other hand, fear of the unknown can often trigger anxiety, stress, and the consequent ineffective and debilitating behavior.

Anthropological data tell us that the family unit was formed thousands of years ago. Throughout history the main goal of the family has been to provide for the physical welfare of its members. Over the years the *structure* of the family has changed very little. The *goals* of the family, however, have been expanded rather significantly. In addition to providing for the physical needs of its members, the family now is expected to provide for their mental, emotional, moral, and cultural well-being as well. Not only must families put food on the table, but they must serve as temples for spiritual guidance as well as provide opportunities for everything from the development of an appreciation of music to the training of future athletes.

The impact of the family on the child's future achievement and quality of life is growing in perceived importance. For some it is never too early—as we can see in the "super-baby" phenomenon, whereby parents frantically attempt to get their toddlers and even infants on the fast tracks of life by teaching them reading, foreign languages, music, and computer literacy and utilization. While most are not as fanatical in their beliefs, there is at least the widespread recognition that the family *does* indeed make a big difference: in schooling, in morals, in wealth, in all-around happiness. Children also have recognized the decisive factor of family: "I enjoy Georgetown University and I am glad to be here. I also know that I probably wouldn't be here if I hadn't had such education-conscious and supportive parents." Elementary school educators continuously stress the role of the home in the child's early development. Physicians, psychologists, and clergymen likewise point out the critical impact of family on the child's physical, emotional, and spiritual development.

Children who are brought up in the family unit automatically look to their parents to provide leadership. Parents by nature have *status* as leaders in the family. This can be a helpful tool in the parenting process. But the mother or father who continually relies on status to get the family goals met ("You will do as I say because I am your father and I have lived longer and know more") will eventually create an atmosphere of animosity and even chaos, because family goals will not be met by uncooperative sons and daughters whose own needs are unfulfilled. To be effective leaders you have to grow beyond this status authority, which is only a natural starting point. As the complexity of family leadership is recognized and appreciated, fathers and mothers come to the realization that effective parentship does not come naturally. To follow your instincts or simply use a trial-and-error approach is not enough in the 1980s. You do not really have to take this risky approach if you choose otherwise. You can make use of validated data to better understand the intricate and delicate task of leading your family. However, like all learners, you have to take the initiative to acquire this knowledge. Research on what works and doesn't work in the leadership of small organizations, including the family, has come a long way. Parents who gain access to this information and use it in their motherhood and fatherhood roles will have families that are much happier and more successful.

Glen is an example of a father who could have benefited from some of the information now available. A successful, hardworking home-builder on the West Coast, he has developed a "do for" relationship with his two teenage children. Since the birth of his son and daughter, Glen has felt that it was his job as a parent to do everything and provide as much as possible. "I really feel down deep in my heart that if I don't give them all I can, I am not really performing adequately as a parent. I have been successful. Why shouldn't I make life easier for them? What am I supposed to do? Let them struggle like I did? No way." Glen admits that some of his attitudes were probably inherited from his own parents, who lived through the Depression years. His father often expressed the hope that his children and grandchildren would never "want" for anything. Glen also admits having a gnawing fear, tucked away in his mind but surfacing occasionally, that all his success could come to a crashing halt at any given moment. "So why not let the kids have their stereos, designer clothes, and fun at the beach house."

Glen is a poor family leader because he is not aware of a well-documented management principle: organization members have a strong basic human need to contribute action and when the opportunity to fulfill this need is not provided in the organization, members will fulfill it elsewhere. In Glen's case the frustration of personal development that his "giving, giving, giving" style imposes on the children will eventually decrease their level of interest and make the family less effective. They will manifest symptoms of the "spoiled child": obnoxious, unappreciative, sassy, and wasteful. They behave this way because they are frustrated and unhappy. While at the conscious level they are taking all they can, at the subconscious level they are crying out in anger at the oppressor-parent who has capped their potential for growth, sometimes for life.

Why is it that so many parents like Glen overlook the thoughts and feelings that they might have experienced in the workplace or in a volunteer organization when they attempt to lead a family? Most of us have had the experience at least once in our lives of working for a boss who wouldn't let us do anything ourselves. The loss of self-esteem and the sense of frustration was overwhelming. Eventually we stopped really caring about that job and transferred out. These same alternatives are available to children as well: they will eventually stop trying to contribute to the family goals as they are systematically disallowed to do so. They will drop out of the family—initially by emotionally withdrawing, and eventually by being physically absent. The older child or teenager who habitually withdraws to his room to read or watch television or is constantly out with friends may be disengaging in this way.

The need to contribute is only one of several human needs that the effective parent will recognize. Others are the need for achievement, the need for self-esteem, and the need for recognition. The effective mother or father will use these needs to motivate members to achieve family goals.

Successful parenting does not mean that all family goals are constantly and simultaneously met. In fact, in later chapters we will discuss how mothers and fathers often have to make trade-offs and sacrifice one goal in favor of another, perhaps more pressing objective. Parents, although they may not be fully aware of it, are always practicing leadership: each time they make a decision about the family, each time they communicate with chidren, each time they coerce or encourage children to behave in a certain fashion. However, this does not mean that parents are practicing *effective* leadership.

The outcome of using effective leadership skills is that *more* family goals will be met *more often.* How parents choose to involve children in decisions, how they motivate, communicate, and deal with members' needs has a lot to do with their understanding of the complex and sometimes mysterious and elusive process we call parentship. Success in the practice of parentship is dependent on a comprehension of the principles underlying the process. We call these the "primitive principles of parentship," in that they are fundamental and basic. They are not necessarily easy to understand or incorporate into one's outlook or lifestyle. However, they are the critical first step in the development of effective parentship. They are the foundation underlying the recommended attitudes, feelings, and behaviors. If they are not addressed, difficulties are likely to ensue. We ask that you read and think about each principle very carefully. Each could serve as a focal point for private thought or group discussion as well as a criterion against which to critique present parenting. These are the primitive principles:

1. EFFECTIVE PARENTSHIP ALWAYS INVOLVES THE DYNAMIC
   INTERACTION OF THREE FACTORS: PARENT, CHILD, SITUATION

Mothers and fathers often think of their parenting style as if it occurred in a vacuum. Parenting programs that attempt to help in the development of skills can make the same error. While learning all about parenting styles and skills is necessary, it is not sufficient. The fact is that mothers and fathers do not function in a laboratory, but rather in a concrete situation with real children, two factors which are always unique. No one parenting style or skill will work with every child every hour of the day. Often one or both of these factors (the children and the situation) influence the selection of the approach to be used.

For a parent to get locked into one style can be disastrous for him or her as well as for the child. Effective parentship is situational. Important questions like the following must be asked by the mother or father: Who am *I*? What are *my* needs? How do these influence my style? Is my parenting behavior directed toward some specific personal goal? For example, a father may be a hard-nosed driver pushing his ten-year-old son to excel more and more in sports so that he can then feel the sense of achievement which is missing in his own work life. Or is it ritualistic . . . am I following a protocol that is more form than function? A mother may feel obliged to overindulge her children with unrealistic amounts of food as a sign of her love for them. Other questions to be raised relate more to the children: Who are they? Do I really know them? What are their needs? How will these needs influence my style? If there is a conflict between their needs and mine, whose have precedence? In our work with parents we have encountered so many well-meaning mothers and fathers who have absolutely no idea of what their own children really need or want. Often the needs of children (of all ages) go unheeded because parents do not understand them or, equally often, deny them. Most of this is done subconsciously, but, some of the information screening can be more deliberate. We know of one Houston mother in her forties who has her husband listen to all "problem information" from their two teenage children first. He then decides what he thinks she can "handle hearing." As she put it, "there are some things that I would rather not know." Although the family is viewed as almost a model by members of their neighborhood, can you imagine the level of relationship between that mother and her son and daughter? Can you anticipate what is coming in the future for this parent? Trouble, certainly! Finally, some questions must be directed toward the situation at hand: Does this call for a unilateral decision on my part? On the children's part? Is the situation an emergency? Is it a long-range task? One-shot deal? Recurring decision? Does it involve others? Who? The key is for parents to be able to gather sufficient information and assess the situation accurately. A misreading of the circumstances, no doubt, will lead to ineffective action.

Once all three of these factors (parent, child, situation) have been understood, then a suitable parenting style can be chosen. While, at first, this analysis may be a tedious process, with practice it becomes much more routine, second nature. Frankly, there is no other way if one wants to be effective. Not to recognize that the chemistry of parentship involves all three ingredients which are always interacting will surely result in a naïve and disappointing approach to family leadership. In Chapter 2, Parentship Styles, this principle will be developed more fully.

2. PARENTSHIP IS AN INTRUSIVE ACT

Mothers and fathers often act, and sometimes actually believe, that they "own" their children—that children are possessions that have been molded somehow into totally controllable beings. There is often the mistaken notion that because parents have authority, they also have control. Automatically, this approach to leadership in the family is too simplistic. Family life does not work that way. It is much more complex.

The reality is that when anyone attempts to lead others, children included, one is literally intruding in their lives. A sign of a healthy person, adult or child, is the desire to control one's own destiny, to follow a selected course of action, to have individual ideas, and to develop one's own values. When someone comes along and attempts to thwart these drives for personal fulfillment and independence, as all leaders must do, the response on the part of the follower is understandably negative. In fact, the absence of such a response is a sure sign of poor mental health. Only those with psychological disorders welcome the frustration of their needs. Parents who anticipate this negative response and who understand the reason for it will be much more effective. Their sensitivity to the fact that they are invading the child's innermost being causes them to pay more attention to the words they use, their gestures, and their tone of voice, as well as to anticipate the potential conflicts between the family's objectives and the child's own personal desires or plans. This is the heart of parental respect for children. It will have significant impact on their ability to lead their families.

Getting another person, including your own child, to accept norms or to do what you want him or her to do is not easy. To approach it in a cavalier fashion will lead to less than rewarding results. Effective parentship is not a simple matter. The first step in overcoming the difficulties is to recognize them and accept the fact that mothers and fathers, like all leaders, must work hard for good results. It is not a two-way street or a fifty-fifty proposition. Parents often have to go 70 percent to 80 percent of the way.

Parents are really not "entitled" to obedience from their children. They have to earn it. Nor are parents anointed leaders of their families. This they have to merit as well. Being loved by their children, a justifiable expectation of parents, is not enough. Love comes from the heart and is spontaneous in parent-child relationships. Leadership appeals to the head as well as the heart and takes more time to achieve.

Love does not necessarily generate followership on the part of the children. Love is easier to attain than acceptance as the family leader, as someone who can be trusted and counted on for the achievement of one's personal goals through surrender to the common good of the family.

3. SUCCESSFUL PARENTS ARE EFFECTIVE NEGOTIATORS

The essence of parentship is the ability to negotiate. This skill is critical for family leadership. As noted above, leadership often involves an intrusion into the lives of the followers and one has to negotiate in and out. While the recognition of negotiating as a key parenting skill is important, it is equally essential to understand the cardinal principle in achieving such competence: get to know the follower as much as you can, certainly more than he or she knows you.

If parents do this, they will be successful negotiators. The better they know their children, the more they will be able to offer something that meets those children's needs. And what they use to satisfy those needs will be magnified in value. Likewise, whatever detracts from the attainment of their children's needs will be magnified as a detriment. If parents allow themselves to get to know their children without prematurely passing judgment, they will be in a good position to negotiate effectively with them. If, on the other hand, they make false assumptions about their children's values, emotional state, knowledge background, or any other factors relating to their needs, they will have difficulty "connecting" in their attempt to negotiate. Parents who have difficulty negotiating often take a textbook approach to their task. They believe that their children "should" be doing, feeling, or believing certain predetermined things that are superimposed by nature, mandate, or custom. For instance, they may assume that all twelve-year-old sons like football or all fifteen-year-old daughters love pretty clothes. Nothing could be further from the truth for some youngsters, and parents who build their negotiating strategy on this assumption will be off the mark. They will appeal to needs that are not there and miss those that are. Not only will leadership fail, but alienation may result as well. Adults know the feeling when a person assumes something about them that just is not the case. It often infuriates them because there is an implicit denial or rejection of their individuality.

Parents can make a very serious error in assuming that their children have the same needs that they had at the same age. This can be a false assumption for one or both of two reasons: times have changed, and/or their children do not have the same interests or needs that they themselves once had. We will never forget the father at one of our New York workshops who threw his hands up in total exasperation: "I don't know what to do to get my fourteen-year-old son to do better in school. I told him that if his grades went up, his mother and I would take him to the Bronx Zoo for a whole day!" While this "reward" might have been attractive in the youthful days of the father, it will most likely fail to compete with the video discs, arcades, and sports events available in the world of today's children.

The better parents understand children's state of mind, the more effective they will be as negotiators with them. The "shoulds," "oughts," and "supposed to's" have no place. Only the "is" counts. Good parent-negotiators take what's there, observe it, listen to it, get to know it, tolerate its existence, appreciate it, and act upon it. In so doing, they are able to make the vital connection between leader and follower, parent and child.

4. Parentship Is a Performing Art

Often the question is asked: Is parenting an art or a science? In other words, is there a knack, that sometimes comes naturally, for motherhood or fatherhood? Is parenting instinctive? A gift? Or is this a role for which we need training? Is there a set of validated, well-defined, and theoretically sound principles, a "science" of parenthood? The answer is that parenting involves all of these: it is an art as well as a science. Or, more accurately, it is a performing art. The script for the parenting role has its foundation in the scientific: there are beneficial and detrimental attitudes to have; there are certain behaviors that lead to success and others that lead to failure almost every time; and there are effective methods for coping with the difficulties of the role. In short, there is a body of knowledge called "effective parenting" and it is growing every day. It can be added to or subtracted from, and men and women can be trained in it. However, every time the script is followed, the role is most likely performed differently. No matter how many times it has been played before, each enactment of the role is unique. There is a sameness, a routine, but also a freshness of approach in each effective parentship act. The scientific dimension of parenting is what allows mothers and fathers to improve upon what they have done in the past and eventually become masters. The artistic dimension contributes the excitement that comes through the wonderment and discovery that results from interaction with children. Effective parents respect and value both of these dimensions.

In our work with parents we notice that it is uncommon to hear mothers and fathers talk about or report or demonstrate successful parenting acts. Usually, the comments and questions focus on the problem areas. If you were to sit in and listen, you could easily reach the conclusion that there is a lot of bad mothering and fathering going on. This couldn't be further from the truth. Most people who attend parenting programs, seek counseling, or read books on parenting, for that matter, are hardworking, dedicated moms and dads. However, they are reluctant to talk about their successes in performance terms: "Let me tell you what I did to motivate my son yesterday . . ." "I tried this discipline approach with my daughter and it worked . . ." "Over the weekend I was able to make a very critical family decision without the usual hassle. It was smooth, crisp, and timed just right." If parents approached their role as a performing artist does, the thrill of accomplishing the near-impossible would overshadow the drudgery of the daily routine.

5. Effective Parents Use the Medical Lens, Not the Moral One
Correcting children's behavior is an integral part of parenting. Mothers and fathers spend much time and energy doing this. Of equal importance to the strategies and techniques used is the attitude toward the problem behavior itself, how it is viewed. There are two basic ways to look at the children's aberrant conduct: one is through the lens of the medical model and the other is through the lens of the moral one. The lens which the parent uses will color the conclusions drawn concerning the nature, causes, and solutions proposed for the problem. Those functioning within the framework of the medical paradigm will attempt to understand the anatomy of the difficulty: "Why is this happening? There is a reason. My task is to find it." The *behavior* is the focal point and not the *child* behaving. The energy is directed toward understanding and correcting the problem, not judging or blaming the child involved. Just as physicians do not get angry at or dislike patients who are ill, parents taking this approach likewise "depersonalize" the curative process. They separate their displeasure with the behavior from the child engaging in it. They recognize that there are not "bad children" but children who behave badly, and that their behavior is not a reflection of some inherently deviant personality. The behavior is correctable if the appropriate methods and resources (time, energy, know-how) can be secured and applied.

Parents who use the moral lens see their children as culpable for their actions. They assume that children have choices and that when they misbehave they have opted to do so. Accordingly, they blame their children for their actions. The children's behavior is viewed as an outward reflection of their internal state. Who they are and what they do become one and the same. As a result, some parents begin to actually dislike their own children. The children sense this immediately and the situation becomes personalized on all fronts. Solutions become difficult to attain because of the "vinegared" relationships permeating the household.

Many parents today think and function within this moral framework. Mothers and fathers, for the most part, are influenced by a set of moral principles which greatly influences how they look at the world and how they react to what goes on. When their children's behavior is not quite up to par, their natural question is "Who's at *fault?*" They wonder: "Is it the kids?" "Is it me?" "Is it their friends?" They may not know the answer immediately, but they know (or at least assume) that *someone* is at fault. Most of the attention is then directed toward the "who?" For the guilty and defensive parents there is the terror that the "who" may be them. For finger-pointing or martyr parents there is the hope that the "who" may be the child himself. For the suspicious parent there is the vindicating pleasure of demonstrating that the "who" is a friend of the child. The moral vision carries with it the need to place blame in the diagnosis. The treatment plan relies on external control through fear of punishment and on internal control through guilt. The moral approach has dominated child rearing in this country and elsewhere only because it has been the major frame of reference for our whole Judeo-Christian culture. Parenting styles simply have reflected this, as have forms of leadership in other kinds of organizations.

While this is understandable, it is also regrettable. Parents and others who can learn to shed the moral perspective in their leadership behavior will be much more effective. They will be more objective and insightful in their analysis of their children's behavior. Their energies will be directed toward skillful family leadership behavior as opposed to coping with frustration, guilt, and anger.

While this primitive principle is by no means a call for the removal of morality from parenting, we recommend that mothers and fathers concentrate on understanding the nature and dynamics of individual and family behavior.

6. LIFE IN THE FAMILY IS PRIMARILY NONRATIONAL

Mothers and fathers do themselves a great service and take a giant step forward the moment they understand and accept the fact that life in the family is very emotional. Parents and children are both mind and body.They think, but they also feel. When it comes to personal interaction between parent and child, feelings tend to dominate. The relationship between children and parents is seldom, if ever, a purely rational affair. There is an awful lot of emotion and passion involved. Parents who do not understand this or attempt to ignore it fail in leadership of the family. By appealing solely to the rational side of their sons or daughters, they are unable to "connect" with them fully. We often find parents and children who are virtual strangers. They really do not know one another, except at a superficial level. It is absolutely amazing what parents do not know about children. A very perceptive and articulate seventeen-year-old boy in Denver put it this way: "My parents really don't know me. They think that they know me. They see what they want to see and hear what they want to hear. They have a picture in their head of what they want me to be. They ignore everything that doesn't fit in with that image of what I should be. I don't think that they will ever know me or see me. That realization is the saddest thing in my life for me." This kind of discovery can generate strong hostility, often accompanied by a need to detach oneself from parents emotionally and deal with them primarily at the intellectual level. Otherwise, the pain of unrequited personal interest is too deep and biting. There are many children in our society today who are lonely, and it is not because they are alone. There are people all around them. However, they are disconnected, psychologically abused in the sense that their parents rarely deal with them on an emotional level. They are starving for attention and affection, not in the form of material goods bestowed, but through acceptance and empathy with their emotional state. "I feel like I always have to say the right thing, act happy all the time, and let my parents think that everything is just great, even when it isn't," a thirteen-year-old girl in a Dallas suburb confided while lowering her eyes in sadness. "My mother and father keep telling me that they're happy when I'm happy. I feel that I shouldn't tell them when I'm sad because it will make them sad. So I only tell them about good things and nice feelings I have. I never tell them about my worries. I just hold them in and keep them to myself." This child, like many others, finds herself in the unenviable position of having to choose between inflicting pain on herself or on her parents. She, like most of her counterparts, opts to spare her parents and suffers in loneliness. The wise mothers and fathers are those who can truly get to know their children as unique human beings and fully tolerate what they discover. Your child's energy can be used up in a struggle (sometimes lifelong*) to gain mommy's and/or daddy's approval and acceptance. Alternatively, your children can direct this energy toward outward accomplishment, building on a foundation of inward peace that results from "settling" with you their parents. The choice is yours.

7. PARENTSHIP REQUIRES ACCEPTANCE OF THE UNPREDICTABLE NATURE OF THE FAMILY

A healthy family has some logic and some illogic, some predictability and some unpredictability, some certitude as well as lack of certitude. This dual nature often presents a problem for the family's leader, the parent.

There are some mothers and fathers who place a high value on logic, order, structure, clarity, and certitude. They don't like fuzziness or complexity in the operation of their households. They like to know that what they plan to have happen *will* in fact happen. Ambiguity and ambivalence are most unwelcome in the lives of these individuals and are often accompanied by discomfort.

Other parents are prone to be more tolerant of the unpredictable and even value it. The fact that the future does not fully disclose itself at any given moment presents for them an opportunity for the excitement of anticipation. The changing nature of the family as well as changing relationships with their children are viewed as a chance for continuous growth.

Parents who are predominantly rational in their perspective have a much more difficult time in managing their families because their way of looking at the world is not compatible with the organizational nature of the family. On the other hand, those parents who are more sensitive to the irrational dimension of family life have an easier time leading in this environment. They are able "to go with the flow" when necessary and eventually influence the course of the flow. While an essential part of parenting involves planning for the future, realistic parents write their plans in pencil. Sometimes parental planning has a functional purpose: "We are saving two hundred dollars a month for his college education." Often it is in the form of hopes or even dreams: "If we enroll him at the institute now he may develop into a concert pianist." It is critical for parents to distinguish between these two types of planning. While planning for the future is certainly prudent, mothers

---

* In our work we have encountered a large number of adults who are still seeking parental approval and acceptance as full human beings.

and fathers must realize and emotionally accept the unpredictable nature of family life as a whole and each child's individual development.

8. Creativity in Parenting Is a State of Mind

Creativity is a key factor in successful parenting; it is an outlook, the ability to see potential in the resources that one has available, a way of adding value. Creative parents are able to look at the available resources and utilize them in the most valuable way possible. What are some of these precious assets that can make the family more successful both in terms of accomplishment and of internal efficiency? Time, human energy, money, and space, are a few of the more tangible ones. Others are more subtle, but nevertheless important: children's interest, curiosity, desire for affection, loyalty, character, wish to achieve, pride, etc. Parental creativity can also be applied to the parent-child relationship. The creative father or mother will look at every child (as the sculptor looks at the block of granite) and see another child waiting to come out. The parent must free the child by inducing him or her to shed the old self. Just as the statue is more valuable than the granite block from which it emerged, even though it is made of the same material, the child that emerges will be more valuable than the original child. Creative parents can set in motion a chain that will enrich the lives of their children for a long time.

9. Parents Generally Get What They Expect

When it comes to parenting, it's not what one *in*spects that counts, but what one *ex*pects. Mothers and fathers generally get exactly what they anticipate from their children. Children have a tendency to meet their parents' expectations of them. We will never forget a young father of two sons standing up at one of our workshops in Baltimore and relating this anecdote: "You know, when I was a kid, my mother would come into my bedroom every morning and give me a few slaps on the behind. She would say, 'I know that I am going to have to do this eventually today so I might as well get it out of the way now while I have some strength.' Of course, you know what I would do? [Comments from the audience] . . . That's right, I would go out and break windows and harass people in the neighborhood. After all, I had already paid the price. Why not commit the crime?"

While this incident, as described, borders on the psychopathological, it is illustrative of the important role of expectations. While parents may not punish their children physically in anticipation of wrongdoing, they may "slap them around" psychologically and emotionally through suspicion ("Are you *sure* that you don't have any homework?"); rejection ("Can't you do anything right?"); comparison ("His father must really be proud of *him!*"); or anticipated disappointment ("I hope that you don't go and get swept off your feet by some boy at college.").

Most people have had the experience of being held in high esteem by somebody even before there was an opportunity to earn that spot on the pedestal. It might have been a relative, a teacher, a friend, or a neighbor. The message was clear: "You are a wonderful person. I like you." Or, "You are quite talented. I admire you." Or, "You are a hard worker. I respect you." The feeling that accompanies such regard is pleasant and invigorating. The last thing that one wishes to do is to let down the person who holds you in such high esteem. Most people will work very hard to stay there. It becomes a top priority in their lives. The same holds for the opposite feeling: if you feel that you are held in low esteem, if you are viewed as untrustworthy, inept, incapable, or not likeable, improvement in the eyes of that beholder becomes a low priority. "Why bother? It's a lost cause." Effort is diminished. It is a classical case of the self-fulfilling prophecy at work: by anticipating something you cause it to happen.

So parents have a great power within them. By merely expecting something they can influence its occurrence. This is wonderful, but also very scary. We have encountered so many mothers and fathers who have sown the seeds for their own family leadership problems through their negative expectations. Often they mean well and their detrimental predictions flow from a general pessimistic personality, deep-rooted fear of personal failure through their children, insecurity, jealousy of their children's success and its implications for them, fear of success, or other factors. Other parents have been very successful in motivating their children toward accomplishment and personal happiness through their positive expectations.

There are two points to remember with regard to this primitive principle. First, children know what their parents expect of them regardless of what is said verbally. They have a perception and it is usually correct. If you were to take an adolescent aside and ask him or her, "What does your dad really think of your ability in sports?" or "How bright does your mom think you are?"—he or she would have an answer. If the answer is a positive one, there is a good possibility that the outcome will be positive. Negative consequences are likely if the answer is negative.

The second point is this: make sure that the expectations conveyed are attainable, that they are realistic. There is often a fine line between underexpecting and overexpecting. While underexpecting can lead to lower than potential results, expectations that are too high can result in stress, frustration, and guilt. Parents have to assure themselves continuously that they are not vicariously fulfilling their own unachieved goals through their children.

10. Parents Must Control Their Resources or Somebody Else Will

Sufficient resources are critical for the successful management of the family. How those resources are used and who is really in charge of them are important factors in parentship. Often mothers and fathers relinquish or abdicate responsibility for or control over time, energy, money, space, and other assets. How do they do this and how can it be recognized? You can find yourselves feeling totally overwhelmed by all your duties: earning a living, chauffering children from school to sports programs to music lessons to the library, cleaning the house, trimming the lawn, contributing to the community. In addition, you may also have many personal development interests: exercising, taking courses, attending music or entertainment or sports events, socializing with friends. In all of our interviews and lectures across the country we have found no parents yet who felt that they had too little to do. Not one person! The list of things to do and the involvements that consume time, money, and energy often appear endless, while the resources available are clearly limited. Often the relationship between pledged commitments and resources available is totally unproportional. You have to ask yourself the following question regularly: "Who is putting things on my list?" If the answer is anything other than "I am," it is the wrong answer. What are the sources of some of the wrong answers? It might be a perceived societal expectation: "All good parents have their children take piano lessons," or "Fathers really should help out coaching soccer. It's good for the kids. They really like it." Or, "Parents really ought to help their children with their homework to give them the edge in this competitive age." It might be tradition as transmitted through grandparents or other family members: "He will be the third generation to attend Exeter if he gets in. So his attendance in the summer tutorial program is really essential." Or, "My mother is appalled that I am not home to give the kids a snack when they return from school each afternoon. Frankly I'm embarrassed about it because she was such a caring mom to me." It might be an immature insensitivity to or denial of the limited nature of resources available: "Well, I know that I'm attempting the impossible, but I'm sure something will work out."

The moment you realize that slowly but surely you have allowed your resources to be committed for you, you must take steps to regain control over the destiny of the family. You must come to realize that the key to successful parentship is to invest resources where they will have the greatest result. As a matter of fact, the only universal characteristic of individuals successful in anything is their ability to invest time, money, energy, interest, space, etc., where it will have the most benefit for them. If you wish to be successful family leaders, you must develop sensitivity to R.O.I. (Return on Investment). You must realize that every time you commit a resource to one possibility, you preclude several others. This is called opportunity cost: "By doing this, what is it that I am not doing but could be?" "By spending money on this item, what am I preventing myself from buying?" "By using my limited supply of human energy on this, what am I not using my energy on?" Mothers and fathers have to sit down occasionally and ask themselves and each other: How are we using our resources? Is this the best use? Can we get a better return on the investment?

There are several dangers surrounding this problem. First, parents usually use resources on worthwhile pursuits—there is *some* positive return. However, it may not be the best return possible. Return on any one investment cannot be truly judged in a vacuum. Its worth is always relative to other options. If you are not aware of all the available alternatives for your resources, you will get limited returns.

A second possible deficiency in the allocation of parental resources is a narrow view of the criteria used to judge investment and return. For instance, there is a dual time dimension: long-term and short-term investment and return. If you focus too heavily on either of these to the neglect of the other, you could invest unwisely. For example, spending money on extravagant vacations or recreation vehicles may allow family enjoyment now, but preclude the availability of tuition for college later. Conversely, miserliness now in the quality of food may lead to health or hygiene problems later. In addition to the criteria of time frames, there are other important variables for selecting how and where to invest, including family financial success, happiness, stability, togetherness, safety, security, health, and growth potential. All of these factors must be considered when resource plans and decisions are made. While this may at first seem time-consuming, it will become instinctive with practice. The important point is for you to begin thinking and behaving in this manner now.

11. The Whole Family Is More Than the Sum of Its Parts

Mothers and fathers often assume that if they know all the individual family members, they understand their family. Nothing could be further from the truth. While each child's behavior may be fathomable individually, the mystery of the family, with all its dynamics, may continue to plague the unwary parent. Behavior in the family is interactive. Very few actions are without impact on others. Each parent's or child's plans, values, priorities, attitudes, and dispositions have implications for the other family members. In the family more than any other place the adage holds: "No man is an island." Parents who are not cognizant of the essential difference between the sum of all the family members' individualities and the family's nature as a whole could be in for a surprise. For example, a financial decision regarding one child (will it be public or private school?) could have an impact on other younger children (will it be dental braces or crooked teeth?). In an earlier period in the evolution of the family unit its collective and communal nature was more obvious. There were certain family goals that could supersede each individual child's goal. For instance, it might have been agreed that the family should "produce" a physician, and one child might be supported through medical school by parents and siblings. This accomplishment was viewed as good for the family as a whole, not for just the one son or daughter. Likewise, children who were working often contributed to the common family coffers. Parents bought land and built homes with the children's future marriage and family plans in mind. Siblings also lived close to one another for economic, emotional, and social support. It was all for one and one for all.

The nature of the contemporary family is such that family members are much less dependent on each other and therefore less sensitive to the fact that the family is more than the simple aggregate of its individual members. This is so because outside organizations (schools, government agencies, health care services) support the family in ways that they did not previously. The individual family members perceive themselves as more capable of survival without the help of siblings and parents. Parents likewise have diminished sensitivity to the importance of the whole because of a possible overemphasis on the development of one-to-one personal relationships with each child. The consequences of this shift in emphasis from the whole to the individual has led to a disregard of the distinction between the two and in some cases the false assumption that the two are one and the same.

As a result, there are many parents with a diminished capacity for understanding and managing the dynamics of the family as a whole. Unfettered, these dynamics could lead to a family state that is totally self-destructive. It happens all too often. Controlled and directed, the dynamics of the family as a whole could become a positive force for growth and development.

12. PARENTS' VIEWS OF THE NATURE OF CHILDREN WILL INFLUENCE THEIR APPROACH TO FAMILY LEADERSHIP

Mothers and fathers tend to view the nature of children in one of three ways: (1) static, (2) mechanical, or (3) dynamic. The static perspective holds that youngsters are born with a certain personality and characteristics and that these stay pretty much in place during the life of the child. Parents who subscribe to this view tend to feel that their children, as well as the children of others, are "programmed" for certain attitudes, behaviors, and dispositions. If parents are optimistic, they express thoughts like the following: "He can't miss. He's a chip off the old block." If they are pessimistic, they might say the following: "I don't know where he got that terrible attitude. He must take after his great-uncle Fred!" This perspective on the nature of children has some serious flaws. It usually brings about a "tracking system" whereby children are truly locked into a lifestyle not because of inherent traits but rather because of parental highlighting of these perceived characteristics. If the perceived attributes are negative, the results could be devastating for the child and parent alike. For instance, if a child is viewed as being clumsy "by nature," he or she will quickly become self-conscious, anxious, and more accident-prone. This in turn will cause the anticipation of more stumbling behavior. Even when children are tracked on the high road, they can lose. The inordinate parental focus on what they see as the positive characteristics may preclude their recognition of other traits that may be more rewarding. For example, if a son were to demonstrate ability in football at an early age and this became a top priority, the rewards might be wonderful, but they might be *more* wonderful if the child's even greater ability in science were to be recognized and developed. Levels of success and achievement are always relative to what else would have been possible.

Other parents look at their children's development within a mechanical or "competency" perspective. The overriding question is not "What are my children's characteristics?" but "What can they *do?*" The focus is clearly on performance, and the child's sense of success is generally expressed in those terms. These "bottom line" parents are generally not too interested in or concerned about genetics, early personality development, or physical, mental, or social traits unless these can somehow be directly related to tangible achievement. They are not so much concerned about inherent abilities as about the expression of those skills in action.

This perspective also carries with it some major shortcomings. First of all, the inference that a child has developed knowledge or an ability because he or she can perform a task may be erroneous. The level of mental or attitudinal or moral development may not be what the performance seems to suggest. Some children are able to learn by rote and recite historical, scientific, or geographical facts with little understanding of the concepts involved. Children can recite prayers and religious dogma with nothing but a superficial knowledge of the real meaning. They often verbalize about world events, sports, lifestyles, and culture at a level that is much more sophisticated than their real knowledge and understanding. For parents to assume that the ability to talk about something implies a true grasp of the issue can be seriously misleading. On the other hand, there are many elements of the child's nature that cannot be translated into specific and immediately observable behaviors. Feelings, emotions, passions, curiosity, understanding, appreciation, internal peace, sense of balance, and connection with the world, for example, are often difficult to translate into specific skills. In some cases the gestation period leading to visible fruition may take years. Children quickly learn "what counts" and "doesn't count" in daddy's and mommy's eyes. Eventually the less rewarding aspects of the child's life fall by the wayside and the more rewarding behavior gains importance. If this continues, children will become partially developed. Their innermost being atrophies and family relationships usually develop at the superficial level only.

Parents with a dynamic view of their children's nature focus on the *potential* that is present in them. These mothers and fathers recognize that important personal traits and characteristics of the children are developed early and that skills certainly must be developed as a part of the growth process. However, they feel that the most important aspect of the child's nature is the possibility of becoming someone more valuable. They recognize that in each child there is another child who may be, for example, more capable, more intelligent, more loving, more creative, happier, or friendlier. Rather than feeling that children are beneficiaries or victims of their genetics or early environment or that growth must always be translated into observable behavior, parents with a dynamic view of children's nature realize that each present state of the child is temporary and that they will have a new child tomorrow. They feel that whether tomorrow's child will be better or worse than today's is largely a function of their leadership role.

While the first two perspectives (static and mechanical) have some merits, the third point of view results in more effective parentship. It focuses on the concept of "value added." All parents have to ask themselves this question regularly: "As a result of interaction with me, how much more valuable are my children? My family as a whole?" If the answer is "Not much" or "Less valuable," then efficacy of leadership must be questioned. If the answer is "Measurably so" or "Appreciably," then the success level of parentship should be clear.

THE FAMILY AS AN ORGANIZATION

Understanding the nature and dynamics of family life is fundamental to laying the groundwork for successful parentship. Very often parent-child difficulties stem from a misunderstanding or overreaction to what may be normal. The more parents learn about families *as organizations,* the more astute their leadership will be. For the parent, knowledge indeed is power. But it must be a knowledge untarnished by faulty assumptions, stereotyping, false expectations, unreasonable "shoulds," and other contaminants. If they are to remain viable, parenting principles and practices must be tested regularly. Fathers and mothers, therefore, do themselves a service by reading about, listening to, and discussing not just ideas with which they agree, but challenging material as well. Permissive parents should expose themselves to material espousing more authoritarian points of view. Parents of a traditional style could sharpen their abilities by learning something about the perspective of the more progressive philosophy. Information is the oxygen of parental ideology. If the same air is breathed over and over again it becomes fetid, and so does that which it nourishes. Fathers and mothers develop confidence not by simply reinforcing old ideas and habits, but by regularly assessing their own basic premises. In so doing they increase the likelihood of their success.

The primitive principles presented here can serve as a guide for parental examination of basic beliefs, attitudes, behaviors, and coping skills. The first important step in parentship is to address and understand the radical (root) issues underlying the process. These twelve principles are primitive in the sense that all parentship ultimately flows from one or more of them. They should be viewed as such and parents will do well to go back to these "roots" regularly as a problem-prevention routine or for recovery purposes whenever they find themselves facing family leadership difficulties.

The next important step in parentship is to know self, children, family tasks and the relationship of all three as much as possible. Chapter 2 provides a framework for further developing that knowledge.

2

Parentship Styles

Phil, a forty-five-year-old engineer in Baltimore, was planning a weekend outing with his two sons, ages fifteen and thirteen. It had been a while since they had spent a Saturday together and Phil was looking forward to their pleased reactions when he would tell them his plans over dinner that Friday night: they would go to the Orioles baseball game and then out to eat at one of their favorite restaurants. However, Phil was totally unprepared for his sons' sullen expressions when he announced his decision to spend the whole Saturday with them. He was even more surprised on Saturday when he found the boys not enjoying the game, being disruptive and rude to him, and not seeming to want to talk to him very much. That night Phil fell asleep wondering why the day wasn't much fun and why things no longer seemed the same between him and his sons.

Sally, a forty-year-old working mother of three, headed home from work in downtown Boston expecting the house to be clean and dinner started. Three months ago when she went back to work, Sally had explained to Kathleen, age sixteen, Donald, age fourteen, and Karen, age ten, that they would all benefit from the extra money she would be making and that they would have to start doing extra chores to make up for her not being there. She let *them decide* which chores they wanted, making only minor suggestions. Sally also let them decide on rules for enforcing their decisions. In the three months since they had started the "new system" it had needed only minor adjustments and had worked fairly smoothly.

On arriving home, however, she found Kathleen, who was supposed to have started dinner, in bed with the flu. Donald, who was supposed to have walked the dog, was surrounded by cookbooks and trying to figure out how to make meat loaf. Karen, who was supposed to have cleaned her room, was frantically chasing the dog who had broken away from his leash. Sally retrieved the dog, started dinner herself, and quickly gave some new directions to Donald and Karen about chores that needed to be done that night since Kathleen was sick. She expected her directions to be met with resistance. Donald and Karen were used to participating in the decision process. To Sally's surprise, they accepted her decisions happily, almost with relief, and the rest of the evening went smoothly with all the new objectives accomplished.

Why did Sally's evening, despite impending chaos, go smoothly? Why did Phil's Saturday, despite his careful choice, turn out to be a disaster? The answer is that Sally successfully chose an appropriate leadership style to deal with her situation; Phil did not.

Appropriate leadership styles will result in the family's objectives being met more often. In Sally's case she used a *participative* style when she needed the children's cooperation when she went back to work. They were mature enough to decide which chores they would do best and aware enough to realize the benefits of her new income. Sally also knew that this change in their lives would require a sense of team work and cooperation. Allowing the children to participate in the decision process was the best way to ensure this esprit de corps. However, when Sally arrived home to find her system disrupted because of unforeseen circumstances, she was forced to switch styles and become *directive.* Her use of a more authoritarian style that evening was the one way she could ensure that all the family's needs were met at the time. And, as Sally discovered, a switch in leadership style does not necessarily lead to the expected hostility and animosity—not if the members of the family perceive that their goals will be met as a result of the switch. Donald and Karen were old enough to understand that following Sally's directions to the letter would get them dinner faster, and get their chores done on time.

Phil, on the other hand, employed an *autocratic* leadership style for a decision which would have been better handled with a more participative approach. His style lowered family morale. His sons were not enthusiastic about their outing with their father because they had no say in how they would spend their time. Their need to have some control over their own destiny (which is a very strong need for fifteen- and thirteen-year-olds) was completely overlooked by Phil even though his intentions were most honorable. The boys' disruptive and withdrawn behavior was evidence of their sense of frustration. In this case, Phil's unilateral decision resulted in more unrealized goals than realized ones. Phil and his sons had their day at Memorial Stadium, but it did not produce the desired goals of family harmony, trust, and relationship building.

Parent leadership styles are not immutable, as these examples illustrate. Some styles work in some situations but not in others. As we have seen, however, effective styles are always the result of three interacting factors: the parent's personality; the children's personality; and the task at hand. Successful leadership on the part of the parent will take place when these ingredients are in balance. For this reason no particular leadership style is, in and of itself, good or bad, appropriate or inappropriate. Rather, styles are relative to the particular situation. Ultimately, leaders, whether in the family or elsewhere, will be accepted or rejected if they are perceived by their followers as meeting each individual's needs. Healthy human beings—and children are no exception—are attracted to those courses of action that are in their own best interest. The successful parent leader is the one who can connect the goals of the family with the needs of each individual member. This is the essence of parentship. For example, while democratic parenting may sound wonderful, it will not work if the children are craving direction from above. It is important for parents to keep this in mind and develop diverse styles which may be used as the occasion warrants. While certain styles may be more "natural" for some parents to use or more compatible with the needs of some children or more appropriate for certain circumstances, each leadership act is unique and must be custom-made. Of course, it must be kept in mind that children often desire consistency of parenting style as a source of security. This need must be respected as well. To be effective, then, family leadership must sensitively reflect the uniqueness of the situation and at the same time recognize the value of the children's quest for parental predictability.

There are several prototype leadership styles for parents: autocratic, bureaucratic, cooperative, and democratic (just remember the initials: a, b, c, d). Each style has its own strengths and weaknesses. Autocratic parents usually get things done quickly and maintain external control over family affairs but often suppress children's growth and alienate them through poor communication, especially in the area of listening. Bureaucratic parents generally establish well-structured family policies and procedures that provide a stability and orderliness in the household, but the rules and regulations can become ends in themselves and serve as a rigid list of "do's" and "don'ts," the original purpose of which can become clouded. Cooperative parents are able to stand back and let family members develop themselves creatively with a minimal amount of interference on their part—at the risk, however, of not providing direction and guidance that are sometimes needed. Democratic parents generate interaction and mutual support among family members through a high degree of participation, but often at the price of too much time and energy that goes into explaining things and reaching consensus.

One leadership style is only preferable to another in terms of whether or not it produces the desirable outcome: the achievement of family goals. As we have seen in the preceding examples, family goals may conflict. In Sally's case the short-term goal of feeding the family (a physical goal) was more immediately pressing than her long-term goal of teaching Donald how to cook (an educational goal).

Parents are always making major and minor leadership style decisions without realizing it. Becoming aware of and remembering those factors which result in the most appropriate leadership style for each task will help make parents more effective in these decisions. These are two of the more important factors:

1. *Parent personality.* The personality of the father or mother will always affect leadership style regardless of the other interacting factors. For example, some parents are high achievers, goal-oriented, and pushy; others are more relaxed, relationship-oriented, and less ambitious. Some are suspicious and distrustful while others are more accepting and open. Some parents rely on reason and logic while others are more reliant on instinct and feelings. Those with authoritarian personalities are often distant or aloof from family members, make autonomous decisions, and rely on the use or threat of punishments. Those with democratic personalities are often socially closer to family members, share decisions, and are less reliant on coercion to meet family objectives. Some parents are future-oriented while others are present- or past-oriented. These are just a few of the factors that describe personality, a complex and unique component of the parent's individuality.

2. *Children's followership style.* It is important for parents to remember that their children generally have ambivalent feelings toward authority. They will tend to place conflicting demands on their parent-leaders: while they want freedom to do things in their own way, they also want to have goals clearly set for them and specific instructions to follow. The children's potentially erratic shifts between these

desires can send shock waves throughout the parents' leadership plans.

Family cohesion and morale are maintained best when there is compatibility between leader and follower styles. For example, autocratic personality tendencies in children show up in their submissive attitudes and need for direction. Democratic personalities exhibit tendencies to take independent action and the need for participation in family activities. Of course, parentship styles will vary between parents themselves, just as followership styles will differ among children within the same family. This is to be expected because the family is composed of unique individuals, each with his or her own personality.

The followership style of children can modify the leadership style of parents, often without the mother or father even knowing it. For example, children can *reduce* the parent's circle of responsibility by completing tasks that the parent may have expected to perform (e.g., making plans and commitments for the weekend without checking with mom and dad). As a result, the parent could feel usurped and may respond by taking more control or reprimanding the guilty child. The opposite phenomenon also occurs, and probably with greater frequency. That is when children *increase* the parent's circle of responsibility by failing to carry out an assigned task like dumping the trash. Children can actually win the war of behavior modification if they continually fail to do an assigned chore and the parent eventually decides "It is easier to do it myself." Whose behavior is really being modified?

The key is for parents to become aware of the assets of each leadership style and develop the ability to use each as the circumstances warrant.

However, before a plan can be designed for developing this multi-style leadership approach, it is important that parents understand which parentship style is most compatible with their own personality, with all its tendencies, dispositions, and needs. It is likewise critical that parents know what styles are compatible with the personalities of their children. Parents must also develop a sense of which family activities and events require which parentship style. If these are known and anticipated, the family will be more manageable, and the greater will be the chances for success.

The following three inventories will assist you in determining your own most compatible leadership style, your children's preferred followership style, and the family events and activities that may be best served by the respective styles. If both parents are completing the inventories, the two scores should be averaged to one for each item on the Parentship Style Inventory and the Children's Followership Inventory. Likewise, a consensus between both parents should be used to complete the Family Task Inventory. The time spent in discussions leading to consensus will help refine the compatibility of leadership perspective between the parents themselves.

PARENTSHIP STYLE INVENTORY

Directions: Indicate your level of agreement or disagreement with the following statements. Think about each before answering. Use the following rating scale.

```
   1      2      3      4      5      6      7
 ─────────────────────────────────────────────────►
 I disagree fully              I agree fully
```

_____ 1. When a parent tells a child to do something, it should be done right away.

_____ 2. Parents should encourage their children to make their own decisions.

_____ 3. Order is very important for the family.

_____ 4. It is important for parents to encourage family members to talk with each other often.

_____ 5. It is important for children to pursue their own areas of interest even if parents may not like it.

_____ 6. Family decisions are best made by parents.

_____ 7. Following a routine is beneficial for family life.

_____ 8. Grievances within the family should be talked out.

_____ 9. Parents should take the responsibility of establishing family goals and seeing that they are carried out.

_____10. Ultimately, each child must find his or her own way in this world.

_____11. Children should be taught that a job is not finished until it is done right.

_____12. It is a parent's job to provide an environment where the children motivate themselves.

_____13. Parents know the real needs of children more than the children know them.

_____14. Family decisions are best made by the entire family whenever possible.

_____15. It is important for all family members to learn to and be willing to compromise.

_____16. Children need a clearly understood set of criteria for rewards and punishments.

_____17. Parents should encourage curiosity in children at a young age.

_____18. Parents should enforce family rules and regulations.

_____19. Children should have the right to question the wisdom of parental decisions.

_____20. Family traditions ought to be preserved and protected.

Scoring and interpretation: The results of this inventory can be used to indicate which parentship style is most compatible with a parent's personal tendencies, expectations, view of family life, and values. In each of the spaces below write in your score for that item. Then, total each column. The column with the highest score will indicate the most compatible style and the lowest score the most incompatible style. If the totals for some or all of the columns are similar, this is indicative of a multistyle approach to parenting. The scale below the columns allows interpretation of the intensity of the styles.

a. *Autocratic Items*	b. *Bureaucratic Items*	c. *Cooperative Items*	d. *Democratic Items*
_____ 1	_____ 3	_____ 2	_____ 4
_____ 6	_____ 7	_____ 5	_____ 8
_____ 9	_____11	_____10	_____14
_____13	_____16	_____12	_____15
_____20	_____18	_____17	_____19
Total _____	_____	_____	_____

Parentship Style Intensity Scale

31–35:	Exceptionally high
26–30:	High
21–25:	High moderate
16–20:	Low moderate
11–15:	Low
5–10:	Exceptionally low

Individuals scoring in the exceptionally high or exceptionally low category should be aware of the possible incompatibility problems that they might encounter with a child who has an opposite set of needs (to be determined in the inventory below) or in a situation that might demand an opposite parentship style. Modification of the intensity of the style should be a top priority in order to improve all-around effectiveness.

There are several issues that parents should consider in assessing their children's preferred followership style. These questions should be asked about every child in the family individually:

1. *How mature is the child?* For example, younger children may respond better to directive approaches. With maturity comes more understanding, motivation, a sense of responsibility, and the need for a democratic style.
2. *What is the child's skill level?* Does he or she know how to do the task? Does the child know how to do it as well as I do? If so, the cooperative or democratic style may produce the best results. If not, perhaps a direct approach is more appropriate.
3. *What has been the child's performance?* Has the child been performing and behaving well? If so, a supportive style may be in order. If performance is poor, a directive approach may improve the probability of reaching goals.
4. *What is the child's interest in the task?* If the child is starting to express interest in *participating* in certain family activities or goals, a cooperative approach will usually suffice. If there is no initial interest, however, a democratic or more direct style which "sells" the child on the issue may be more beneficial.

CHILDREN'S FOLLOWERSHIP INVENTORY

Directions: Think about each of your children's personality, temperament, behavior pattern, and disposition. Indicate the accuracy of the description using the following rating scale. Do an individual assessment for each child.

```
     1     2     3     4     5     6     7
  ────────────────────────────────────────────→
  Inaccurate description      Accurate description
```

_____ 1. My child likes to be given reasons for family rules and regulations.
_____ 2. My child is very creative.

_____ 3. My child has a tendency to ask a lot of questions about how things should be done.

_____ 4. My child gets easily bored by routine.

_____ 5. My child pays a lot of attention to detail in performing a task.

_____ 6. My child likes decisions to be made quickly.

_____ 7. My child cherishes independence.

_____ 8. My child likes the security of knowing that I am in charge.

_____ 9. My child seems to enjoy and benefit from family discussions.

_____10. My child often does things without checking with me first.

_____11. My child is a self-starter.

_____12. My child usually assumes the leader's role with his or her friends.

_____13. My child is usually willing to compromise.

_____14. My child seeks my advice often.

_____15. My child resents any unexpected changes in routine.

_____16. My child likes to know what is expected of him or her.

_____17. My child's motto is "live and let live."

_____18. My child is well organized and neat.

_____19. My child is a very good listener.

_____20. My child likes to share.

Scoring and interpretation: The results of this inventory can be used to indicate which parentship style is most compatible with your child's personal tendencies, expectations, view of family life, and values. In each of the spaces below write in your score for that item. Then, total each column. The column with the highest score will indicate the most compatible style and the lowest score the most incompatible style. If the totals for some or all of the columns are similar, this indicates acceptance of more than one parentship style. The scale below the columns allows interpretation of the intensity of the styles.

a. Autocratic Items	b. Bureaucratic Items	c. Cooperative Items	d. Democratic Items
_____ 6	_____ 3	_____ 2	_____ 1
_____ 8	_____ 5	_____ 4	_____ 9
_____12	_____15	_____ 7	_____13
_____14	_____16	_____10	_____17
_____19	_____18	_____11	_____20
Total _____	_____	_____	_____

Followership Style Intensity Scale

31–35:	Exceptionally high
26–30:	High
21–25:	High moderate
16–20:	Low moderate
11–15:	Low
5–10:	Exceptionally low

PARENTSHIP STYLE COMPATIBILITY PROFILE

What is your dominant parentship style?_____
(from the *Parentship Style Inventory*)

What is (are) the desirable style(s) for each child?

Child #1:_____Child #2:_____Child #3:_____
(From the *Children's Followership Inventory*)

Are these compatible? If yes, fine.
If not, problems are likely to occur in several areas. A change in parentship style or children's followership style may be necessary.

In our experience with mothers and fathers, we have found several factors underlying the development of leadership and followership styles and causing most of the problems in this area. Personal needs relating to these factors as well as incompatibility between parent and child continue to cause much difficulty in families. Often discrepancies in these areas are not recognized or their importance is overlooked as parents focus more on the behavioral or verbal aspects of life. As we will see in Chapter 3, these factors are often the basis for the family climate as well. But here we address them as they affect parents' and childrens' personalities and relationships. They are: achievement orientation; time framework; materialism; structure and order; need for certitude; definition of completion and precision; trust levels; and dependency.

These factors can serve as good reference points for you in considering and analyzing existing difficulties in your leadership style or your children's followership style. Also, an understanding of these issues as of difficulty can lead to the prevention of parentship

....NT ORIENTATION

....nts and children sometimes differ in the value they assign to
..chievement. Achievement may be their whole life, and they are then
driven to accomplish more and more. There is no end and seldom a
feeling of total fulfillment. For these individuals, whether they be children or parents, no day is considered a success unless there is some
tangible accomplishment—some result that they can show for their
time and effort. They also tend to judge other people within this
framework: they value those who are able to and do achieve and frown
upon those who do not, according to their standards. If they have any
tolerance at all, it is in the type of achievement regarded as acceptable:
money, fame, scholarship, craftsmanship, entertainment, cooking,
physical prowess, etc. They virtually translate a person's worth into
how much has been achieved. The two factors become one and the
same. Achievement-oriented parents are often more interested in what
their children have done than in who they are, although they will deny
this vehemently. "My son, the doctor, or the lawyer, or the stockbro-
ker" lives on in the hearts, minds, and words of many parents. Likewise, greeting cards sent by parents to children often imply parental
pride because of what the children have "done," or "accomplished,"
or "achieved."

Parents have not cornered the market on achievement orientation.
Children, too, can be performance-centered, even more so than their
parents. The causes of this tendency vary and could possibly include
genetics, peer pressure in the neighborhood or at school, the media,
role models in sports or entertainment, folklore, and/or home environment. Some children equal or surpass their parents in this quest to
succeed and are never satisfied.

While there is nothing inherently wrong with achievement orientation, trouble does begin when the focus on achievement interferes with
or even precludes the recognition of other personality factors . . .
trouble for children as well as parents. We remember the commentary
of a fellow air traveler on a trip to Detroit once who confessed that he
really felt his twelve-year-old son was turning out to be a "dud," as he
put it. "He can't play ball; he can't make anything with his hands; he
can't play a musical instrument. Nothing. I hate to say this about my
own son, but he is really a loser. What a disappointment!" Notice how

this forty-year-old construction equipment salesman defined worth: being able to *do* something. When we responded by saying, "But surely your son must have *some* good qualities and must be enjoyable just to behold as a budding young adult," he countered, "Yeah, yeah, of course, but he's not turning out the way I expected. I don't know what the hell went wrong!" This man will most assuredly never know his son as a total person. We would be amazed if serious trouble between them didn't arise.

Another father that we encountered at one of our workshops in Wilmington, Delaware, pointed out a similar pitfall for parents who are achievement-oriented and live or work in such an environment. He explained that all of his fellow engineers at work continuously bragged about the accomplishments of their children: "Whose daughter got all A's, whose son batted .350 in Babe Ruth League, whose children all went on to become computer experts . . . on and on. I have to talk about my kids' achievements, otherwise they would all think that I am raising a bunch of incompetents. It would make *me* look bad. And, frankly, I think even my supervisors would notice and wonder about my own ambition and drive. I find myself hoping more and more that my kids will do something that I can talk about. I am internally angry that they are not doing more and I think that they know it. The strain in the household is getting heavier and heavier." Unfortunately, this father is getting himself and his family into a double bind. He feels that if he doesn't play the game at work, he will lose out. However, by playing the game he will most likely lose out at home. The only way to end the game is to get out and not play anymore. This father will have to ask the question: What will happen if I do not play, positively and negatively? On close analysis we think that he will find more pluses resulting than minuses. He will feel more relaxed, as will his children. He will get to appreciate them for who they are and not for what they do. The children will respond in kind and see their dad not as simply someone to please, but as a whole person. The authenticity of their relationship will increase tenfold. The superficial relationship of pleaser–pleased will be replaced by an association akin to a strong marriage, characterized by mutual respect, "for better or worse."

Another potential problem flowing from an achievement orientation on the part of parents is the tendency to discount other characteristics and qualities of children that cannot be translated into performance terms or short-term accomplishment. Because children will have to make choices concerning the use of their time and energy, they most likely will do things "that count"—things that will earn for them their parents' praise and sense of satisfaction. Those aspects of their lives that may not be put into measurable terms could easily fall by the wayside, which could be tragic for many. These might very well include intellectual, moral, spiritual, and aesthetic development. A heavy emphasis on achievement is likely to result in partially developed children whose sense of worth will crash if achievement diminishes or ceases as they mature. They will have little else to draw on for strength and self-confidence.

Finally, when there is a serious discrepancy between parents and children in the value placed on achievement, the likely consequence is a lack of mutual respect or, at least, the perception of such. Children become self-conscious and anxious, embarrassed because they see themselves as not living up to their parents' expectations, or hurtfully angry because their dignity is being diminished by those whom they love most.

TIME FRAMEWORK

While many parents have a past or future time orientation, children generally focus on the present. Parents have lived longer and have a personal historical reference point which often influences what they do today. Supposedly mothers and fathers are able to learn from the past. This is the essence of wisdom and maturity. Likewise, parents often think about the future. If they are optimistic, they may think, for example, "I can't wait until . . ." If they are pessimistic, they may be haunted by notions like "What will happen if . . . ?" In contrast, children tend to be oriented to the present. "What's happening now?" is their motto. First of all, they have a limited past. They have only been around for a few years and a good part of that time is fuzzy and unfocused. They forget it quickly. One Baltimore father told the story of his eight-year-old son asking him and his wife what they were going to do now as they were "literally driving out of the gates of Disneyworld after just having spent three eighteen-hour days totally immersed in the Magic Kingdom and Epcot . . . I couldn't believe it. I thought that this would satisfy all of us for at least two years!" For children, the question often is "What have you done for me lately?" They get bored easily if the present is not stimulating. Parents often do not understand this. They are so preoccupied with the past or future that they do not have time to deal with the present.

Many parents interpret this attitude and behavior on the part of children as being signs of an ungrateful nature. They often confuse conscious intent with time perspective. This confusion can create problems between parents and children if parents assume ill will when there is merely a difference in the focus of attention. Parents have difficulty understanding the children's perspectives, and the children can't quite comprehend what the parents are so upset about.

Just as referring to the past with children ("Look how much I have done for you!") does not often work, references to the future can likewise cause frustration for mothers and fathers. Saying to a fifth grader, "Study hard so you can go to college someday" is like using a foreign language. Saying, "Practice your piano Tuesday so that you can enjoy the weekend" to a seven-year-old generally will not work either. College for the fifth grader and the weekend for the future concert pianist are light-years away. The future for them is tomorrow or maybe the next day at best, and they have difficulty relating in any meaningful way to anything beyond that.

Another important distinction in time frame relates to conceptions of when things should be done. For some, "mañana" is the watchword. Others, of course, are much more punctual and, in fact, like to get things out of the way. Children, who have a tendency to be less sensitive to the finite nature of time and its constraints, are more prone to delay, postpone, procrastinate. After all, schedules only make sense because we do not have all the time in the world. If we did, we would not need a timetable. Parents know too well the limits of this precious resource; respect for its value increases with age. Children, on the other hand, often view time as limitless and indefinite: there will always be a tomorrow, so what's the big hurry? In exasperation, mothers and fathers will cry out: "How many times do I have to ask you to clean up your room? . . . put the trash out? . . . study your Spanish?" In most cases, believe it or not, children do have good *intentions*. There is often a compatibility in the acceptance of *what* has to be done. The discrepancy lies in *when* it needs to be done.

The key point for reducing parent-child conflicts in this area is for parents to understand and tolerate the differences in outlook and to phrase commentary in a manner that recognizes children's time perspective. This will call for more specific requests, rules, and family policies: "Jimmy, I want you to put the trash cans out at the sidewalk by seven-thirty this morning . . . not a minute later. The truck always comes by at that time." Some parents post a schedule of music practice, study, room cleanings, etc., on the refrigerator door or home corkboard after developing it together with the children. They state what they want done in concrete terms. These parents accept the need to do this because of the nature of children and refrain from immediately personalizing the situation by becoming angry or disappointed.

MATERIALISM

The value of material objects and their role in one's life can be a major cause of difficulty between parents and children. If there are differences, they can vary from family to family. In some cases, the parents are more materialistic than the children. In others, it is just the opposite. The reasons underlying materialism are complex and usually deep-rooted: sense of earlier deprivation, security, fear, lack of interpersonal skills (it's easier to deal with objects), early values development, or just plain greed. While the causes differ from individual to individual, the attitudes and behaviors of the materialistic person are quite universal: you are what you *have.* The accumulation of money, objects, space, pets, anything is what counts. If some idea, value, concept, or principle cannot be translated into concrete matter it doesn't really mean very much.

Contrary to popular opinion, not all children living in the 1980s are materialistic. Even those living in a household headed by materialistic parents may not be, although it is unlikely because children generally emulate their parents' behavior up to a certain age. Discrepancies, however, will appear as children move into their late teens. There may be a rejection of their parents' materialistic values particularly if they are extreme and have been the cause of family discord. A son or daughter who has been deprived of affection because his or her parents were too busy working day and night to accumulate more and more wealth might see these values as harmful and reject them completely, no doubt sending shock waves through the family structure. We have counseled and trained a significant number of professionals and businesspersons whose children have developed lifestyles that are much less materialistic. Not a few have actually taken on rather spartan lives either through choice of occupation and personal interests or by actually joining spiritual groups and cults where they own very little. Several parents related that everything that they gave to their children was, in turn, given away to the group with which their children were affiliated or to other people. Some parents have been forced to change their wills and modify trusts.

If parents are extremely materialistic, it is important for them to realize the damage that they may be doing to themselves or their families. Their very acts of accumulating things to improve the quality and "quantity" of their children's lives may very well backfire and cause the downfall of the entire family. "I don't remember my father once taking me to a baseball game, going fishing with me, or even seeing me play soccer on my recreation league team. I think that he only came to my school events twice or maybe three times. And most likely, he came late or left early," the twenty-year-old son of the owner of a large, well-known Florida restaurant told us at a recent stress workshop. "My sister, brother, and I all split from that scene as soon as we could. My parents couldn't understand how ungrateful we all were for everything that they had *done* for us. What they didn't realize is that we really didn't *want* what they were killing themselves to attain. What we wanted and needed badly they didn't provide. Now my dad sits there and bemoans the fact that none of us are interested in taking over the business. Frankly, I think he blew it all the way around!"

Of course, there are children who are more materialistic than their parents. However, sometimes children may take on the trappings of materialism (valuing clothing, automobiles, stereos, etc., on the surface) without being materialistic *per se*. The nature of our contemporary society is so materialistic that this may be difficult to escape for children. It's the "in" thing to do. Parents will do well if they empathize with their children's situation without necessarily condoning it. Showing them the higher value of other dimensions of life, by their own example, rather than condemning materialism, will do more to eradicate a narrow perspective.

Materialism need not be a source of contention in the family if there is a sense of moderation and perspective. Rather than condemning lifestyles and values, both parents and children must be sensitive to differences in experience and outlook.

STRUCTURE AND ORDER (THE ROLE AND VALUE OF ORGANIZATION)

Every family, no matter how small, is a social organization. This organization has two dimensions: structural (rules, expectations, chains of command, roles) and personal (individuals' needs, likes, dislikes, points of view). Behavior of the individual family member is a result of these two aspects of the social organization. The impact each dimension has on the life of the family is governed by the leadership style of parents. Some mothers and fathers lean heavily on structure for controlling behavior of family members. We call them maintenance-oriented family leaders because their driving force and top priority is to preserve the family structure at all costs. Other parents use the personal dimension for controlling behavior of family members. They sit down with their children, listen to their personal interests and needs, and try to incorporate these in the life of the family. We call them mission-oriented family leaders because they believe the family unit exists to serve the objectives of individual members. Maintenance-oriented parents believe that the individual family members will be successful if the whole unit is well organized and controlled. Mission-oriented parents believe that the whole unit will be successful if the individual members fulfill their own needs. Maintenance-oriented parents direct their attention to the rational/logical and formal side of family life. They prefer certitude, predictability, consistency, and stability. Mission-oriented parents are more appreciative of the nonrational side (feelings, emotions) and more tolerant of change. They are innovative and pursue new objectives regularly. Maintenance-oriented parents place a very high value on structure and order. They like to have their households well organized and predictable. Punctuality, routine, consistency, neatness, are considered virtuous characteristics of the family as a whole as well as of individual family members. Parents who are maintenance-oriented generally run a "tight ship," and are more prone to use an autocratic style of parentship. They believe that structure and order are functional in that family goals are best achieved that way. They also feel psychologically comfortable in this situation. They know what is to be expected and they are in control. They are often convinced that this is the way the world was meant to be. This desire for and eventual dependence on structure is generally learned and is often the result of formal education and social conditioning. It is therefore primarily adult behavior.

Children, on the other hand, are more creative and less in need of structure and order. They are able to look at the world in a more holistic fashion and often feel bored and unchallenged by routine. They like change and generally find it stimulating. They also feel free to exploit the world around them and reshape their environment in a way that is more attractive to them. Toy rooms do not look that way by accident! Children are not as threatened by disorganization as adults are.

Accordingly, parents have to keep two things in mind when it comes to structure. First, there is a fundamental difference in how grownups and children look at the world: mothers and fathers by nature generally gravitate toward order and structure; children tend to want to hold onto their sense of flexibility and excitement that comes through the freedom to control their own environment.

Secondly, parents must keep in mind that structure and order are creations of the mind and are therefore introduced from outside the situation. While there are legitimate reasons for the imposition of order in the family, the degree of value placed on it as well as methods used differ from person to person. It can never be assumed by the parent that his or her perception of order is shared by all of the children—or by any of them, for that matter. A helpful set of questions for parents to ask themselves is: Why do I want structure? Do *I* need it? Do my children need it? Does it serve a purpose? If yes, what is it? If not, why do I have it? What will happen if it is removed? Can I live with that?

Successful family leaders balance the structural and personal aspects of family life. Distorted family organizations generally result from an inordinate dosage of maintenance or mission orientation.

NEED FOR CERTITUDE

The need for certitude, like order and structure, is a factor that is differentiated among family members. Here the differences may not necessarily fall along chronological lines. Both parents and children have varying degrees of need in this area. In most cases, emotionality more than practicality triggers the need. Parents and adults who value certitude have difficulty tolerating mystery, unpredictability, change, complexity. Situations, relationships, or plans that are ambiguous or ambivalent are stressful for them. They will often, therefore, force a decision by another person prematurely by hounding them incessantly, often to their own detriment. Their "need to know now" supersedes their sense of prudence and even political strategy. Good timing leading to success becomes secondary to the satisfaction of their need to be certain. Parents will often force children to make decisions that are destructive for everybody involved by painting them into a corner. How many teenagers, especially young women, have been forced to elope because an intolerant parent could not bear even the remote possibility of a daughter marrying the young fellow that she was dating? And how many children have forced their parents to make negative decisions concerning their requests because they could not wait until their parents gathered more information in order to make a responsible decision?

Those parents and children who have an inordinate need for certitude or who even become obsessed by it are highly ego-centered. In a sense, their world revolves around them. They declare reality to be what they would like it to be and attempt to get everybody to promise to go along. They will constantly seek reaffirmation of their declared reality from other members of the family. They often begin questions or seek advice with the following introduction: "Don't you think that if I . . . ," thereby setting up the respondent for agreement with them. Other family members will often go along with them or tell them exactly what they would like to hear. It is often easier to do this than to have to put up with all the denial, questioning, and whining. Children who know that their parents are pained by the lack of certitude will often refrain from sharing with them any problems they have that may bring about this anguish. A whole mechanism of denial and censoring of information is established whereby only issues characterized by certitude are transmitted. The mental twisting and turning that accompanies uncertain situations or choices is seldom shared with parents who have made it clear that they really do not want to know about such experiences. Their message often is: "Tell me about it when the difficulty is over . . . when there is certitude." As a result the child suffering through the quandary has to go it alone. Opportunities for development of close, binding relationships through empathy building are missed because of this. Eventually children develop a sense of isolation and resentment toward those parents who are supposed to be there to assist, support, and comfort, but instead have set up a neat self-protective shield which blocks requests for their involvement in working through the uncertainties. Most children put in this position will suffer in silence. Some high school students, for example, often complain that their parents have a low tolerance for their apparent indecision in thinking about colleges and majors that they may want to pursue. Parents will often sigh in exasperation, "One day it's this and the next day it's that. He doesn't know what he wants. First, it's the state university, then it's Duke, then it's Georgia Tech. Who knows what he'll do?" While parents often intellectually recognize the difficulty and complexity of these kinds of decisions, they may not have the emotional ability to go along. This internal dissonance between what they know and how they feel causes some parents to attempt to remove the perceived source of pain, the lack of certitude: "Look, son, you have to make up your mind by March 15 or I will do it for you . . ." Others will withdraw from the situation: "Look, dear, you do whatever you want to do. Just don't bother me with it. The less I know, the better for me." Both responses represent the typical "fight or flight" reaction to stress.

However, the stress in this situation is self-imposed because of the parent's artificial and unrealistic expectation of an absence of ambivalence.

Parents (and children) need to remember two points to minimize the potential damage resulting from this need for certitude. First, there should be a recognition that this need is based in the individual and not the situation. Certitude is a human condition and therefore it is fully within the control and responsibility of each person. While the causes may be deep-rooted, the attitudes, behaviors, and dispositions can be modified with introspection and the desire to change. It is not enough to throw up your hands and say, "That's just the way I am!" The damage that may be inflicted on those around you is too overwhelming.

Secondly, it is important for parents who find themselves with this need for certitude to recognize this as a personality characteristic that others may not have to the same degree. They must understand how this can be a source of contention between themselves and their children. If they convey this knowledge of themselves to their children, many interpersonal problems and hostile feelings can be precluded: "Mommy can't help it, but I *have* to know things are going to be o.k., and that's why I may seem like I'm bugging you all the time with so many questions. I am trying to change a little bit, so can you put up with me until I do? Be sure to tell me if you think that I am pressing you too much and we'll see what we can work out." If parents take this approach of sharing knowledge of themselves and its potential pitfalls for relationships with their children, many conflicts will be avoided and their role as a leader will be legitimized. If parents deny or are ashamed of who they are or feel obliged to defend themselves, the gap between them and their children will widen.

COMPLETION AND PRECISION

Differences in the concepts of completion and precision can also interfere with successful leadership on the part of parents. The father who asks his son if he has finished mowing the lawn may be totally exasperated to find, after his son has answered "Yes," that the yard still needs trimming and the lawn mower is still sitting out in the backyard instead of in the shed. The notion of what defines completion and levels of precision expected will often differ in parent and child. Children often are less precise because they are more awkward physically and are so anxious to complete their tasks that they are likely to rush it, prematurely declaring themselves done. They often see completion time as a symbol of success (the quicker, the better in terms of pleasing dad and mom). They may want to get it done so that they can go play with friends. They may, like many youths, just work at a fast pace because of their vast amounts of energy.

Parents have to keep in mind that children do believe that they *are* in fact done and that the level of precision is acceptable to them. We recall one mother of two adolescent boys telling about the time when she was hospitalized for a few days for a minor ailment and her sons decided to clean house for her and tidy up: "When I came home everything looked great . . . I was pleasantly surprised . . . until I opened the closet doors. There it was: old newspapers, soiled laundry, even a dirty pot or two. Of course, they meant well and were so cute and sincere." While this case may be a little dramatic, the attitude of that mother is healthy. She realized that there was good intent and that her boys had tried their best. With physical, mental, and social maturity, children's concept of what it means to complete a job at an acceptable level of precision will be crystallized. The key is for parents not to become impatient or to assume ill will or a lack of cooperation. Reprimanding or shouting will not help matters. Children want to help and do the right thing. Believe us, nothing makes them happier. Rather than judging the child's performance against the criteria of what they consider a job well done and criticizing it, effective parents will focus on what the son or daughter has done right and guide the child in improving upon and eventually fine-tuning that. The parent can truly become the mentor. The worst thing that parents could do is to complete the task themselves. This would severely undermine any confidence and motivation that the child has developed. The message would be clear: "You have failed." This is another example of an occasion for potential contention or an opportunity for parents and children to grow closer.

TRUST LEVELS

In the family, trust has traditionally been the cement of relationships . . . that is, *mutual trust.* This means giving the best of yourself, but expecting the best of the other family members in return. It is an all-inclusive pledge. It involves everything. The opposite of the trust framework is the contract mentality, although a breach of contract could indeed stem from or result in a lack of trust. Some families use actual written contracts; others don't. Whether they do or not, however, this approach to family relationships usually involves more specificity and has limitations as well as exclusions. It precludes total mutual giving and expecting. There are distinctions made concerning what is to be expected from each party. Whereas the trust relationship is like an invisible bond between family members—a bond which, for instance, emerges from the establishment of a love relationship between husband and wife and is present at the moment of birth for a child—the contract relationship is much less nebulous.

While traditionally family relationships have been characterized by trust, the contract approach is gaining in popularity in many quarters. Young men and women more and more are approaching marriage with actual written contracts defining who owns what, who will do what, and who will get what if the marriage were to be dissolved. This signed-sealed-and-delivered ethic, established early, permeates the household. As children are born and live in the family they, no doubt, will begin to think and operate within this framework.

Problems can arise when parents and children alike begin to mix the two frameworks (trust and contract), hoping to have the best of both worlds. In short, if parents go the contract route, then they had better be prepared to live with it and be willing to translate most family matters into this quid pro quo structure and climate. Likewise, if they go the trust route, then they should be willing to exercise their choice fully, tolerating the lack of specificity in mutual expectations. But can parents use both, trust and contracts? The two approaches are not mutually exclusive, but they do serve different purposes. When the purposes are not distinguished, difficulties can arise. Trust is in the category of virtues and values. Like love, respect, admiration, and loyalty, individuals extend it to each other because they feel compelled to or find doing so personally rewarding in some way. The key is that there is an option, and the choice is not forced. The mission of trust in the family context is the building of strong and permanent relationships among parents and children that will hold them together in good times and bad.

Contracts serve more of a logistical purpose. Parents develop them to control broad areas of responsibility that could be unmanageable and elusive. Contracts are useful to clarify relationships, to crystallize objectives, to break down work, to assign tasks, to provide a time frame, to evaluate performance, and to record the progress and growth of individuals as well as the family as a whole.

If both are used, it is absolutely essential that parents make very clear to children what is sealed by trust and what is governed by contract. For example, "I know that you will not have wild parties with your friends when I am not home" is a trust statement, while "If you want to go to summer camp again this year, you must maintain at least a B average in school" is an expression of contract. A violation of the former statement would be a breach of trust. To disregard the latter would be a breach of contract.

While most healthy parent-child relationships will include both types of agreements, it is important for you to make this distinction because your response to the violation of trust and contract should differ. Breaking of trust generally involves intent and reflects a defect in the personal relationship, at least on the part of one of the parties involved. Corrective behavior must center on the people involved and their relationship. Trust will be mended when the cause of the breakdown is determined. Unfulfilled contracts, however, come about for many reasons: children may try the best they can, but still fail to accomplish what they set out to do; situations could change from the time the contract was made; the terms of the contract might be unclear; or, of course, your child may have willfully neglected his or her promise. While an *inter*personal issue between you and your child could be involved in contract violation, a personal or situational cause is more likely: maybe your son has taken on too much; maybe you expect too much; maybe your daughter tends to feign understanding of what is expected when, in fact, she really doesn't understand.

Parents can use trust and contracts to cement relationships with their children and operate effective and efficient households if they are able to distinguish the role of each of these ingredients and to use them judiciously. An inappropriate expectation or response, which often occurs when trust and contract relationships are confused, can lead to seriously damaged relations between parents and children.

DEPENDENCY

The extent to which children are dependent or independent can often be at odds with parents' needs and expectations. While some aspects of dependency levels can be a result of personality, most is learned behavior or situational. Some boys and girls seem to have an independent nature from birth, manifested by behavior that is often unique and creative and by a yearning for autonomy. Parents have two choices when confronted with independent children: fight them or join them. Those who choose to fight generally frustrate and repress their offspring to the point of confrontation, which may come early and continue even into adulthood. Some children accept or cannot escape the frustration of independence imposed by their parents and practice their autonomy outside the home while imploding in the presence of their parents. These are the sons and daughters who usually cannot wait to "fly the coop," often too early as far as parents are concerned, but much too late for the children's own liking.

Those parents who decide to join their children in their quest for independence will provide avenues for them to exercise this need, without abdicating their parental responsibilities. They can allow their children to have increasing control over their own lives; they might even challenge them to develop their sense of independence further. For example, a parent might ask the teenage son or daughter to actually decide which television set or stereo system or even computer the family should buy within given budget and size constraints.

Dependency in a family setting has to do with whether the individual members contribute as much energy and other resources as they take from the other members collectively or individually. If the resources taken and given are equal or in favor of the family, then the individual member is self-dependent. If the balance favors the individual family member, then he or she is other-dependent. Any member of the family can be characterized by this balance or imbalance. It can involve many kinds of resources, such as money, time, interest, emotional support, or helpfulness.

The causes of dependency vary as well. Some parents or children are just plain takers and not givers. Some are fearful of self-dependency because of low self-image: they value other members of the family more than they do themselves and would prefer to identify with them ("If you don't watch it, I'll tell my brother about this!"). Some family members have a need to give and/or suffer (through giving) and therefore force others to become receivers, sometimes just to please them. ("I killed myself, son, all day making this meal because I know you like this kind of fish . . . so eat all three pounds of it!"). Some parents (and children) define their family role in terms of dependency: there is meaning in their lives because somebody is dependent on them.

Whatever the cause, low self-reliance and high other-dependence generally lead to problems among family members. In cases where the dependent one is the perpetrator, the depended-on feels anger, resentment, dislike, and confusion because of the ambiguity of feeling exploited by someone whom he or she loves. Even in cases where the depended-on causes and maintains the imbalance of giving and taking, there is difficulty. In this case, the self-imposed dependency is most likely based on some inordinate sense of virtue or unhealthy need to be needed, the effects of which will ultimately be viewed as an emotional drain and burden on the bearer. Parents who feel compelled to "do, do, do" and "think, think, think" for their children eventually reach a point of resentment which can lead to either emotional or physical abandonment.

A strong family is one that is composed of self-reliant parents and children, who contribute more to the common good than take from it, who avoid parasitic relationships, and who view helplessness with disdain. What family members must realize is that by giving more than they take from the family they, in turn, get the security and longevity that comes with growth and love.

FAMILY TASKS: WHO SHOULD DO WHAT AND HOW SHOULD IT BE DONE?

In addition to parentship styles and children's followership styles, a final consideration in developing effective leadership acts in the family is the accomplishment of tasks. This could outweigh the other two factors. Some tasks are best completed by certain parents or children. Matching task with appropriate parent or child can be beneficial not only in the accomplishment of the task, but also for the individual family member's growth and sense of contribution to the family's common good.

The inventory that follows will assist parents in analyzing task assignment. We use as an example "household chores." Other recommended tasks for analysis include educational decisions, family budget decisions, vacation planning, safety and security policies, clothing purchases, etc.

The same sample format can be used to analyze any of these family tasks by comparing the strengths and weaknesses of each of the four styles. For example, it may become clear on analysis that family safety decisions (fire escape routes) or meal planning (to ensure good nutrition) may best be made using an autocratic style, while family recreation plans would be served best by a cooperative or democratic style.

FAMILY TASK INVENTORY

Here is an example of an important type of family task, along with illustrations of possible strengths and weaknesses accompanying each of the following parentship styles:

a. autocratic style   c. cooperative style
b. bureaucratic style   d. democratic style

(Sample Format for Analysis)

Designated task:
Household chores (e.g., washing dishes, mowing lawn, trash collection)

Styles	*Strengths*	*Weaknesses*
a.	1. Don't have to bargain with kids	1. Can be arbitrary
	2. Each task covered by someone	2. Resentment builds up in children
	3. Fast response in emergencies and crises	3. Encourages overdependency on parents
b.	1. Orderly and structured	1. Can be boring
	2. Everybody knows the rules of the household	2. Low communication among family members
	3. A lot of things are done automatically	3. Doesn't allow for give and take
c.	1. Most family members get to do what they like best	1. Tasks will "fall through the cracks"
	2. Places responsibility for task equally in each family member	2. Older kids might exploit younger ones by getting them to do all the hard work
	3. Flexible	3. Too little direction

Styles	Strengths	Weaknesses
d.	1. Encourages group participation	1. Makes it hard for parents to step in and assert control
	2. Is perceived as most fair	2. Promotes bickering
	3. Teaches bargaining skills	3. Could be too slow in an emergency situation

Analysis of results: An analysis of strengths and weaknesses of each style for the given family task will help parents to approach each activity in the most productive manner.

3

Family Climate

Every family has a climate, a general atmosphere which influences values and ways of operating. Climate is to the family what personality is to the individual. It is something that develops early, becomes well entrenched, is complex, and changes slowly. It often has a kind of mystique attached to it. The climate of the family is pervasive and affects all the members. It is difficult to escape its influences and constraints. Children are immersed in the family climate from birth. Most incorporate it permanently into their very being: "You can take the boy out of the Hanson family, but you can't take the Hanson family out of the boy." Family life is the first organizational experience for most people. Its effects are long-lasting and influence much of what goes on later in adult life. Family climate is a composite entity. Just as human personalities have several dimensions (self-esteem, need for approval, etc.), the presence or absence of which define particular personality types, family climates have several components.

We can identify ten dimensions of family climate. The degree to which these are present will determine which of eight climate types best characterizes the family. The ten factors are:

1. *Goal orientation:* the degree to which the family is future-oriented and focuses on moving toward preestablished objectives; the amount of time and energy devoted to planning; the tendency to evaluate the success of the family and its members in terms of accomplishment and development.
2. *Tradition:* the extent to which customs, habits, and rituals affect family life; the value placed on doing things as they have always

been done; the role of religious, ethnic, socioeconomic, or cultural practices in family behavioral patterns.

3. *Control:*   the degree to which family activities are regulated and governed; the rigidity of the parent-child chain of command; the amount of freedom allowed members of the family for discretionary behavior; the role and value of conformity.

4. *Dependency:*   the value placed on the independence of the individual family members within the family; the independence of the family as a whole in the greater society; the need to be depended on by family members.

5. *Security:*   the need to put physical safety and financial security above all else; devoting large amounts of family resources to protection; establishing family policies and habits based on criteria of security.

6. *Conservation:*   the tendency to save resources, especially financial ones; degrees of thrift; levels of delayed gratification.

7. *Pleasure:*   the role of enjoyment, fun, rest, relaxation, and recreation in the life of the family; the amount of individual and family resources (time, money, etc.) devoted to this; the place that diversions have in family schedules.

8. *Interpersonal relations:*   the value placed on harmony, congeniality, and mutual support in the household; the importance of resolving conflicts peacefully; levels of respect among family members.

9. *Sharing:*   the equity with which the family distributes its resources; the degree of exchange of material goods, experiences, knowledge, feelings, concerns, etc.; levels of mutual communication (telling and listening).

10. *Perspective:*   the degree of parochialism in the family's operating context; the extent to which the family exists in isolation; the breadth of the perspective of family interests and concerns.

While stereotypes always have some shortcomings (all families, like people, are really unique), there are certain *general types* of families. And these types are prone to hold certain values and attitudes and behave in a predictable way. Types, like personalities, are neither good nor bad, although each has strengths and weaknesses in a given context. Their value is relative to the situation in which they find themselves. To determine the climate of your family, complete the following scale.

FAMILY CLIMATE SCALE

Instructions: Rate the degree to which these statements describe your family. If two parents complete the scale, use the average of the two ratings.

1   2   3   4   5   6   7

Doesn't describe   Fully describes

_____ 1. We encourage our children to think on their own.

_____ 2. We do things the way they have always been done.

_____ 3. We ordinarily save up to buy things.

_____ 4. We usually do things in a step-by-step fashion.

_____ 5. We do very little on impulse.

_____ 6. There is a lot of confusion in our household.

_____ 7. We usually examine as many options as possible when buying a new car.

_____ 8. Members of our family rarely eat together.

_____ 9. Work is a high value in our family.

_____10. We are often short of cash.

_____11. We share family problems with friends.

_____12. We have many visitors and social gatherings at our house.

_____13. We usually do not know how much money we have in our checking account.

_____14. Members of our family like to go to parties.

_____15. All of us love to travel for pleasure.

_____16. We have a high-quality burglar alarm system for our house.

_____17. There is only one boss in our household.

_____18. At least one neighbor has a key to our house.

_____19. We often buy things that we like even though we really can't afford them.

_____20. We own a recreational vehicle.

_____21. We prefer to have a few good friends rather than many acquaintances.

_____22. We don't feel obliged to attend neighborhood or community events.

_____23. We have a watchdog.

_____24. We tend to borrow and lend with our neighbors.

_____25. We go out to dinner at least once a week even if it's just a fast food restaurant.

_____26. We live in the same geographical area (within 75 miles) of most of our extended family.

_____27. People are surprised to hear where we live.

_____28. Our children have lots of toys.

_____29. We seldom feel guilty about buying luxury items like stereos, expensive lawn furniture, household gadgets, etc.

_____30. We allow our children a lot of freedom.

_____31. Our family philosophy is "go for it . . . enjoy life."

_____32. We lose a lot of things in our household.

_____33. Children are generally kept out of parents' space in the house (bedroom, work areas, etc.).

_____34. Parents and children have their assigned chores in our household.

_____35. Our children often ask us to protect or defend them.

_____36. Family members belong to many clubs and are involved in many activities.

_____37. We don't have a systematic savings plan for our children's education.

_____38. We don't expect all of our children to like the same things.

_____39. Children are not encouraged to ask too many questions until they are in their teens.

_____40. We see no reason why children have to go to college out of state.

_____41. We often resolve family conflicts and tensions by going out to dinner, taking a trip, or buying something nice that will divert our attention.

_____42. We carry quite a bit of life insurance.

_____43. We are not very fashionable in our dress.

_____44. We usually have a maximum credit-line balance on our credit cards.

_____45. Our children know exactly what is expected of them.

_____46. In our investments we go for high return rather than safety.

_____47. Our children's friends often play at our house.

_____48. We always like to meet the parents of our children's friends so we can get to know what kind of family we are dealing with.

FAMILY CLIMATE PROFILE

Your family climate will be one of eight possible types: (1) monarchs; (2) randoms; (3) high rollers; (4) independents; (5) steadfasts; (6) good-timers; (7) sociables; or (8) protectors. Remember, none of these types is inherently good or bad. All have their strengths and weaknesses. To determine your family's climate type, complete the following steps:

1. Transfer the ratings for each of the items in the Family Climate Scale to the corresponding spaces in the following table.

FAMILY CLIMATE TYPES

Monarchs		Randoms	
Column A	*Column B*	*Column A*	*Column B*
Item #	Item #	Item #	Item #
4_____	1_____	6_____	2_____
17_____	6_____	8_____	4_____
33_____	8_____	10_____	16_____
34_____	11_____	13_____	17_____
39_____	13_____	32_____	33_____
41_____	30_____	37_____	34_____
Total_____	Total_____	Total_____	Total_____

Profile score:_____
(Subtract B total from A total)

Profile score:_____
(Subtract B total from A total)

High Rollers

Column A	Column B
Item #	Item #
7_____	5_____
19_____	16_____
29_____	21_____
41_____	26_____
44_____	33_____
46_____	42_____
Total_____	Total_____

Profile score:_____
(Subtract B total from A total)

Independents

Column A	Column B
Item #	Item #
1_____	2_____
22_____	3_____
27_____	11_____
30_____	12_____
38_____	14_____
43_____	24_____
Total_____	Total_____

Profile score:_____
(Subtract B total from A total)

Steadfasts

Column A	Column B
Item #	Item #
2_____	6_____
3_____	7_____
5_____	8_____
9_____	10_____
21_____	13_____
26_____	19_____
Total_____	Total_____

Profile score:_____
(Subtract B total from A total)

Good-Timers

Column A	Column B
Item #	Item #
14_____	3_____
15_____	9_____
20_____	21_____
25_____	40_____
28_____	43_____
31_____	48_____
Total_____	Total_____

Profile score:_____
(Subtract B total from A total)

Sociables		**Protectors**	
Column A	Column B	Column A	Column B
Item #	Item #	Item #	Item #
11_____	5_____	16_____	1_____
12_____	21_____	23_____	6_____
18_____	22_____	35_____	11_____
24_____	23_____	40_____	18_____
36_____	26_____	42_____	24_____
47_____	35_____	48_____	46_____
Total_____	Total_____	Total_____	Total_____

Profile score:_____
(Subtract B total from A total)

Profile score:_____
(Subtract B total from A total)

2. The highest profile score will indicate which climate type best describes your family, and the lowest profile score or a minus score indicates which of the climate types your family least resembles. In some rare cases the profile scores may be identical or extremely close (within 2 points), indicating that the family has a dual personality. If this is so, it is important that parents examine the consequences of this confusing state and attempt to find out the reason for it. Situations involving multiple climates are generally stressful.

FAMILY CLIMATE PROFILES

The eight family climate types are described below. These behavioral profiles include indications of likely strengths and weaknesses.

1. MONARCHS

The most obvious thing about this type of family is its high degree of internal structure. Family rules, regulations, policies, and chain of command are valued. There is usually one parent who dominates the entire family: whether patriarchal or matriarchal, this family rarely has coequal leaders. Family members are expected to know their roles. Predictability in family functioning and relationships is emphasized. It would be uncommon and hardly acceptable for family members to make impulsive decisions. In the parent-centered environment, planning is important and decision making is based on precedent and order. Communication is generally top-down (from parent to child).

Challenges to the family power structure are rebuffed quickly and often viewed with disappointment, anger, and disdain.

Strengths of this climate include the provision of a stable and secure environment characterized by certitude. Standard operating procedures prevail and little time is spent debating issues (*Cheaper by the Dozen* style). Likewise, decision making is usually quick and unfettered by differing opinions or difficulties in understanding the content of the decision situation.

Possible weaknesses include repression of family members' egos to the point where members stop growing as persons or decide to do their growing someplace outside the family. Creativity is reduced in this sheltered, structured, and often rigid environment as children become drone-like in their obedient quest for parental approval. Another cost is the encouragement of dependency on the part of children: "If I play by the rules of the game, I will be taken care of." Eventually this "service" provided by the parent becomes a "need" for the child, and the albatross of dependency wears down parent and child alike.

2. RANDOMS

This climate is characterized by unpredictability, ambivalence, and ambiguity. Change is rather constant and family rules, policies, and even schedules are written in pencil, always tentative and temporary. It's a "hang loose" atmosphere, where the extemporaneous is highly valued. There is minimal routine, and generally physical order is not a top priority, although household clutter is not always present. There is very little long-range planning and little time is spent in short-term planning. "As the spirit moves us" might be the theme for a family with this climate.

Some benefits of this type are the allowance made for spontaneity among family members, the sense of freedom to exploit the moment; a sense of independence on the part of children; the development of an atmosphere of fun and adventure through the occurrence of the unpredictable in the family. Likewise, family members have a tendency to be more imaginative and creative because they are not shackled by the protocol of internal family structure.

Potential weaknesses of this climate include high degrees of stress due to frequent change; insecurity on the part of young children in particular; a high incidence of misplaced household items; much inconvenience imposed on family members due to the unpredictability of the other family members' behavior. In addition, family expenses are often increased because of the low regard for logistics: parents may find themselves driving to the supermarket five times a day, each time buying only one or two items. The cost in time, energy (human and auto), and emotion could be heavy.

3. HIGH ROLLERS

This type of family is well aware that risk and reward can be directly connected. Often high risk can mean high reward. The motto of this climate is "go for it." Family members are not likely to feel restricted by the fear of failure and are willing to take chances. An attitude of "nothing ventured, nothing gained" permeates the household and underlies the family philosophy. Material standards of family life tend to be cyclical . . . here today and gone tomorrow . . . easy come, easy go. The possibility of short-term gains generally outweighs the probability of long-term returns. This type of family wants to go first-class all the way.

One key strength of this climate type is eternal optimism: there is always a tomorrow, and it is bound to be better "if we play our cards right." Because they think big, these families sometimes accomplish big things and are very successful. They usually share good times and children often enjoy family life. Family structure is flexible and individual members are encouraged to develop as much as they can. Success and achievement are seen as virtuous. Competition and envy *among* family members is highly discouraged and is viewed as "loser" mentality.

Families with this climate also have some severe weaknesses. The "what's there to lose" attitude, if overdone, can create insecurity and anxiety in spouses and children. The overemphasis on "hitting" success often causes foolish decisions that can lead to flirtations with bankruptcy. The seesaw financial picture that is often present causes confusion for children as parents "borrow from Peter to pay Paul," creating a roller coaster atmosphere for a family spending-saving policy. The father who flashes $100 bills one week might be walking around the house flicking off light switches in anger the next week. While stakes are attractive for high-risk family winners, the penalties are equally heavy for the losers: financial, emotional, interpersonal.

4. INDEPENDENTS

For the independent family, autonomy is the highest virtue. Not tied to conventionality, family members are often mildly sociable. They tend to make decisions on merit rather than tradition and they usually have a high need for variety. They stress individual responsibility and self-dependency and believe that strong families are made up of strong individuals. They are minimally influenced by social pressures, fads, and cultural values although most function well within the mainstream of American family life. Independents are unique and idiosyncratic in their values and behaviors. As a result, they are difficult to predict.

A key strength of the independents is their low vulnerability to environmental pressures which causes them to control their own resources (money, time, energy) to a high degree and increases greatly their probability of success. Because they are less sensitive to societal approval or rejection, they are able to devote their energies to the accomplishment of goals. Families with this climate are often free-spirited, and children enjoy the opportunities for self-development. The members of the family collectively and individually develop a sense of self-worth and dignity as they recognize their independent nature.

Problems for independents can abound. Because of the ethic of individuality and self-reliance, there can be low family cohesion. The potential for isolation is always present as family members feel obliged to "go it alone" because they have difficulty asking for help. Likewise, it is taxing for family members, especially children, to understand or cope with what appear to be contradictory behaviors: one family member may be doing something that is out of synchronization with other family members, or the family itself may do something that violates family precedent. The changeable nature of family patterns and customs makes it uncomfortable to initiate permanent commitments.

5. STEADFASTS

This climate describes those families that are conventional. Dependability, reliability, and tradition characterize them. They generally follow a social, economic, and political middle of the road. "Moderation in all things" is their motto. They rarely act on impulse, so that family attitudes, values, and behaviors are highly predictable. Individual family members are urged and expected to be good citizens inside and outside the home. The pace of change is slow and the level of risks taken by the family is low. There is a more than moderate degree of self-reliance, but trust in extended family and friends for social and emotional support is present as well.

The strength of the steadfast climate lies in its stability, security, mutual support, and predictability. The individual family members have a high degree of understanding of who they are and what the family is like. Their expectations of family life are congruent with what happens. They are usually relaxed, sociable, and not driven by a need to achieve. They enjoy a high degree of support in a family environment that is often congenial and empathic.

This climate does have its weaknesses. Family life can be viewed as boring, rigid, and narrow-minded. Because they value stability to a high degree, steadfasts can be easily threatened by change. Parents sometimes feel the need to control children to make them conform to family living patterns. Children, in turn, often become vulnerable to this manipulation and either aggressively resist or become complacent and lethargic. The family becomes a place of doom and gloom for the member who wants to grow.

6. GOOD-TIMERS

Families characterized by this type of climate place a very high emphasis on enjoying life and having fun. Their motto is: "You only go around once, so you might as well enjoy it." Family life centers on weekends, vacations, recreational activities, social gatherings, travel, and the like. The physical setting of the home, inside and out, is generally geared up to support this lifestyle. Many of these families have boats, vacation homes, several televisions, stereos, radios, and other kinds of entertainment paraphernalia. Individual members often equate the quality of family life with these kinds of activities and possessions. Likewise, family relationships are also evaluated in terms of enjoyment: "I don't know what's happened to us, dear . . . We haven't been out to a night club in months!" Or, "I really have got to take the kids someplace nice for vacation this summer. I haven't been able to take them too many places this past winter and spring." Good-timers are constantly on the go, planning, enjoying, and talking about the pleasures of life.

The benefits of this family climate are the immediate gratifications that abound. Children often develop very positive feelings about home life: it is a nice place to be. This image also lives on in their memories, which in itself could be a source of joy to parents and children alike for years to come. Likewise, the family becomes a respite from the difficulties of the environment that the children may be experiencing: school, friendships, social pressures to achieve, etc. Children love to see their parents enjoying life and are themselves pleased by this sight. In the good-time family a spirit of joy and happiness can bring about some very positive psychological results as well as family and individual achievement.

Good-time families can also get into serious trouble as they become addicted to pleasure. The disappointment and eventual desperation, if pleasure is withheld for a long period of time, can take its toll on the health of the family. If the worth of the family is defined in hedonistic terms alone, what happens to the family's worth when fun and games diminish or disappear? The good-time climate is truly a double-edged sword: it can be the thread that weaves a strong, happy, and loving family, or it can, by default, allow disintegration.

7. SOCIABLES

This climate is characterized by a dynamic atmosphere inside and outside the family. Family roles are not at all static, as children and parents transfer responsibilities and tasks. The family is very communicative, freely exchanging ideas and opinions. Family members do a lot of things together and look forward to meals as well as household work and recreational activities that involve all of them. This type of family is also interactive with the neighborhood and the greater community. They often discuss world events. Parents are most likely members of service clubs, civic groups, church organizations, or PTAs. Children likewise tend to join athletic teams, scout organizations, or other cultural and social groups. A sense of internal and external community is important for the members of this kind of family.

The strengths of this climate type include a healthy sense of place in the world, and a recognition that the family is not an island. Its internal flexibility provides all family members the opportunity to grow and change while having the support and encouragement of the other family members. Usually family members are able to experience a wide range of ideas, feelings, and emotions. Because of the high internal and external value placed on people, this family climate most often provides a pleasant surrounding for children.

Some of the potential weaknesses include a lack of privacy for family members coupled with pressure, sometimes only subtle, to conform. Confidentiality relating to family matters can be jeopardized as individual family members feel the need to share the plight of the family with friends, neighbors, or relatives. Because of the value placed on openness to the environment the family can be victimized by social or economic pressures that may even seriously wound its basic values. In some cases the individual family members may lose their own identity as they blend with the family as a whole, and the family itself may lose its individuality as it attempts to fully mingle with the greater society.

8. PROTECTORS

Families with this climate operate a tightly controlled system. Their basic motto is "Good fences make good neighbors," and they see family health as founded on safety, security, and vigilance. Members of the family often view their home as a safe harbor for loved ones. Parents feel that their major obligation and top priority is to protect, defend, and provide for their children. They do not take what they consider to be unnecessary risks. Therefore, social interaction is generally guarded and limited. They often feel obliged to keep a protective weapon in the home. Ideas that are foreign or that challenge the family's status quo must meet a stringent test of validity before they are incorporated into the family value system and structure. These families do not change easily and are fad-resistant.

The benefits of this family climate include the comfort of a secure and safe home environment as well as a sense of a stable community. Life in this family environment is cohesive, dependable, and predictable. Family members know that someone is looking out for them at all times. Fears and anxiety about the risk of being harmed physically, socially, or mentally are low. The high focus on strengthening the family creates a feeling of unity and common purpose: "It's all for one and one for all!"

Protector families are not without shortcomings. A "bunker mentality," characterized by an "us against them" attitude, can isolate and insulate the family and its members. The spirit and practice of group thinking (with pressure to conform to the family norms) can slowly but surely permeate the family, leading to a state of righteousness and moral indignation at the rest of the world. Lastly, parents in protector type families can unknowingly starve the children's potential for developing self-sufficiency skills. By doing and thinking for them, parents can set their sons and daughters on the road to stagnation and dependence. In so doing, they create children who are fearful of and incompetent to deal with the external world and who will, no doubt, continue to seek the protection of the womb when seriously challenged.

HOW CAN KNOWING THE FAMILY CLIMATE HELP?

The chief benefits accruing from a knowledge of the family's climate are threefold: diagnosis, treatment, and prevention. First, such knowledge provides a framework for understanding the nature and dynamics of what goes on in the household. Just as certain personalities tend to behave in a certain fashion, family types follow a predictable behavior pattern. When the cause of the behavior is known, much of the mystery is taken away and along with it the fear and anxiety that accompany the unknown. Parents who understand the concept of family climate and know their own family's type will recognize that there is a reason for what takes place and that they are not alone.

A second benefit of knowing family climate and understanding its components is the corrective potential. If the present climate is viewed as dysfunctional and troublesome, it can be changed (albeit slowly) by systematically modifying some or all of the ten dimensions. A plan to modify the family's climate over time can be developed and implemented by the family members alone or with the help of an outside expert (e.g., a family counselor), just as personalities are successfully modified through therapy. The following Matrix of Family Climates is presented as a general guide which relates the ten dimensions of family climate to the eight types.

To modify the present climate of the family from one type to another, parents should increase, decrease, or stabilize the factors accordingly. Specific behaviors to bring that about can be planned and designed around the definition of each of the dimensions as presented above. For example, if a family needed to increase its goal orientation, parents might institute the practice of forced savings of a fixed amount of money through payroll deduction or the practice of having children establish concrete objectives for their school grades each quarter. Slowly but surely, as family behaviors change, the family's climate will change as well. But parents must remember that just as personalities do not change overnight (an introvert can't become an instant extrovert by simply wearing flashy clothes and driving a sports car!), modifications in climate take time. Family members have become accustomed to the old way of doing things. They will often resist change at the emotional level even though they agree at the mental level. Change is always stressful; and often, no matter how bad the situation, it still appears easier to keep the status quo. This is all the more reason for maximum involvement in the change process by *all* the family members. If any are left out or choose not to participate, they will surely attempt to sabotage the planned changes, often unknowingly.

Finally, understanding climate can help prevent the family's becoming something that would be detrimental to its well-being. Awareness of the factors that compose the various climate types can help mothers and fathers avoid certain behavior patterns and ward off temptations to respond to the family's environment in counterproductive ways. It is

MATRIX OF FAMILY CLIMATES

	Goal Orientation	Tradition	Control	Dependency	Security	Conservation	Pleasure	Interpersonal Relations	Sharing	Perspective
Hierarchs	H	H	H	H	M	M	L	L	H	H
Randoms	-	L	L	L	L	L	?	?	?	L
High Rollers	L	M	L	M	L	-	H	M	H	L
Independents	M	L	L	L	L	M	?	M	L	L
Steadfasts	H	H	H	H	H	H	?	M	H	L
Good-Timers	L	L	M	M	M	L	H	H	H	L
Sociables	L	L	L	L	L	M	H	H	H	H
Protectors	M	M	H	H	H	H	H	M	H	H

Symbols:
H = present to a high degree   - = not present
M = in a moderate fashion   ? = irrelevant (may or may not be present)
L = present to a low degree

beneficial for parents to study and get to know the various climate types and then to lead the family in its quest to remain what it is or become what it would like to be.

Climate, then, can change. But parents must remember that it is an interactive process: the change agent affects the climate, but the climate affects the change agent. Parents are immersed in the climate, at the same time a cause and a product of their family's personality. Objective analysis of what is going on is critical to success. In a sense, the parents have to step outside their own families and serve as consultants to them. Attempting to lead that of which they are an integral part is no easy task. We ask of parents that they defy conventional wisdom: "He who treats himself has a fool for a physician" and "He who is his own lawyer has a fool for a client." Parents do indeed need a special power to overcome this wisdom! That power is love.

4

Communication: The Lifeline of the Family

In private interviews with parents and in discussions with groups of mothers and fathers across the country, we often ask the question, "If you had to select only one skill that you would consider to be *the* critical one for success as a parent, what would it be?" The response is nearly unanimous: COMMUNICATION. As an experienced and emotionally scarred Rhode Island father of three children in their early twenties put it, "If you can't communicate with your kids, you know, connect with them, you're dead in the water as a parent. Forget it. You don't stand a chance. I learned that the hard way. I wish that I had known this twenty years ago." Unfortunately, many parents have difficulty with this skill even though they intellectually recognize its value. Communication is the lifeline of the family, but it is indeed a fragile one. It can be easily frayed and even snapped completely. As we have seen, the family is constantly changing. The family that exists today will not be the same as it was yesterday or the same as it will be tomorrow. If a parent were to snap a picture of his or her family and then take another one a year or two later, a marked difference in size of children and other physical attributes would be noticeable in contrasting the two photographs. In a sense, each picture is outdated the moment it is taken because the family is continuously evolving. The same would be true if parents were to take mental and emotional pictures and contrast them:

"What are my children thinking and feeling that they were not thinking or feeling last year?" The only thing that keeps parents' understanding of the family up to date and allows mothers and fathers to stay "connected" is communication. Most parents, however, are untrained in these skills, a critical dimension of parentship. It is small wonder, then, that an overwhelming percentage of parent-child problems stem directly from a breakdown in communication.

In order to improve communication skills it is important for parents to understand the process as it takes place in the family. On the surface communication is a simple process, but in reality it is most complex. For this reason, improvement in communication is not a two-way street between parent and child. Parents, because they are generally more mature and wiser, have a much greater obligation than their children do to establish sound communication in the family. Children cannot be expected to understand the process as well as adults.

Communication can be defined as "any interchange of a message between two or more people." It is a constant process; there are not time-outs. Whenever parents are with children, they are communicating the whole time: speaking, listening, acting, reacting. Silence itself conveys a message. Even when parents are separated from children the process goes on; messages are transmitted through letters, notes, phone calls. Likewise, the environment itself can send many messages between two family members when one is absent: a mother sees her daughter's messy room while she's in school; a boy finds his favorite snack tucked in the lunchbox he had packed himself; the spotlessly clean, beautifully decorated living room says, "Do not enter" to the children, even when mom and dad are away.

Everyone has communication strengths and weaknesses that have been developing throughout one's life. Any time one needs or wants to interact with another person at work, at school, or in the community, communication skills can help or hinder relationships. But nowhere is effective communication more essential than in the family. The ability to communicate well is strongly linked to emotional well-being: people who feel good about themselves generally are better able to express themselves and to listen than people with poor self-concepts. And family members' emotional growth is enhanced when they are in frequent contact with people who express themselves openly and honestly—and really listen. Parents who communicate well create an environment that encourages emotionally secure children and a stable family. At the same time, they teach their children essential communication skills which will benefit them throughout their lifetime.

While parents understand the importance of effective communication, most also have a few of those bad habits that cause communication problems. Mary, a Phoenix mother of two sons, eleven and eight, said, "I know I've always been a poor listener, but lately it's gotten even worse with the boys. I find myself nodding absently, saying 'uh-huh' and 'oh really' as they talk to me, and when they're finished I have no idea what they've said. It just seems like I've heard it all so many times before. I know what they're going to say before they do. They seem so hurt when they realize I'm not really paying attention and I really don't want them to stop talking to me. But I'm not sure I could change now; I've always had trouble listening to teachers at school, my boss and co-workers, my husband—just about everyone. It's just the way I am." This concern is very frequently expressed in our parents' workshops across the country.

It is true that eradicating bad communication habits and replacing them with more effective skills is not easy. But it is possible and will be worth the effort in terms of increased effectiveness as a parent.

The process begins with an awareness of existing bad habits. This calls for a really objective self-analysis, often a very difficult task. The following inventory will help you assess your strengths and weaknesses in this critical skill.

PARENTAL COMMUNICATION INVENTORY

Directions: You can evaluate your skills in communication by honestly responding "yes" or "no" to the following questions. To check your perceptions of yourself, have at least one other person (spouse, older child, etc.) respond to the questions as they relate to you. If there are serious discrepancies, discuss the differences in perception with your evaluator.

_____ 1. Do I select my words in a way that is appropriate for each child's age, experiences, educational level?

_____ 2. Am I aware of the real purpose of each message I send?

_____ 3. Am I sensitive to the emotional impact of the messages I send?

_____ 4. Am I direct, honest, and open?

_____ 5. Do I view communication as a shared activity between parent and child?

_____ 6. Do I express myself well nonverbally?

_____ 7. Are my nonverbal signals compatible with my verbal messages?

_____ 8. Do I ask questions appropriately to enhance my understanding of what my children are communicating?

_____ 9. Am I a good listener?

_____ 10. Can I keep an open mind when communicating with my children?

_____ 11. Am I sensitive to where and how I attempt to communicate with my children?

_____ 12. Do I interpret correctly the feedback that children give to me?

Once you have an idea of what your strengths and weaknesses are, you can then begin to examine alternative ways of communicating. In order to do this, you must know the components of the communication process.

FAMILY COMMUNICATION COMPONENTS

At a PTA discussion one evening, Frances, a mother of two junior high age children, expressed some thoughts that are common to many parents: "It seems like my kids speak a foreign language or something. I am having more and more difficulty getting through to them. And frankly, half of the time I don't know what they are talking about." On the surface, communication seems like such a simple process: one person says something and another person says something back. But a true understanding of the process of communication depends on a more thorough analysis. Let us begin by examining a model of the communication process:

ENVIRONMENT

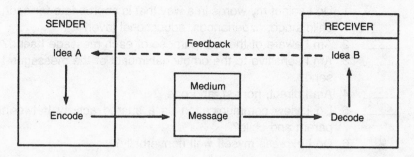

The interaction begins with a thought (Idea A) in the mind of the sender that he or she wishes to transmit to the receiver. Suppose a mother wakes up ill and wants to ask her son for some support. Since direct mind-to-mind telepathy is not possible (as far as we know!), some indirect path to the receiver's brain must be used. The sender (the mother) must *encode* her message into some symbol that can be understood by the receiver (her son): spoken or written words, gestures, or postures that will convey the meaning of "Idea A." She may decide to say, "Sam, I'm not feeling well and I'm going to need some extra help today." Along with this verbal message, the tiredness in her voice and droopy eyes may transmit the unspoken message: "I really feel rotten." Another *medium* or communication channel could have been chosen. Rather than this face-to-face verbal-nonverbal message to Sam alone, the mother might have written a note and gone back to bed, telephoned from work, or addressed the whole family at breakfast.

After the message has been sent, the receiver must *decode* it, or translate it into a thought that is meaningful. We call this "Idea B," because although it may be very close to the sender's original Idea A, it can never be an exact match. Even when the communication is excellent, there just simply are not enough codes (words, questions, gestures, etc.) to express every idea totally, and no two people interpret the same code in exactly the same way. When the receiver has decoded the message, his or her reactions transmit *feedback* to the sender. A concerned look on Sam's face and his quick "Sure, Mom. What can I do to help?" let his mother know that her intended message had been received.

BARRIERS TO EFFECTIVE COMMUNICATION

Barriers to effective parent-child communication can exist within the environment, in the sender or receiver, in the encoding or decoding process, and in the sending or receiving of feedback.

One of the most common obstacles is an unfavorable setting. Normal family life today is full of distractions that make it difficult for any two people to concentrate on each other. Even when the setting appears quiet, the hidden distractions of trying to accomplish much in limited time can make communication hard. For example, it would be most difficult for a father and son to have a "heart-to-heart" discussion concerning an intimate issue while sitting in a crowded fast-food restaurant with other young people all around them and within earshot.

The emotional environment can be another barrier to effective communication. Past experiences—recent or of long standing—may make sender and receiver fearful or distrustful of each other on a certain topic. If Sam's mother, for instance, frequently pleads illness to get Sam to help her so that Sam feels resentful of her dependence on him, their communication on this subject is hardly likely to be successful.

Other emotional factors within sender or receiver can hamper communication. Often either or both have mixed motivations to exchange a certain message, especially when it is a negative one. Matt, the single father of thirteen-year-old Jason, had received a substantial reduction in pay due to a reorganization at the company where he worked. A drastic cutback in their life-style would be necessary for some time to avoid serious financial problems. This was a message that Matt, a proud man, did not want to send—any more than Jason, a boy who needed very much to keep up with his peers, wanted to receive it. Matt's idea, "We must cut our expenditures by one third," was softened to the spoken message, "We'll probably have to cut back spending a little." With the message further softened by his father's casual attitude, Jason decided, "We might have to give up a few things, but not much and not for long." This is quite a far cry from the intended message.

With communication so strongly linked to the emotions, many other factors can become communication barriers. The sender may be afraid of the receiver's reaction to the message or feel inadequate as a communicator. The receiver may react to an assumption or inference made about the message (or sender), rather than to the actual message. A child may say, "I really don't feel like going to school today," fully intending to go but needing to express negative feelings about her teacher. If her mother assumes the child wants to get out of school to avoid a spelling test, she may respond, "I don't care, you're going anyway." Not only has this interchange been unsuccessful; the possibility of future positive communication on the subject has been greatly diminished. Reacting to assumptions or inferences instead of the actual message is a fairly frequent problem in family communication. Familiarity may not always breed contempt, but often the frequency of contact between parent and child leads them to form conclusions about what the other is saying and feeling—and why. Often these conclusions have little merit and could be completely erroneous.

To avoid such problems it is important for the receiver to try to discern the purpose for the sender's message. There are four basic communication purposes: social (to maintain a relationship but not exchange any meaningful message); informational (to give, receive, ask for, or exchange facts or knowledge); expressive (to convey feelings or attitudes); and persuasive (to convince the receiver to change his attitude or behavior). If the receiver is to understand the sender's message, it is important for him or her to understand why the message is being sent. Many communication misunderstandings occur when the purpose is misunderstood. When a mother asks, "How was school today?" as a social question, she needs to be aware that the purpose of a message that she receives in response may not be obvious. "O.k., except for English" could simply be a social answer to her social question. Or it could be meant to convey information ("Something happened in English") or perhaps express a feeling ("I'm upset about English class") or even to persuade ("I want you to talk to my English teacher"). If the child's purpose was to express feelings and the mother perceived the message as a social one, further communication could be cut off, at the expense of both parent and child.

Problems with encoding and decoding messages can also create barriers to effective communication. While our supply of words, symbols, and gestures is quite rich, it does not come close to the full range of ideas, feelings, thoughts, and attitudes that can exist within any individual's mind. It is impossible for any message—even a verbally explicit one combined with expressive nonverbal communication—to transmit the exact idea. And since each individual's past experiences with ideas and words are different, the meaning he or she assigns to any word may be different from another person's. When a young child looks miserable and says to his father, "You hurt my feelings," the father must try to understand this message from the child's frame of reference, not his own.

The limited number of available codes and differences in frames of reference can present barriers to effective communication between any two individuals, but can cause even more difficulty between you and your child. Your child's limited vocabulary must express ideas and feelings far more complex than the codes the child has learned to use. The most extreme example is a newborn baby; crying is the only "code" babies can use to express hunger, discomfort, pain, fear, or anything else. Most parents realize that they must work hard to "decode" the message in this case: How long since he's been fed? Is she wet? cold? hot? bored? Could a diaper pin be pinching her? As a child learns to use more and more words, it is important for you to remember that his or her range of words is still limited. Does "I'm hungry" mean "I'm faint from lack of food," "I'm bored and I need something to do," or "I know there's ice cream in the refrigerator?" Not until your children reach late adolescence will their vocabulary equal yours; but, by then, their frames of reference are likely to be vastly different. Only a mother who understands her teenage son's frame of reference would take "That's a really mean outfit, Mom" as a compliment.

Children often have trouble decoding their parents' messages, too. Their minds interpret unfamiliar words according to their own experience, and their interpretation can sometimes be inaccurate. Joan had difficulty understanding why her three-and-a-half-year-old son was suddenly afraid to go in the car with her until, as she was discussing her recent "crash diet" with her friend, her son cried out, "Please don't crash the car, Mommy!"

Another barrier to effective communication is the failure to see that sender and receiver share the responsibility for achieving that goal. The parent who laments, "Why can't that child ever listen? I know I told her she had to be home at three-thirty sharp today," when her thirteen-year-old daughter forgets to come straight home from school to babysit for her little brother, is not entirely blameless in this failed communication. Could she have chosen a better time and place to have asked her daughter to babysit in the first place? Could she have been more aware of other things in her daughter's mind that could have provided mixed motivation for receiving the message? Could she have been more alert to feedback from her daughter that might have indicated her message wasn't totally received? Would an additional communication medium—maybe a note on the refrigerator that morning —reinforce the message? But it is important for parents not to go too far in accepting total responsibility for communication effectiveness. Even small babies learn to take some responsibility for communicating with their parents when they begin to cry differently when they mean "I'm tired" than when they mean "I'm hungry." So when communication fails, it is important for *both* sender and receiver to ask: What could I have done to improve this communication? While parents and children speak and listen to each other with varying degrees of success, much of what is transmitted is never put into words. A major part of family communication is nonverbal in form.

NONVERBAL COMMUNICATION

"I know as soon as my dad walks in the door in the evening what kind of mood he is in; in fact, even before he comes in the house I can tell what kind of a night it is going to be by the way he opens the door." A youngster once shared this insight with us at a recent presentation to high school students. Words are not the only tools parents and children have to convey meaning to each other. Tone of voice, the position and movement of the body, and facial expressions are elements of nonverbal communication. The relative importance of the nonverbal dimension varies according to the purpose of the communication; it is usually much more significant in expressive and persuasive communication than in social or informational. In some cases, the nonverbal elements convey much more meaning than the words themselves. Imagine a nine-year-old boy coming home with a hard-earned B+ on a science project. His mother's response, "Nice job," could express many very different things depending on the nonverbal message that goes with the words. A brief glance from her work and flat tone of voice might say, ". . . but it's not really very important." A sarcastic tone and disgusted look could mean "Couldn't you have done better?" A warm smile, a hug, and an excited voice could tell the child, "You're fantastic!" A hand on the shoulder, a soft voice, and meaningful eye contact might say, "I know how hard you worked. I'm so proud of you."

It is important for parents to be aware of the nonverbal messages they send and receive in order for communication with their children to be most effective. Nonverbal messages are tricky business. There are many standard misinterpretations. For instance, parents often construe lowered eyes as a sure, telltale sign that the child is guilty or attempting to hide something. In some cases this may be an accurate interpretation. But in others it could be the furthest thing from the truth. As a matter of fact, exactly the opposite could be the case: pathological liars tend to boldly look their victims directly in the eyes, overcompensating for their lack of veracity. Likewise, arms crossed over the chest could be interpreted as a sign that the receiver is "closed" to the message. Parents who would directly interpret this gesture to mean "I don't want to hear this" may be harming rather than helping the communication. The child's arms may be crossed because he or she is cold or has a stomach ache!

A more effective way to utilize information from nonverbal messages is to learn from experience how each individual child uses nonverbal means of expression. How do his face and body look, how does her voice sound when she means "I don't care," "This is very important," "This makes me angry, sad, happy, uncomfortable, etc."?

When parents feel that their own messages are not getting through, frequently it is because too little nonverbal communication is being used, or because the words and nonverbal messages do not match. Margery, the mother of six-year-old twin sons, often found that the boys did not respond to her directions to get ready for school, pick up their toys, or come to dinner. She felt that they saw her directions as casual requests rather than directions they were supposed to follow. Margery asked her husband and her best friend, "How do I look and sound when I really mean what I say?" Her friend said that she noticed Margery tilting her head downward and raising her eyebrows slightly when she wanted her message to be more emphatic, and her husband explained that sometimes, when she said, "I want you to clean up your room right now," her tentative tone of voice added ". . . if it's not too much trouble." After practicing a more emphatic expression and tone of voice with her reflection in the mirror, Margery became more aware of her nonverbal communication with the boys and was able to increase the effectiveness of her messages.

Since the nonverbal messages we send are less intentional than the words we speak, actions often do speak louder than words. When a child's nonverbal behavior conveys the same message as his or her words, parents can be fairly sure they have gotten the real message. But when they perceive an inconsistency between the verbal and nonverbal message, it is important to get some clarification: maybe they have misread the nonverbal signals, or perhaps the child's words are not expressing the tone or total message. Phillip's teacher had told his mother Maryanne that some of the boys in Phillip's class were suspected of vandalism at the school. When Maryanne discussed the matter with her son, he said he knew nothing about the incident, but he began squirming nervously in the chair. Maryanne knew that this was the way Phillip acted when he was not telling the truth, but she wisely avoided jumping to the conclusion that he had been involved in the vandalism. Perhaps his nonverbal behavior indicated that he knew who had done it but didn't want to "squeal." He might have been very uncomfortable about being questioned by his mother. Or maybe he felt guilty about some escapade he had participated in but hadn't been punished for. The wise parent avoids assuming that a child's nonverbal behavior has a definite meaning. When parents observe inconsistencies in a child's verbal and nonverbal communications, they should try to clarify the true meaning. Maryanne could try addressing the situation directly by commenting, "You seem uncomfortable about discussing this," or she could try bringing up the subject later in a different way.

If you tune in to the nonverbal messages sent by children as well as by yourself, you will have a powerful tool for improving communication skills. But you must be careful to avoid the pitfall of jumping to premature, inaccurate conclusions based on nonverbal behavior.

SELF-EXPRESSION

"I don't understand it. My kids will look me right in the eye and shake their little heads like they understand me. Then within minutes they go off and do exactly what I told them not to. They do this all the time and it is driving me crazy!" Evelyn, a mother of three youngsters in a Philadelphia suburb, shared her exasperation with other parents recently as many others in the workshop nodded their heads and rolled their eyes in agreement. How many times have you been certain you've gotten your messages across to your children, only to have their behavior indicate they didn't hear you at all—or didn't remember it for very long? For most parents, this is a fairly frequent occurrence. Once they have sent a message they assume that it has been received. Quite often that is a false assumption. Sometimes, parents become so frustrated by unsuccessful communication that they stop trying, or allow their irritation to show in their messages, which further decreases their potential for effectiveness.

There are many guidelines you can use to enhance the effectiveness of the messages you send. The first is to know the purpose of your message. Do you want to build or maintain your relationship with your child? Do you want to give or receive some sort of factual information? Do you want to express feelings or encourage the child to express his? Do you want to teach something, reinforce a value, change an attitude or behavior? Only when you have the purpose of the communication very clear in mind can you evaluate its success and change tactics if it is not working.

Some communications require more planning than others, especially when the purpose is to discuss a difficult subject, express strong or negative motives, or effect some type of change. It is sometimes helpful in planning very important or sensitive communications to clarify thoughts in writing before talking with the child. Fallacies in arguments and potential barriers to effective communication can become clearer, and parents can be more certain that they will achieve the purpose of the communication.

Tom and Susan, the parents of two bright teenagers, take this writing-planning stage one step further. When any family member has something important or sensitive to discuss with another, he or she tells the other what the subject is, and both of them write a one-page statement about their thoughts, opinions, and feelings on that subject. Then, before any verbal discussion on the subject, they exchange and read their statements. This process proved very helpful when Tom wanted to express his concerns and persuade his son to be cautious when he obtained his driver's license. He wanted his son to know that his fears were based on his love for him and concern for his safety and well-being, not on a lack of trust. Writing about his thoughts and feelings ensured that Tom expressed all that was on his mind. Giving the statement to his son to read before their discussion prevented him from backing down or becoming defensive if he felt his verbal message was not well received. And because his son followed the same procedure, Tom was forced to focus on his son's thoughts and feelings as well as his own.

Besides knowing the purpose of the message, it is important for parents to know their intended receiver as well as possible. It may seem silly to say that parents need to know their children in order to better communicate with them; after all, what two people spend more time together or share a deeper relationship than parent and child? However, it is precisely this closeness and familiarity between parent and child that often makes communication difficult. We are so close to our children that we often erroneously assume we know how they are thinking and feeling.

As we have mentioned before, each individual has a unique combination of background, experiences, personality, and other characteristics that influence everything he or she perceives. When the sender and receiver of a message have similar frames of reference, effective communication is much easier than when the area of shared experience is small.

Until children are well into adulthood their parents' frames of reference are much larger than theirs. A newborn infant has a tiny frame of reference that consists of inborn traits and intrauterine experiences; most of the baby's very narrow frame of reference is shared with the mother. As children grow, their frame of reference increases in overall size, and they begin to collect information and develop personally in areas outside the experiences and characteristics they share with their mother and father.

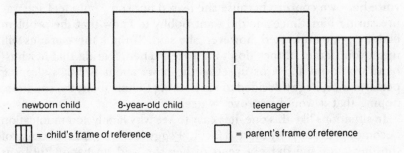

newborn child   8-year-old child   teenager

▯▯▯ = child's frame of reference   ▯ = parent's frame of reference

While the child's growing experiences and knowledge make it easier in some ways to communicate as the area of shared experiences and characteristics increases, the potential for communication problems increases too. The child's frame of reference outside the mother's experience is growing at the same time, and with it the chances for misunderstanding and false assumptions.

As children's experiences and personality outside the parents' frame of reference grow, they are more likely to have mixed motivation to receive parental messages. They may be so preoccupied with their own ideas, thoughts, and feelings that they are unable to pay attention to the parents'. When a three-year-old is so absorbed in his play that he ignores his mother's calls to get ready to go shopping, or when a teenager swears that dad never told her about the upcoming business trip he has been talking about for days, their inability to listen well is often not deliberate. Becoming angry and resentful at the child's inattention to the messages is counterproductive. Screaming or moaning, "Can't you ever listen to me! How many times do I have to tell you . . ." is likely to get the child's attention, but may actually decrease his or her motivation to listen to what parents want to say. Use of emphatic (but not angry) nonverbal communication, finding a more appropriate time when the child is less preoccupied, or asking the child to repeat the message can sometimes be effective.

Another way to increase the effectiveness of messages is to strive to be direct, honest, and open in what you say to your children. Because many parents have been socialized to be indirect, or to soften the blow of difficult messages, this is sometimes difficult. Peggy, a Cleveland mother of three children, spent much of her life feeling hurt and resentful that no one in her family seemed to listen to her or take her seriously. When Bobby, her eight-year-old, began bringing papers with slipping grades home from school, she couldn't bring herself to voice her own concern because she feared her son would feel she was pressuring him. Since she did want Bobby to know that the problem had not gone unnoticed, however, she said, "I think these grades will upset your father, if they don't improve." Then, fearing that her husband would be angry or upset at the news about Bobby's slipping performance, Peggy decided to say nothing to him about the situation, hoping that it would improve by itself.

In situations like this one, it is easy to see why family communication becomes progressively more difficult. Peggy feels resentful because of the messages she did not send to her son and husband; Bobby is confused about both of his parents' feelings and expectations; and his father may sense that something is wrong but feel left in the dark about it.

Peggy's nonassertive, indirect communication habits were particularly hard to break. Her mother had always hidden her own thoughts and feelings in a misdirected attempt to maintain a harmonious family atmosphere. Peggy learned from her mother's example to suppress her own ideas and feelings much of the time and, when she did try to express herself, to attribute her thoughts to someone else, or to "drop hints" rather than express herself directly. When the anger at herself and her family became almost intolerable and was overtly expressed by increasingly bitter statements of resentment about her family, a close friend suggested that she take an assertiveness class at a local college. There Peggy learned that she had a perfect right to have and express her own ideas, and that direct communication often need not be seen as horrible or selfish. In fact, Peggy found that as she began to express herself more directly, not only did she feel better about herself, but her family seemed less confused and resentful.

Understanding the communication process and respecting its complexity, then, is critical for effective motherhood and fatherhood: it is one of the cornerstones of parentship. In addition to a knowledge of the nature and difficulties of this process, parents need to develop specific communication skills, some of which will be addressed in the next chapter.

5

Parent-Child Communication: Key Skills

We have found several communication skills to be most important in parent-child relations. If they are performed well, they can be the foundation for success in parenting. However, if executed poorly or if completely absent, the seeds of much discord are sown. These communication skills include asking questions; listening; feedback; and group communication.

ASKING QUESTIONS

The right questions asked in the right way can greatly facilitate the exchange of information between parent and child. Parents can learn this skill by understanding the difference between various types of questions and when to use them. A closed question is one that requires a "yes" or "no" answer or asks the child to select from a few choices: "Did you put on your boots?" "Would you prefer rice or potatoes with chicken for dinner?" Closed questions are good to use when parents need a limited amount of information. If rice and potatoes are the only choices available, it makes sense to limit the answer to that question. Information gained from closed questions is likely to be concise and fairly easy to interpret, but it is also quite limited. It is often important to get at information that remains unexpressed in response to a closed question.

Susan's nine-year-old daughter, Ellen, had been very unhappy after the family's recent cross-country move to Oregon. She cried often, lost her appetite, and began having nightmares. One morning after Ellen had eaten a little more breakfast than usual, Susan asked, "Are you feeling better, honey?" Ellen's response, "Yes, a little," was true: she did feel a bit better, but she still ached for her old friends and missed her former teacher terribly. She had mixed feelings about sharing her emotions with her mother, but since Susan seemed satisfied with her answer she decided to keep the rest of the information to herself.

Susan would have had a better chance of hearing this if she had asked a more open-ended question. She probably would have understood what was going on with Ellen much better if she had asked, "How are you feeling about our move now?" or "Tell me how things are going for you at your new school?" These broad, general questions allow the child greater freedom of response and almost always yield more information than closed questions. Sometimes new and valuable information previously hidden from the parent is uncovered. One afternoon when Ellen came home from school, Susan could tell she had been crying. She guided her to the couch, sat down with her, and asked, "Tell me, what made you so unhappy today?" Through a torrent of tears, Ellen revealed her feelings about her new school, classmates, and teacher, and told her mother about two problems she had not discussed before: her New York style of clothes made her feel out of place and she was bored with several school subjects that had already been covered in her old school. It became very apparent to Susan that Ellen really needed much more support and help from her parents than she had been able to ask for before.

Open-ended questions do not always work so well with a child who is reluctant to share information. If she had felt guilty about her feelings or wanted to keep them from her mother for some reason, Ellen may have responded to her mother's question (as many children would have) with a noncommittal "Oh, nothing." When a parent realizes that there is more important information hidden below the surface of the child's answer, probing comments and questions can be helpful: "Tell me more," "I don't quite understand," or "Could you explain what you mean?" are examples. Clarifying questions, such as "Do you mean that your teacher doesn't listen to you?" or paraphrasing or repeating what the child has said not only encourages the child to open up, but also gives both parent and child the chance to verify that the right message has gotten through. When a child seems reluctant to respond to an open-ended question, following up with a well-chosen closed question that gets to the heart of the matter often works. By varying the mixture of open-ended questions to get at important, hidden information and closed questions to keep the conversation on track and to keep it going when the child begins to close up, any parent can become an effective interviewer.

Using open-ended, closed, probing, and clarifying questions appropriately, the dialogue between Ellen and her mother might have gone like this:

SUSAN: It looks like you've been crying. Tell me, what made you so unhappy today? (Open-ended question)

ELLEN: Oh, nothing.

SUSAN: Did you have science today? (Closed, probing question)

ELLEN: Yes—we did the same stupid experiment we did at my old school in second grade. This is a really dumb school.

SUSAN: You feel your new school is too easy, is that it? (Clarifying question)

ELLEN: It's so boring.

SUSAN: Could you tell me what makes it boring? (Open-ended probing question)

ELLEN: Everything is boring.

SUSAN: How about your teacher? Is she boring? (Closed probing question)

ELLEN: Yeah, in a way. She just doesn't seem to care about the kids the way Mrs. Wilson did.

SUSAN: She doesn't care about you? (Paraphrase)

ELLEN: No—she hardly ever smiles or talks to anyone except about schoolwork . . .

Through this "interview" with Ellen, Susan was able to gain much valuable information about just what was going on with her daughter and so was much better able to understand and support her. Ellen felt relieved to get it "off her chest" and thankful that her mom really cared about how she felt.

There are other types of questions that can also be helpful to parents. Third-person questions, which ask children to express how someone else feels about a situation, can get them "off the hook" if they are reluctant to express their own feelings. When asked, "How do some of the other kids seem to feel about this?" a child may project his or her own feelings and express them indirectly, since it is sometimes safer to say, "Some kids are really angry" than "I'm really angry." Skillful probing and clarification are necessary to ascertain whether children really are expressing their own thoughts. "How about you?" or "Tell me about a time when you felt angry" could be good questions for Susan to use to find out if Ellen was one of the kids who felt angry.

Hypothetical questions often help both parent and child to better understand a situation and to explore alternative ways of dealing with it. With a brief analysis of the situation, most parents can set up a situation indirectly related to the topic under discussion. Susan might ask, "What advice would you give one of your friends before she moved across the country?" or "If you could start over on moving day, what would you do differently this time?"

We rarely think of silence as a questioning technique, but silence can often be used as a very effective means to uncover additional information—or, used improperly, can cut off communication altogether. Whether silence is effective or destructive depends on the nonverbal communication that accompanies it. Silence works because it causes some amount of discomfort during a conversation; both parties feel compelled to fill up the silence by saying something. Most adults and children can tolerate only a few seconds of silence before they are affected emotionally and feel uncomfortable. This is why the so-called pregnant pause is so powerful a rhetorical device. If the parent's nonverbal message during a period of silence says, "I'm interested, I care, and I will accept whatever you have to say," the child's discomfort will be softened by the encouragement to open up. On the other hand, if the nonverbal message is "I'm tired of talking about this and want to stop," or "Well, spit it out, I don't have all day," the discomfort will be intensified and the communication closed.

There is one type of question that parents need to avoid: the leading question. These questions telegraph to the child the response wanted and often lead to misinformation. When Ellen is asked, "Are you feeling happier at school, now?" she may think to herself, "My mother wants me to be happy at school" rather than "My mother wants to know how I'm feeling at school." Her response will most likely be quite different than if she had been asked, "How are you feeling about school now?" Any time parents begin a question with "Isn't it terrible . . ." (or "wonderful," or "exciting," etc.) or "Don't you think that . . . ," they should be aware that the response they get might often be a reflection of their own feelings or thoughts, and not the child's.

Throughout any "interview" with a child, no matter what the purpose, it is necessary to recognize and avoid a few questioning pitfalls. First, avoid interrogating a child. Anyone can become defensive and uncommunicative when one is the target of a series of rapidly fired questions. Children are particularly susceptible to feelings of powerlessness and will often clam up at the first hint of an inquisition. You should strive for a natural, conversational tone interspersed with some anecdotes and personal reflections, careful that your own comments do not lead away from the child's own thoughts. If there is some give-and-take in the interviews, rather than the parent constantly talking and child constantly giving information, both will feel more comfortable and more information will be exchanged. Second, you must be sure to exercise sufficient "wait time" after asking a question. Most fathers and mothers do not provide enough time for a well-thought-out answer. It generally takes your children much longer to formulate a meaningful response than you estimate. When wait time allowed by parents is not compatible with the time needed by children, two possibilities are likely to occur: parents will manifest impatience and/or children will blurt out a half-constructed answer just to please the parent and avoid verbal or nonverbal reprimand and rejection.

Third, you must keep an open mind. Many fathers and mothers, even experienced ones, tend to form a quick judgment about what they are hearing and block out any information that does not go along with that judgment. Parents are notorious implementors of "selective perception," the tendency to magnify information that supports their beliefs and viewpoints relating to their children and minimize contradictory evidence. This happens frequently in parent-child communication because parents think that they know their child so well. Furthermore, they have arranged this knowledge into a set of beliefs and expectations. If you find yourself forming a judgment or coming to a conclusion about what a child is saying, you should try to ask questions that will *disprove* rather than *confirm* your judgment. For example, if a child says, "Maybe I need glasses—I get headaches sometimes and lots of kids at school have been getting neat glasses," you might conclude that the child wants glasses as a status symbol. Rather than assuming that you have gotten the message or asking a leading question to confirm your judgment ("So you think glasses would be neat?"), you should try to ask a question that might prove the conclusion wrong, such as "Tell me more about your headaches." Remember that getting the complete, accurate message is far more important than being right —and will be greatly enhanced by the "other side" of communication:

listening. The best answers to the best questions are useless if fathers and mothers do not really listen.

LISTENING

"Frankly, my dad drives me absolutely crazy because he never really pays attention to me when I'm trying to tell him something. He looks spaced out or yawns or looks out the window right when I'm at the high point of my story or problem. Half the time I end up mumbling to myself and he doesn't even realize that I've stopped talking to him. He always looks so bored with me. I can't wait to get out of that house. I guess that I'll be doing him a big favor." As he wiped away the tears coming down his cheeks, these innermost thoughts were shared by the fifteen-year-old son of a Washington, D.C., attorney. The father was astounded to learn of his son's feelings and wept even more profusely when learning of them in a family counseling session.

Listening is the most difficult communication skill to master, but it is also the single most important one. When parents listen—really listen —to their children they give them the greatest gift a parent can bestow: attention. They show love, caring, and support; they let their children know that they are valued and important; and they get to know who the children really are. When parents listen to children, two important things happen: (1) they gain information about them, a distinct advantage when we consider that the essence of parentship is being able to negotiate effectively through a knowledge of the children's real needs; and (2) they develop an emotional bond with their children—it is psychologically impossible for a child to dislike a parent who really listens to him or her. They will always want to go back for more. Parents will often throw their hands up in exasperation and sometimes desperation: "How do you get through to these kids? They listen to their friends more than to me. How am I going to compete with tapes, records, movies, video discs? How?" We often ask in response, "Have you tried listening?" Parents can always win the "communication battle" by listening. The greatest psychological reward for children is attention, and no one is capable of giving them more than their parents who, after all, have the most interest in them.

If parents put their mind to it, no friend or peer of their children can successfully compete with them when it comes to granting attention through listening. Video and audio technology, no matter how sophisticated, is only capable of sending messages; it doesn't have the capacity to receive them actively. It takes attention and does not return it. It offers a nonreciprocal relationship with which parents can no doubt compete if they try.

Very small children are excellent listeners. They have to be; listening is their major way of making contact with the world. As children learn to talk, read, and write, they concentrate on these new skills, and as they grow up their listening acuity gradually diminishes. Public and private schools teach reading, writing, and public speaking, but classes in listening are extremely rare, if they exist at all.

Listening is hard work. Unlike hearing, which is involuntary, listening requires concentrated effort. Human nature, the environment, and the unique characteristics of parent-child communication cause many problems for the parent as listener. For one thing, parents are often too busy talking to listen. Parents must teach, advise, explain, inform, discipline, and motivate their children. Sometimes so much time and energy is spent sending these important messages that there is no time or energy left to allow messages to flow back the other way. Even when they are not talking, parents' minds are often preoccupied with their own concerns and interests, and it is often difficult to put these aside in order to concentrate on what the child is saying.

Human beings can hear at the rate of 400 words per minute, while the normal speaking rate for adults is about 125 words per minute; for children the rate is much slower. The brain of the listener, then, has some extra time and tends to keep busy by thinking of other things instead of concentrating on the message. And children—as much as parents love them—can sometimes be—well, frankly, boring. Their monologues about what they saw on an excursion through the neighborhood, questions such as "How do they make highways?" and naïve impressions of the world can often seem trivial and easy to ignore in comparison to parental thoughts about work, family finances, relationships with spouses, etc.

Research indicates that people of higher status tend to spend less effort listening to people of lower status and that they tend to interrupt them more often. Children obviously have a lower status than their parents. Their limited vocabulary and relatively inferior speaking ability often makes it difficult or uncomfortable to listen to or understand them. There is also a physiological dimension to listening: it is one of the most exhausting in which a parent can engage. When a parent truly listens to a child intently and actively, pulse rate and blood pressure may increase as it would if he or she were engaging in physical exercise. It is a tiring experience and in fact is one of the more energy-consuming activities in which parents engage. However, parents can get themselves into good "listening shape" by gradually training themselves to build up the energy needed to listen effectively, just as joggers condition themselves to jog longer and longer distances by expanding the capacity of their cardiovascular and aerobic capacities. Listening, then, is by no means a passive event. Parents who listen are not spectators; they engage in very strenuous action.

With so many factors that can present barriers to effective listening, it is easy to see why listening is so difficult. But your listening skills can be improved by doing a number of things which anyone can learn. The first is to pay attention to how much time is spent talking and how much is spent listening. Although there is no specific rule about what percent of time should be spent listening, parents must remember that they cannot really listen when they are talking. If you find yourself doing half or more of the talking in your conversations with your children, you may not have enough time to listen well. You should make an effort to put aside some of the less important things you have to say so you can pay more attention to the children. Patience is a real virtue when it comes to listening to children. You must remember that you can hear much faster than the children can talk. You have to work hard to resist the temptation to get mentally sidetracked. You must keep your mind focused on the child and what he or she is saying and use any extra mental time to check on how you are listening.

It is much easier to listen when you look as if you are interested. When the body is in a position that shows you want to listen, it becomes easier to concentrate on what the child is saying and it is actually much more difficult to become distracted. You can look ready to listen by turning away from anything else you might be doing and leaning slightly toward the child. Establishing comfortable eye contact is also important, but you should avoid constant staring which can make both you and your children feel uncomfortable. While every mother and father must establish their own pattern of eye contact that feels right with each child, most children generally respond best to the eyes meeting briefly, then breaking away but staying in the vicinity of the other person's face, and then meeting again.

Keep in mind that the first goal in listening is to understand, not to evaluate. Forming judgments about what a child is saying not only distracts parents from really listening, but their judgment is often transmitted to the child through nonverbal signals, and communication could be cut off. If it is necessary to evaluate what the child has said, remember that there will be time for that later, after the child has finished talking.

Listening is also facilitated when the parent truly empathizes with the child. You should try to put yourself in your children's shoes; strive to be aware of their own point of view in order to understand what they are feeling and thinking. Most parents see themselves as sensitive to their children's thoughts and feelings, but true empathy is very hard to achieve. It is difficult to strip away your own feelings, thoughts, and personality to be able to see things from a child's frame of reference. It is often helpful to practice empathizing with children when one is not actively listening to them. As you watch your child at play with other children, eating lunch, getting ready for bed, etc., you might try to remember what you were thinking and feeling at that age. Since no two people are alike, what is going on in the child's mind now is somewhat different or perhaps very different from your thoughts at that age. Getting away from your own adult perspective can be very helpful in enhancing the empathy you feel with your children.

True empathy is impossible without accepting one's children and their right to think and act as they do, regardless of how one feels about it. This is hard enough to do with acquaintances, but when the other person is your own child, it is sometimes next to impossible. It is not easy to say, "I accept my child as he is despite the fact that I don't like his poor grades" (or insolent attitude, or choice of friends, or careless behavior, or thoughtlessness). As a matter of fact, parents *are* responsible for guiding the child's behavior and trying to change it when he or she behaves inappropriately. But before any change is possible, it is necessary to understand the child as the child is. Often, the only way parents can hope to do this is to look at their children as persons separate from their own behavior. The love and acceptance a parent feels can remain constant, even as the child's behavior fluctuates from stellar to unacceptable.

Separating facts from inferences is another skill that can help you become better listeners. When individuals interact as frequently as most parents and children, the natural tendency is to shortcut the listening process by taking something that the child has said, interpreting it mentally, and then reacting to that interpretation. Though making inferences about messages is an important aspect of communication, it can often cause problems, as in this illustration:

CHILD: "You're late coming home from work today."

PARENT'S INFERENCE: (I'm sure the kids resent my spending less time with them since I took my new job. He's pointing out that I'm late to make me feel bad about working so much.)

PARENT'S RESPONSE: "You've got to understand how hard it is to juggle working and caring for a family. I do my best but I can't be in two places at one time."

The only fact here is that the child has pointed out that his mother is late coming home from work. The parent's inference that the child resents her working and wants to make her feel guilty may or may not be correct. He may simply be using small talk as a conversation opener, or he may want to express his sympathy for the difficulty he sees his parent facing. If the parent had added ". . . but my inference might be wrong" to the assumption she made about her child's statement, it would have been easier to avoid a possible misinterpretation of the child's intent. She might have simply said, "Yes, I am late today." If she felt that this was the right time and place to discuss their feelings about her work, she could have added, "Tell me how you feel when I'm late."

Children can often tell how well their parents are listening to them by the responses they get from them. Carl Rogers, one of the fathers of modern counseling techniques, has strongly emphasized the importance of this factor in successful helping and supporting relationships. It is no less critical in the parent-child interaction. Most parental responses fall into five distinct styles. You can determine your own dominant style by completing the exercise below.

PARENTAL LISTENING-RESPONSE INDEX

To determine how your children might perceive your listening-response style, for each lettered statement select the response that is closest to the way you would respond to your child. Be frank and honest. There are no absolutely correct answers.

A. Your preschooler says, "I never want to learn to read."
  1. "Don't worry, honey. Teachers know how to teach children to read and you'll have me to help you."
  2. "Why not?"
  3. "It's silly to worry about it. You're a bright child and you won't have any trouble."
  4. "You feel that you don't want to learn to read?"
  5. "You'd better learn to read. I won't raise an illiterate child."

B. Your third grader says, "I got a D on my spelling test."
  1. "Let me see your paper."
  2. "We'd better spend some extra time on spelling homework tonight."

3. "That's terrible. You can do better than that."
4. "After all the help I've given you on your homework, I can't understand it."
5. "You seem to be concerned about your grades."

C. Your teenager says, "I just can't ever talk to you about my boyfriend —you don't even try to understand me!"
1. "Do you feel that I'm not listening to you?"
2. "Give me an example that shows what you mean."
3. "That boy is not good for you."
4. "I'm trying as hard as I can."
5. "If you would just sit down and talk to me like an adult, maybe it would be easier to listen to you."

D. Your preschooler says, "I'm leaving—I'm not gonna be your little girl any more!"
1. "You're too little to be able to take care of yourself."
2. "You feel like running away from me?"
3. "You'd have to look pretty hard to find someone to care for you as well as I do."
4. "Why don't you think about what it would be like without your family?"
5. "What makes you feel that way?"

E. Your ten-year-old says, "Nobody likes me—I'm so unpopular."
1. "I think you should be more friendly with the other kids, then they'd be nicer to you."
2. "Oh, no, honey—lots of people like you."
3. "It seems that you feel you don't have any friends."
4. "Tell me more about it."
5. "I do all I can to help you make friends."

The five listening-response styles are judgmental, advisory, probing, understanding, and defensive. This is the key to the responses:

Parent-Child Situation

Style	A	B	C	D	E
judgmental	3	3	3	1	2
advisory	1	2	5	4	1
probing	2	1	2	5	4
understanding	4	5	1	2	3
defensive	5	4	4	3	5

If you selected one type of response style three or more times, your children most likely perceive you as listening and responding to them that way even when you are using a different style. To check your objectivity it is a good idea to ask your spouse, a friend, or even your children to indicate what responses they think you would make.

In general, no one listening response style is better than the others all the time. To be an effective listener, it is important to know what style you tend to use most often and become aware of how this affects the way your children communicate with you. The ideal response style is one that varies appropriately depending on the situation. You need to be able to use (and be perceived as using) all but the defensive style.

As a parent who is responsible for shaping a child's behavior it is often necessary to be judgmental. There are times you must tell your children: "You're right" or "That's wrong." But if children see parents as primarily judgmental listeners, they may communicate very well with them when they think the evaluation of their message will be positive—and hide when they think it will be disapproving.

You also often need to advise your children. Adult experiences and insights can be instrumental in helping a child grow and learn. But a dependent child who views Mom or Dad as an advisory listener may come to them to solve every problem he or she has rather than trying to deal with it alone. A very independent child, on the other hand, will often avoid communicating with a parent who is perceived as an advisory listener; advice is the last thing this child wants or needs.

Probing is also important, as we discussed in the questioning section. Parents often need to know more about what their children are thinking and feeling; asking probing questions can demonstrate parental concern and interest. The child who sees the parent as a probing listener, however, may feel that the parent is intruding in areas he or she doesn't really want to share. Everyone, even the youngest child, has a right to some privacy. When children feel that parents consistently violate their privacy, resentment often builds to the point where they avoid communicating.

Responses that demonstrate understanding or that reflect or paraphrase the child's feelings are also a good way to encourage children to feel comfortable and continue talking. Children are often so relieved and happy that their parents are just trying to understand them—not judge, advise, or probe—that they want to express even more. Even an encouraging "Oh" or "I see" can be viewed as an understanding response. But there are times when all children need to hear their parents' judgments, to get advice from them, or to have them probe for more information. If a parent is viewed mostly as an understanding listener, this may cause frustration and resentment if some of the child's other needs are not being met.

The only type of listening-response style that serves no useful purpose in parent-child communication is the defensive style. Parents often receive messages from their children that they would really rather not hear. Sometimes they feel that their skills as parents are being questioned or that their values or egos are threatened by a child's remark. Although it is human nature to defend ourselves against anyone or anything that threatens us—even our children—defensive responses are likely to cause a potentially productive discussion to disintegrate into an argument.

The best way for parents to continue to evaluate their styles is to check themselves after conversations with their child: Which style(s) did I use? Would another style have been more appropriate in this situation? How do my children view me as a listener, and how does that affect the way they communicate with me? The key is to be able to respond in a judgmental, advisory, probing, or understanding style at the appropriate times and to remember that if one style is used at least half of the time, the child will perceive that you always use that style, and communication in other areas will be adversely affected.

As communication is the most crucial parenting skill, listening is the most important aspect of communication. The time and effort any parent invests in becoming a better listener will pay rich dividends in terms of improved communication, greater satisfaction in being a parent, and a richer parent-child relationship.

FEEDBACK

The complexity of the communication process may seem overwhelming and impossible to master. Some parents may liken it to walking a tightrope. However, all communication has a fail-safe device that can help to evaluate and improve any interaction: feedback. This is the point at which the parent uses the child's verbal and nonverbal signals to determine how the original message has been received. If the feedback you receive says, "O.k., he got the message I sent," you can be pretty sure the communication has been successful. When the feedback indicates "He didn't really hear me," or "He got the wrong message," you must restate, clarify, or find some other way to get the message through. The problem is that you are often in too much of a hurry to take the time for feedback, the last step in the communication cycle. It is too easy to assume that if the message has been sent, it has been received. Most parents have learned only too well how false this assumption can be!

There are many things you can do to become more receptive to feedback—and to give feedback more readily yourself. When you are the speaker, you can actively seek feedback in several ways. You might ask, "How do you feel about what I've said?" or "I'm not sure I've said everything I meant to say. Could you tell me what you heard?" Simply asking, "Do you understand?" is often ineffective: children may respond, "Sure," to avoid admitting they didn't understand or weren't listening. You cannot assume, just because you have asked for feedback, that you will get it. It might take time for your child to collect his or her thoughts or to feel comfortable expressing them, especially if he or she disagrees with you. The ability to wait patiently in silence for feedback is often difficult to learn, but well worth the effort. Be sure, however, that silence communicates encouragement, not impatience or criticism. Likewise, you must be alert to both verbal and nonverbal feedback from children. Just recognizing the importance of feedback is a valuable first step. However, nonverbal signals that don't match the spoken words must be recognized as well: "O.k., Mom, you're right," spoken in a flat tone with eyes averted, probably means the child doesn't really agree with what the parent has said, despite the spoken words.

One of the best ways for you to encourage feedback from a child is to give it yourself when you are on the receiving end of a message. When children are used to having parents say things like "Let me repeat what you said so I'm sure I got it right," or "This is what I think I heard . . . ," they are more likely to provide feedback for the parents' messages without even being asked.

Finally, feedback must be rewarded. It becomes less threatening for children to give feedback actively when they understand it is honest feedback the parents are looking for, not agreement or understanding. If parents solicit feedback and then become angry or defensive when the forthcoming feedback is not what they were looking for, children feel punished rather than rewarded for giving feedback. Comments like "No, that's *not* what I said. *Listen* to me this time," or "Well, even if you don't agree with me I'm still in charge here," will discourage the child from giving honest feedback next time. You can reward honest feedback, even when you disagree with a message, by saying something like "I'm glad I understand you," or "Thanks for being honest with me."

It may take some time to pay more attention to giving and receiving feedback. But the increased effectiveness of communication with feedback actually saves time in the long run. After all, if you do not have time for feedback the first time, when will you find time to correct misunderstandings and get the message straight later?

GROUP COMMUNICATION IN THE FAMILY

We have been looking at communication between two people. But most families have more than two people in them; and a large part of the communication that goes on involves several people. In two-person families, say a single mother and her daughter, there are two possible interaction directions: mother to daughter and daughter to mother. But in a three-person family, the possible combinations increase rapidly: mother to daughter, mother to son, mother to son and daughter, son to daughter, son and daughter to mother, etc. For a five-person family, the total number of possible communication patterns increases exponentially! The communication in each of these combinations will be slightly different than all the others. Family group communications can be very informal (casual mealtime conversations, discussions in the car), or they can be very formal (a serious family discussion about an impending move or a child's discipline problem). Some families even hold regular family meetings complete with their own rules and procedures. No matter what the purpose or setting of a family group discussion, all the techniques for self-expression, nonverbal communication, listening, and feedback apply. The message sender must remember that he has more than one listener to consider, though, and everyone must concentrate a little harder to avoid distraction by the larger group. Effective family group communication is a crucial part of establishing a positive home environment. There are some techniques and rules that will enhance the family's success in this area. First, every participant has the right to be heard. For large active families, at the dinner hour this seems next to impossible. This is how Sylvia, a Ft. Lauderdale mother of four who attended one of our workshops recently, described the situation: "At our house it always seems like there are six senders and no receivers! Everyone comes home from work or school excited or upset about something and anxious to talk about it. We start out with everyone talking, then the noise gets louder and louder as everyone tries to shout down everyone else. But the meal often ends in silence—everybody's sulking because they couldn't get anyone to listen to them." Sylvia decided to initiate a new rule about family conversation at dinner. Starting with whoever went last the previous night, each person has two minutes to talk, uninterrupted, about anything he or she chooses; then the rest of the family has two minutes to respond to what the speaker has said. Sylvia frequently turns to her six-month-old son in the high chair to ask, "And what do you think about this?" Although his "comments" make no verbal sense, his obvious delight in having his whole family's attention focused on him is readily apparent as he makes his contribution to the discussion. Sylvia reports that their dinner discussions are quieter, more satisfying—and longer; they often linger after the meal is finished to discuss a topic of particular interest. "It's not easy," Sylvia says, "but we're all trying harder to listen to each other."

Just as important as the right to speak is each person's right to be silent. Everyone is entitled to some privacy; any person who doesn't want to participate in a particular conversation should be allowed to be silent, without being criticized. Reluctance to participate in family communication over an extended period of time may be a sign of a larger problem that the parents need to address, but this must be discussed privately with the child. And every person has the right to call a halt to any conversation that threatens his or her privacy or self-esteem.

Most family discussions require some leadership to make sure that the rights of every individual are upheld and that the conversation stays on track. When the children are small, it is usually the parents who take the leadership role. But as children grow, they should be taught and encouraged to be leaders themselves. Families with older children who have regular formal meetings sometimes rotate leadership among all family members. It is important not to think of the leader as the chairperson of a meeting with all communication directed to or from that person. Whoever is "leading" a family discussion must be very careful not to monopolize the conversation or impede the free flow of communication among the others. Effective family discussion leaders would not be easily identified by outside observers; they would be careful not to speak more than their share.

Probably the most important task for the parent in leading family group communication is to make sure it happens. Communication in the family—whether one-to-one or group discussion—is the training ground for each child to develop communication skills. The pressures and distractions of contemporary life often make it difficult to get everyone together with enough time and energy to communicate. Many families are so busy with work, school, sports, friends, and activities that they rarely all sit down to a meal together. Family communication is so important to the climate of the home and each child's development that it is essential to find the time, at least a few minutes each day, for the family to get together. Some busy families must actually schedule times for family communication. This time should be sacred. The phone can be taken off the hook, no visitors allowed, and no one excused except in special circumstances. As children participate in family communication they develop their own skills in self-expression, listening, and empathizing with others; they become more alert, aware, and caring. And isn't providing these opportunities what parentship is all about?

FAMILY MEETINGS AND COUNCILS

A growing number of parents feel a need to control the dynamics of their families in a more structured manner, through the establishment of a regularly held meeting or council. Such formal gatherings can be beneficial for family dynamics. They can also serve as a lightning rod for family tensions. First, the meeting can be used for reinforcing the good works, good behavior, and accomplishments of family members. Secondly, it provides a controlled mechanism for airing gripes and complaints. Family members have permission to express openly negative feelings, perceptions of inequity, annoyances, and other grievances. Thirdly, families can use the meeting to plan and discuss future activities, such as outings, camps for children, or family vacations. A fourth purpose of the family meeting is to disseminate information to family members, letting everybody know, if appropriate, what is happening. The family meeting is also a good forum to discuss family business—for example, cash flow problems, unexpected increases in family expenses, or ways of decreasing costs. Another way to use family meetings is for socializing and having fun. With the whirlwind schedules that many families follow it is often difficult to get the family together for even a short period of time. The regularly scheduled meeting could fill the need to share experiences, recount stories, tell jokes, etc. As the children approach adolescence and the teen years, topics such as sex, drugs, or alcohol could be well handled within the context of the family meeting. The final reason for establishing family meetings has more to do with process than content. When families are in crisis, especially if they have been traumatized (e.g., by illness or death of a family member, dire reversal in financial stability, or serious failure on the part of family members), two possibilities are likely with regard to family structure and stability. First, there may be a tendency for the family to fall apart, for the members to pull away from one another as they individually adjust to the new reality. If the trauma and assault on the family unit is sudden and/or from the outside, the tendency to disintegrate is even greater. During such distressful situations families may attempt to come together in a meeting-like setting, but may find this awkward and more stressful as they attempt to experience the dynamics of the family in interaction perhaps for the first time in many weeks, months, or even years. Because of the crisis or emergency nature of the meeting (e.g., after learning that a family member is seriously ill), the dynamics of the interpersonal family relationships will no doubt have some rough edges that could trigger serious, long-lasting difficulties among family members. It is not uncommon, for instance, for trouble among siblings, no matter what age, to begin or crystallize immediately after the death of a parent, sometimes during the funeral preparation itself.

Some families, on the other hand, pull together and become closer in the face of family adversity. Family members become mutually supportive, comforting, and empathic. They get their heads together and develop the determination and strategy to cushion the impact of the trauma, if it is anticipated, or to cope with the consequences which might even be calamitous. Families that are used to meeting regularly will have a distinct advantage when in crisis or at risk. Because they have met together regularly, the basic dysfunctional wrinkles of family meeting dynamics have most likely been eliminated or controlled; members most likely know that other family members will tend to behave in a certain way, say particular things, and react in a certain fashion. Families which meet regularly already have a cohesive ongoing unit that will have to spend less time and energy on the dynamics and maintenance of the family meeting, and more on the mission.

RECOMMENDED RULES FOR FAMILY MEETINGS

If the family meetings are going to be productive and emotionally beneficial for all family members, certain guidelines should be heeded:

1. The setting for the family meetings should be the most comfortable and pleasant space in the house. An occasional meeting at a restaurant or other location conducive to discussion is permissible as well.
2. The meeting should be scheduled for a fixed length of time (forty-

five to sixty minutes) and should be held weekly at a regular, predetermined time (e.g., Fridays, 7–8 P.M.).

3. The agenda for the meeting should be well planned and either read
   or distributed to family members. Any family member may recommend agenda items. Some parents post a blank agenda sheet on the
   bulletin board or refrigerator door and family members write in
   what they would like to hear discussed at the next meeting. Fixed
   amounts of time should be assigned to each agenda item.

4. The schedule should be adhered to closely. However, a few minutes
   off schedule here or there will not matter too much, especially if a
   family member needs a little more time—for example, to complete
   a thought or to understand a concept.

5. The family should keep a record of what goes on at meetings. These
   "minutes" should be written in a notebook or binder so that they
   can be easily stored, retrieved, and referred to as the need warrants.
   When possible, different family members can take turns serving as
   recorder. Some families prefer to audiotape or videotape their
   meetings. This may provide more accuracy, but be less convenient
   for reference.

The family meeting can be a most useful practice for ensuring family
closeness, stability, and strength, and also for teaching children how to
conduct themselves when interacting with others in a formal setting.
Because childhood is indeed the period of apprenticeship for adulthood, the example that parents give to children during family meetings
can affect them throughout their lifetime: how to listen to others; the
role of nonverbal communication; seeing several sides of an issue;
resolving conflicts; follow-through; principles of equity; politeness;
honesty of expression; power of persuasion—all these can be learned
in family meetings. Contemporary fathers and mothers may be well
served in their parentship function by installing the family meeting as
an integral part of their family's dynamics.

6

Planning: Controlling the Family's Destiny

Effective planning ensures control and eliminates surprises. Families that get what they want experience this success because they have invested some time and energy in planning. Parents who do not plan follow a pattern of crisis management and often find themselves playing "catch-up." Lack of planning is symptomatic of being disinterested in or having given up on managing the family's destiny. Every family should engage in short-term and long-term planning and have a micro-plan (six months to one year) and a macro-plan (two to five years). Although parents cannot predict the future perfectly or control everything that the family may encounter, they can chart their family's course to a high degree through planning.

Parents should perform two kinds of planning: long-term and short-term. An integrated family plan would have a high degree of consistency between the two types. The establishment of the long-range plan would set the framework for the short-range ones, and the accomplishment of the short-range plans would bring about the fulfillment of the long-range.

Parents do not plan well for several reasons. First, planning involves thinking and contemplation, which are sometimes difficult to do in the action-oriented environment of the family. "Think? You've got to be kidding! Who's got time to think?" is the response of many mothers and fathers we know. Parents often convince themselves that thinking is impossible, and before one knows it the tail is wagging the dog— their behavior is dictating their objectives. Parents can overcome this barrier by envisioning the action outcomes of both the planning and lack of planning. What will happen if planning takes place? If it doesn't take place? If they concentrate on these behavioral outcomes they can override the temptation to equate planning with an ethereal, speculative, impractical, even dreamy function, a waste of time and energy.

A second barrier to parental planning is the lack of immediate reward. The benefits of planning activities, particularly long-range ones, come to fruition in the future. Parents often feel so inundated with competing pressures for their time and energy that they feel obliged to take care of what they see as immediate concerns first. Planning is often viewed as a luxury that they will "get to" later. Of course, they seldom do because there is always something more pressing. As a result, planning does not take place. To overcome this, parents must carefully analyze their priorities and ask themselves what gives them the greatest return on their time and energy over the long run, not just the short run. If they do, they will find that planning should be near the top; and, if done properly, it will preclude much of the time and energy that they are now expending to deal with crises and problems.

A third barrier to planning in the family is that the beneficiaries of the planning seldom are appreciative of or reward parents for their efforts. Because planning generally has no directly observable and connectable output, children often do not give parents the intrinsic reward and psychological charge that motivates them to do more of it. "If I spend a Saturday working at the plant and earning some extra money, I can buy my kids new bicycles. They can see that and will love me for it. But if I spend a day doing long-range planning for the family, they won't know what I'm doing and that it is for them ultimately," one father in Milwaukee pointed out, shrugging his shoulders. "My kids would much rather have me skate and slap the hockey puck around with them on Saturday morning than sit and plan for the future," another dad quickly added. "Given the choice, I'm probably going to go play with them," he concluded, and most parents in this workshop nodded in agreement. In order to overcome this potential obstacle to planning, parents have to recognize the futility of expecting children to understand or appreciate their planning efforts. In some cases, the beneficiaries of this task might not even be born! Instead, parents must look inward for the rewards that they need to be motivated to plan. The satisfaction that comes through the confidence of knowing that they are indeed doing the right thing and that it will have a payoff is what must keep them going.

Vernon and his wife Dolores live from day to day and spend very little time planning for the future: "Our philosophy is one of enjoying the moment to its fullest. Who knows what's coming? We have no control over it even if we did. Oh, yeah, we save a little money like most folks and have our concerns about the future. But we focus on the now. Tomorrow will take care of itself. Our kids certainly like us this way. We have very little anxiety about what might be coming in our family." This "micro-mentality," as expressed by this Colorado couple, focuses primarily on the short term and has its psychological rewards of enjoying the present, but, if overdone, can have serious managerial deficiencies. Because there is a low investment in the future, there will be minimal returns when they are needed.

Floyd and Marie, a Seattle husband and wife, on the other hand, espouse a "macro-mentality"; they think long and wide: "We certainly try to enjoy the present, especially when it comes to our kids. And it's tempting to spend more time enjoying life now. However, we also feel obliged to look at the whole picture, to develop some long-term goals, and do all that we can to make them happen. As coleaders of our family, we feel that it is the responsible thing to do. We owe it to our children, even our grandchildren in some ways." This point of view and sense of priorities is much more sound and will contribute significantly to effective parentship. If parents can defer the immediate gratification that comes from children's expressions of appreciation so that they will be rewarded by greater appreciation later, they will conquer this serious roadblock and pave the way for a successful future for the family.

When parents do take time for planning and when they are motivated to continue to engage in planning activities, they often make several errors. These are some common ones. First, plans are often unrealistic, usually too optimistic and grandiose. Parents sometimes feel ashamed of modest plans. There is often the feeling that one should think big and somehow it will all happen: "Nothing ventured, nothing gained." Parents must remember that planning, a management skill, is not hoping, a virtue. While hope is a fine personal trait it must be tempered with realism in parentship. A good family plan is not a fantasized notion of the future, or a master wish-list. Rather it should be a workable description of the projected future. To have a plan to accumulate one hundred thousand dollars in the family nest egg during the next five years on a combined present yearly income of forty thousand dollars is not realistic, unless the parents plan to eliminate food, clothing, automobiles, taxes, and entertainment completely! While the plan is noble, it is also quite unattainable.

A second shortcoming in the parental planning process is that of ill-defined objectives. Because family life is so broad in scope and whirlwind-like, the process of family living often gets ahead of the goals. Parents may have a vague concept of mission, but it is often not translated into concrete terms. "I want my children to be well educated" is nice, but what does it mean? "My objective is to have my two daughters reading at least one book every month by the time they are twelve years old" is much more meaningful. The more objectives are crystallized, the greater the probability of attainment by parents. The success of clarification also makes parents think through the feasibility of the achievement of the objectives.

Thirdly, plans often fail because they are too rigid. This usually happens when parents attempt to overcompensate in reaction to a crisis situation which has resulted from poor planning. For instance, a father may have cash flow difficulties and be under stress because of his inability to pay bills on time. In response, he may establish very tight plans to cut household expenses to increase the availability of revenue and eliminate bills completely within two years. The pressure imposed on the family to cut electricity costs, not waste food, and reduce entertainment spending could be so overwhelming that it brings the family to the point where it either disintegrates or abandons the plan. One Cincinnati father in such a situation said he found himself "getting angry at the kids when they would get sick. In fury, I would yell at my little five-year-old, 'Why are you sneezing and coughing? You better take care of yourself or else. Do you think that money to pay the doctor grows on trees around here?' She would sit there crying and crying, totally puzzled. My wife would become upset with me and the situation. All hell would break loose. Our marriage came very close to an end."

Plans sometimes fall flat when parents begin to act prematurely—that is, before the plans are actually completed. Parents who have a "fast track" mentality or behavioral style often are victims of this plight. Anxious to get going and implement what they have planned, these mothers and fathers must learn to be patient more than anything else. Also, it is important for them to learn the importance of testing out the plans to identify any possible wrinkles. All plans are tentative and are always subject to change. They should be written in pencil, not indelible ink. Parents who act prematurely find themselves going back and redoing what they had attempted too soon. It is the old story again: haste makes waste.

Lastly, parents' plans sometimes fail because they are built on faulty assumptions or erroneous facts. Mothers and fathers who incorrectly assume that their children will be interested in what they have planned —as Phil, the father of two teenage sons, did in Chapter 2—find their plans of little value. Parents continuously have to test out their assumptions and perception of "facts" in planning. This is why unilateral planning in the family generally results in problems for all. The time for reciprocal communication is when the plans are being made, not when they are ready for implementation.

How, then, should parents plan? Is there a course of action that fathers and mothers can follow to develop realistic, workable strategic and operational plans for the whole family? The following step-by-step process will be helpful. More than a process, though, it is a way of thinking. Parents will get good at it by practicing it. The more they use it, the more proficient they will become. Eventually it will be second nature. The procedure for parental long- and short-range planning can be used in a very deliberate fashion, whereby parents move through the steps slowly and thoughtfully, or it can serve as a guide for more quickly developed daily plans. Furthermore, the approach allows the coalescing of the family's three-to-five-year long-range plan with day-to-day plans. While this process may seem awkward and time-consuming for parents initially, they will feel more comfortable with it if they practice and if they resist the temptation to see contemplation and deliberation as unprofitable and the antithesis of the more rewarding action.

SYSTEMATIC PLANNING MODEL FOR PARENTS

Effective and efficient planning for parents should include the following phases carried out in sequential order. The amount of time spent on each phase will vary depending on the scope and purpose of the planning; however, some time should be spent in each phase before going on because of the cumulative nature of the process. It is equally important that, in a two-parent home, both father and mother as well as older children (age twelve and over) participate in the construction of the strategic plan. After all, this is the projected big picture and it is beneficial to have as much insight on this as possible from those whom it will affect the most and who will have to carry it out.

PHASE A: DEVELOP IDEAL OBJECTIVES
Parents need to construct an ideal set of goals initially. What is it that you would really like to have happen, the best-case picture?

What would make you totally happy as the leader of the family? It might be to have all your children get all A's in school. It could be to have seventy-five thousand dollars invested. It could be to have children who are always volunteering to help out around the house; or children who express appreciation on a daily basis for all their parents' hard work. It could be all of these. This phase serves two purposes: (1) it brings forth the values that you consider most important; and (2) it allows and forces you to be imaginative—it is always easier to tame a wild idea than to invigorate a meek one. Often parents prematurely screen out possibilities by focusing too heavily on the "can't do's," "ought not's," etc. There will be time enough to do that in phase B. For now, though, you should be as imaginative as possible and feel free to dream about how life could be. Imagination is the spice of the parental planning process. Without it the end product will be bland.

For example, the Reynolds family of Boston established the following ideal objective: to own a three-bedroom summer home on Lake Winnipesaukee, two hours away in New Hampshire, that they could live in from mid-June to late August.

PHASE B: IDENTIFY OBLIGATIONS AND CONSTRAINTS

After establishing a picture of the ideal world, you now must come back to earth and take a close look at the obligations (have to's) and constraints (can't do's) of your family situation. Obligations could include those imposed by law, social customs, family tradition, or health and safety. Constraints could include the obvious ones: time, money, space, and human energy. The more subtle ones are exemplified by lack of interest, unsupportive attitudes, or lack of readiness in terms of knowledge.

It is critical that you recognize all the obligations and constraints that are present. Factual judgments describing what *is* the case, and not value judgments expressing what *should* be the case, are needed here. For instance, while you may feel that your children *should* be interested in going to college, if they are not interested then *that* fact should be included in current plans for the family.

For example, major constraints on the Reynolds' ideal goal (the two-and-a-half-month stay at the lake) were the hardship and expense of Dad's commuting to the office each day in Boston; the initial cost of the property; and the task of maintenance and protection of the property during the months that the family wouldn't be using the summer house.

PHASE C: ESTABLISH ATTAINABLE GOALS FOR THE FAMILY

By meshing the ideal objectives and the constraints you are able to establish goals that are reachable. These are the things that can be done by your family collectively and individually. It is absolutely critical that you set out to reach only those goals that have a high degree of probability of accomplishment, thereby building in success which will trigger more success in an ongoing chain. When unrealistic goals are set, families and their members experience failure and frustration. Robert Browning's "Ah, but a man's reach should exceed his grasp, or what's a heaven for?" may be good poetry but it is not a sound maxim for the leader of the family. Rather, goals should be set after the imagined ideal picture has been tempered by the real world situation. For example, the ideal objective of having all four children attend prep schools and Ivy League colleges might be modified to having only one attend prep school and other private colleges; having all four forego prep school and attend the local state college; or any of a number of alternatives. However, whatever is established as a goal should be possible.

An important part of the process of establishing attainable goals is an audit of resources available to reach those goals. Without the resources (time, money, people, outside institutions, etc.) the goals are meaningless. One useful approach for the linking of goals with resources is matrix management. This method allows you to look at your goals realistically and to develop some new goals that you may not have thought of previously, but for which you have resources. A matrix and the steps to implement it are demonstrated here:

MATRIX MANAGEMENT FOR THE FAMILY

RESOURCES AVAILABLE

	1.	2.	3.	4.	5.
A					
B					
C					
D					
E					

(OBJECTIVES)

1. List one family objective next to each letter (A, B, C, D, E).
2. List each resource available next to one of the numbers.
3. Put a check mark (✓) in the block in the matrix to connect the objective with the resource available.

The summer home idea was the Reynolds' Objective A. When they examined the resources critical to the achievement of their goal—namely, money and time—they concluded that they had eight thousand dollars in cash (outside of emergency funds, college tuition savings, and retirement funds) and that the most that Dad could take off during the summer months was three weeks.

The amount of money available precluded the possibility of a down payment for a three-bedroom home on the lake itself, and the amount of time available for vacation eliminated the dream of having the whole family spend from mid-June through late August there. In addition, the problem of taking care of the property in the interim months was recognized as a financial cost because someone most likely would have to be paid to perform that task.

In light of these constraints, the ideal goal of the Reynolds was then modified to the following: to spend *three* weeks living on *or near* Lake Winnipesaukee between mid-June and late August.

PHASE D: DESIGN ALTERNATIVE METHODS OF REACHING GOALS

Few goals can be reached by only one means. Parents must use their imagination and consider as many alternatives as possible to attain each goal established. If you find yourselves locked into the old conventional ways of doing things, you will not be as successful as you could be. You must break through the shackles of conventionality and not be afraid to brainstorm together and/or with the children and come up with new courses of behavior. In this phase it is important to refrain from prematurely blocking out or discounting what may appear to be "far out" ideas. To do so limits the creative potential of the individual family members to the point where significant self-screening might set in ("I better not say that. It may sound dumb!"). Once again, it is important for you to remember that it is much easier to tame a wild idea than to invigorate a lifeless one.

The Reynoldses considered several options for reaching their reformulated goal of spending three weeks on or near Lake Winnipesaukee: (a) establish a family vacation fund and draw from principal and interest to rent a three-bedroom summer home right on the lake each summer; (b) put a down payment on a smaller home on the lake; (c) put a down payment on a three-bedroom home in the vicinity of the lake, but not right on it; (d) purchase a three-bedroom time-sharing unit near the lake; or (e) find another family who would be interested in sharing in the purchase of a home of the desired size and right on the lake.

PHASE E: DO A COST-BENEFIT ANALYSIS

Once the alternatives have been established it is time for parents to compare and contrast. This is done against two key criteria: (1) What does each alternative cost? (2) What are the benefits? There are several kinds of costs and benefits: money, time, energy, space, happiness, interpersonal relationships, social relations, precedent establishment, dependency, etc. The task in this step is to identify that alternative which has the least cost but the most benefit. In so deciding, all the costs and all the benefits must be considered. Sometimes a trade-off among several alternatives can lead to the formulation of a new, hybrid alternative that has the best components of all the previous ones.

Underlying this step of the planning process is the recognition that the various aspects of family life cannot be dealt with in a vacuum. Each decision will have repercussions on other dimensions of family life. While one course of action may save money, it may in so doing cause severe stress and tension among the family members. What is the greater cost? While another course of action may take more time than alternative ones, it may bring family members closer personally. What is the greater benefit? The answers to these questions will depend on the value placed on each cost and each benefit by the family involved. And the value can change through the history of a particular family. For instance, money could be seen as more valuable than time spent together when Mom is not earning that second income and there is a substantial mortgage to pay. However, the value of money may drop and the value of time increase when there is less of it because Mom is working outside the home and the adolescent children are in need of an empathic listening ear. The following step-by-step process can be used to determine costs and benefits for each alternative. As outlined here, the procedure would be most useful for parental planning at the broader level, where major long-term decisions are made. However, the spirit, if not the detail of the steps, can be used in a crude form at the day-to-day level. Again, the key is to see it less as a mechanical process than as a way of thinking.

PARENTAL COST-BENEFIT ANALYSIS

Step 1: Rank the following factors in terms of their *least value* in your family *at this time*. It will be hard to rank them because they are most likely all valued by you. It is difficult to eliminate good things, but you must force yourself to do so (e.g., if the family factor valued *the least* by you is "money," rank it "1," and if the next least valuable is "happiness," rank it "2," and so on).

Cost-Benefit Factors
(sample)

	Rank		Rank
Achievement of family members	____	Moral principles	____
		Neatness	____
Autonomy	____	Obedience	____
Comfort	____	Peace in the home	____
Confidentiality	____	Perfection	____
Cultural enrichment	____	Physical fitness	____
Enjoyment of money	____	Pride	____
Financial security	____	Privacy of family members	____
Formal education of children	____	Religious faith	____
Fun	____	Rest	____
Good food	____	Safety	____
Happiness	____	Sociability	____
Health	____	Social acceptance	____
Honor	____	Time	____
Human energy	____	Togetherness	____
Knowledge	____	Tradition and customs	____
Material possessions	____		

These factors and rankings can now be used to do a cost-benefit analysis of the alternative courses of action. Factors such as autonomy, enjoyment of money, financial security, fun, privacy of family members, and togetherness are among the most important in the Reynolds family, while perfection, pride, and social acceptance are among the least critical. The relative weight of these factors influenced their choice among the various alternatives which they considered.

Step 2: *List the alternative courses of action being considered and the perceived costs and benefits for each.* After listing the costs and benefits for each alternative, follow steps 3, 4, and 5 to fill in the remaining columns. These are some of the costs and benefits that the Reynoldses considered for the alternative ways of reaching their objective.

Alternative A: Establish a vacation fund and rent a summer home on lake for three weeks.

Costs	Rank	Intensity Rating	Value	Benefits	Rank	Intensity Rating	Value
1 (e.g., lack of ownership may threaten financial security)				1 (e.g., will be right on lake)			
2 etc.				2 etc.			
3				3			
4				4			
5				5			
		Total				Total	

Step 3: In the "Rank" column indicate the relative value of that factor in your family from the procedure completed in Step 1. Remember, the *least* valuable factor is ranked first, the second least valuable second, and so on by process of elimination.

Step 4: In the "Intensity Rating" column indicate the intensity of costs and benefits listed for each course of action, using the scale below:

Costs	**Benefits**
4 = exceptionally costly	4 = exceptionally beneficial
3 = very costly	3 = very beneficial
2 = costly	2 = beneficial
1 = not too costly	1 = not too beneficial

Step 5: Determine the "Value" column by multiplying the "Rank" times the "Intensity Rating" determined in Step 1.

For example, if "Money" was ranked "1" and the parent feels that it would be "very costly" if Alternative A were implemented, "3" (1 x 3) would be written in the "Value" column. If the Reynolds family ranked the lack of ownership as "3" and gave it an intensity rating of "2," the value for this cost in Alternative A would be "6."

Follow the same procedure for each alternative.

Difference between total cost values and total benefit values = _____

Alternative B: Put a down payment on a smaller home on the lake.

Costs	Rank	Intensity Rating	Value	Benefits	Rank	Intensity Rating	Value
1 (e.g., family members' privacy and comfort threatened)				1 (e.g., build financial equity)			
2 etc.				2 etc.			
3				3			
4				4			
5				5			
			Total				Total

Difference between total cost values and total benefit values = _____

Alternative C: Put a down payment on a three-bedroom home in the vicinity of the lake, but not right on it.

Costs	Rank	Intensity Rating	Value	Benefits	Rank	Intensity Rating	Value
1 (e.g., lack of view of lake)				1 (e.g., size will provide comfort and more privacy)			
2 etc.				2 etc.			
3				3			
4				4			
5				5			
		Total				Total	

Difference between total cost values and total benefit values = _____

Step 6: *To determine which alternative (A, B, C, etc.) should be selected, add up the cost and benefit values for each alternative and subtract the total cost value from the total benefit value.* The alternative with the *greatest positive difference* will be the preferable one in light of the total situation.

The Reynolds family, using this approach, ended up deciding to purchase a time-sharing three-bedroom condominium unit approximately one half mile from the lake. This option provides them with equity, comfort, family member privacy, and proximity to the lake. It also eliminated the problem of maintenance and security during the interim periods when the family would not be utilizing the property.

PHASE F: DEVELOP A SCHEDULE FOR THE PLAN

Once the preferable course of action has been selected by means of cost-benefit analysis, it is necessary to develop a time schedule for implementing the plan. What is the target date for the goal? The projected completion time should not be too optimistic nor too pessimistic. It should be based on a careful and deliberative estimate of the length of time needed to achieve each task. By adding up all these individual times, the total projected time will be determined.

PHASE G: CONSIDER POSSIBLE CONTINGENCIES FOR FAILED PLANS

If the plan has been carefully thought through and developed realistically, it should be implemented smoothly. Of course, because plans are basically forecasts, they are very sensitive to changes that may be unpredictable. Good plans always include some contingencies and "fallback" positions: "What will happen if such and such a thing were to occur?" or "What will happen if this plan fails?" While all threats to the plan cannot be uncovered ahead of time, the more parents think about them the better. In thinking about potential threats to family plans, you should consider how much control you would actually have over each: total, some, or no control? It would also be wise to describe each threat, consider its consequences, determine its probability, know what the family has at stake, and plan ways to ward off the threat, if at all possible.

PHASE H: IMPLEMENT THE PLAN

At this point planning ceases and operations begin. Most plans are phased in over a period of time following the schedule established in Phase F. The key task for you will be to closely monitor the plan as it is implemented.

PHASE I: EVALUATE RESULTS

After the plan of action has been implemented it is critical for you to assess results. The key questions to be answered will be: Were the objectives reached at the level expected? Were the goals as worthwhile as anticipated? Should the goals be sought again? Should they become an ongoing part of family life? Should anything be modified: goals, process, priorities, cost-benefit factors?

In conclusion, you need to motivate yourselves continually to spend the time and energy needed to plan effectively. You must remember that planning is the parentship function that is the most tempting to abandon. When you plan, you should be sure that specific family goals are consistent with overall long-term objectives and strategies; are specific in terms of accomplishments desired; are realistic and attainable; have a time frame; and are consistent with each other. If these principles are kept in mind, the plan should be a living document capable of guiding the family into the immediate and long-term future, allowing it to determine its destiny and not to simply react to the surrounding environment.

7

Decision Making: The Who, What, When, and Why of Family Life

Family life decisions are increasingly complex: Should I have another child now or go to graduate school first? Which nursery school should I select for my daughter? Should we buy that summer cottage at the beach or save the money for Jimmy's college education?

Key words for family leaders in the 1980s and 1990s will be "alternatives" and "choices." Because of responsibilities, obligations, time pressures, and the scarcity of other resources, parents will have to become more adept at making effective, efficient, and timely decisions. These decisions are often complex and involve children, spouses, money, space, jobs, personal development, education, family goals, and values. The decision process will involve tradeoffs and the need to establish priorities. If approached haphazardly, unsystematically, or spontaneously, decision making can lead to disaster for the family. Poor decision making inevitably results in high anxiety among family members, confusion over goals, poor communications, and low confidence in parents by children. A key characteristic of the successful parent is the ability to make sound decisions.

Fathers and mothers do not make good decisions for several reasons. First, some parents just do not know how. They have never been expected to make them. Or they simply make decisions as they witnessed their own parents making them, which might have been seat-of-the-pants style. How to make decisions, particularly in a family setting, generally has been something learned by imitation. And the chain of unenlightenment in this area can continue generation after generation.

Secondly, some parents are afraid to make decisions because of a fear of failure, a failure that may reflect on their sense of self-worth. Almost every decision involves making a choice among possible courses of action, resources to be allocated, even competing values. It is by no means an exact science and there is always the chance of error, no matter how small. Qualms about possibly making wrong choices immobilize parents and cause them to refrain from decision making.

Thirdly, some parents are chronic procrastinators. They often mean well and want to decide, but keep putting off the actual decision until a crisis forces them to act or it is too late to do anything. Then they usually rationalize to themselves and family members, explaining why they "really could not have" made a decision. They sometimes vow to themselves that they will never procrastinate again. Of course, these vows are usually broken. Parents procrastinate for several reasons: fear of failure ("If I try this, I may fail. It is better to be called a procrastinator than a failure"); fear of success ("If I try this, it may succeed. Then my family will no longer need me. As long as there is no closure to this issue I'll be needed"); perception of the task as overwhelming ("Let me get all the little things out of the way so that I can have the time to tackle the big project": of course, the time never comes as it continues to be chewed up in little morsels by the "small stuff"); and the tendency to engage in pursuits that provide immediate gratification and a sense of accomplishment, delaying those that may have a greater long-term return. Procrastination, then, results from psychological as well as logistical barriers. The correction of this deficiency will have to center on the appropriate causes.

The last important reason for not making decisions is the tendency, once again, to value action more than thought or feel compelled to respond to action items rather than deliberation items in the family. "Who's got time to sit and decide? I've got to take action!" is often the lament of fathers and mothers. These parents have not come to appreciate the potential return on their time and energy investment and the loss that no doubt will result from their lack of careful decision making.

They do not realize that they will have to make new decisions to correct faulty ones, thereby doubling and tripling their efforts.

What then should parents do to make a sound decision? The process involves several steps, which are listed below.

THE ANATOMY OF FAMILY DECISION MAKING

1. IDENTIFY THE NATURE OF THE DECISION

Parents must know what they are deciding. Often they may think that they are deciding one thing when in fact it is something else. For instance, an affirmative answer to a sixth-grade child's request to go to a school dance may set a precedent for future such requests by that child and by younger siblings. "Opportunity cost" is another consideration here. Deciding to spend money or time on one thing may preclude expenditures on other possibilities. Purchasing a new luxury car may be more important to a family than not being able to have a vacation for the next two years because of limited funds—a direct result of the decision to spend so much money on the automobile. Parents have to look at the whole picture, realize and accept that every decision they make within the family setting most likely will have an impact on other aspects and dimensions of living. The key question, then, is: Do I really know what I am deciding? A very common error on the part of parents is their focus on answers when in fact they should be directing their attention to asking the right questions.

2. COLLECT INFORMATION CONCERNING THE DECISION SITUATION

After parents know what they are really deciding they ought to collect as much information as possible concerning the decision situation. What is at stake for the family as a whole? For the individual members? Who are the people—all of them—involved in this decision? It is important to recognize those indirectly affected by the decision. The decision to help son Frank through medical school—because he now needs additional funds because of his recent marriage to girlfriend Linda after she became pregnant—may preclude second son Tom from going to a more expensive private college out of town, or may eliminate plans for the purchase of a beach home, or may cause Mom to leave her current job which she likes and find a new one that pays more. Information from all the people involved is critical if a workable and fair decision is to be made.

Knowing as much as possible about the case to be decided will help the parent formulate a course of action that is the most beneficial for all. Parents should not feel obliged to go on with the process if they do not feel that they have enough information. A decision not to make a decision is a decision in itself! If information is not available or accessible, or is withheld by members of the family or others, parents have every right and even obligation to refrain from the decision-making process. Often children wishing to influence the process will present only that information which they would like the parent to have. *Fourteen-year-old child:* "Mom, can I spend the weekend at Laurie's family's ski lodge?" *Mother:* "Well, who will be there?" *Child:* "I really don't know. Why does it matter?" *Mother:* "Will Laurie's mom and dad be there? Her brother and his friends?" *Child:* "How am I supposed to know? I'm sure that somebody else will be there. We have to get there some way. Neither one of us drives and it's about a hundred miles away." The mother cannot make a sound decision in this case because she does not have the information needed. The child is controlling the information flow.

Parents must be careful not to succumb to the social pressures of giving in or going along just to be pleasant. How many times have parents made foolish decisions to let their children do things that could have been and sometimes were in fact truly harmful? One father and mother in New Hampshire recounted an episode in which they allowed their eleven-year-old son to go out boating and scuba diving in a large lake with a group of virtual strangers. "We were strolling on a dock looking at all the beautiful boats when we came across a family that we had met three or four times before at our condominium's swimming pool. They were just about ready to go out in their 24-foot Baysider and spend an afternoon on the lake. We chatted for a few minutes. As they were about to pull out they asked if our son Danny would want to go with them and spend the afternoon swimming off the boat and diving. Of course, our son responded affirmatively and was ecstatic. We looked at each other somewhat perplexed, didn't know what to say, embarrassed to ask too many questions of the family, like 'Will you be careful? Do you have life preservers? Is the diving dangerous?' So we kind of nodded in agreement as our apparently responsible hosts took the initiative to assure us our son would be fine. As the boat sped off with our jubilant Danny waving to us excitedly we stared at each other with the same obvious thought: 'How could we have allowed this? We don't really know those people, where they are going, what their sense of caution is, how responsible they really are, how trustworthy they are.' Needless to say, it was a long afternoon. We were quite happy to see them arrive back at the dock almost exactly at the promised time. Of course, Danny couldn't stop talking about what a wonderful day he had had. We both needed a couple of good stiff drinks. The next day in discussing our decision to let Danny go with them we both pointed out that even though we are pretty intelligent and generally wise parents, we really responded prematurely at the dock. While everything worked out fine in this case, it might not always."

Just as this set of parents did not have enough information to make a decision at dockside, many other parents find themselves pressured, because of time limitations on data gathering, to decide on the spot. This is a serious deficiency in the protocol that many parents *allow themselves* to follow. Remember, no one forces them to make a decision. They respond to the pressure resulting from the socially imposed or situational pressures and make the decision themselves. Often, less important factors, like fear of embarrassment, fear of being disliked, not wanting to be different, or the possibility of their children being viewed as outcasts, override prudence. The cost of not having all the facts usually far outweighs the potential benefits of deciding absent this information. Of course, the cost of gathering information in terms of time, energy, etc., must be weighed against the benefits. To spend a whole afternoon deciding which fast-food restaurant to go to for dinner would be unjustifiable!

3. Look at Possible Options

Once parents have collected sufficient information to understand the decision situation as well as they can, they then should consider possible avenues for deciding. Rarely will it be a simple matter of yes or no. In family affairs there are bound to be many gray areas. Parental decision making is always going to be cast within the framework of "the best possible in light of the situation and what we know." Which of the options is the best—not perfect, but the best of what is available? This is not to say that a choice must necessarily be made if all the options are unrewarding, too risky, irresponsible, or counterproductive. Again, parents should feel free to cease the decision-making process at this point and, in effect, not decide. This is legitimate and may be the only sensible course of action. Parents who feel compelled to pressure themselves into making a decision should ask themselves these questions: "What will happen if I do not decide now?" Surprisingly, the answer is often "Nothing . . . at least nothing worse than exists now, which is not necessarily pleasant, but at least tolerable." Another im-

portant question is "What could happen if I decide without much
understanding of all the other possible options?" The answer often
resembles one of the following: "Things could get better, but who
knows? It's a gamble." Or, "Things could get worse than they are now.
You really don't know." Or, "I just don't have time to consider all the
angles. I'll just take my chances." Parents must ask themselves which
type of response would be the most comfortable for them.

4. CONFIDENTLY IMPLEMENT THE SELECTED OPTION

After considering the pluses and minuses of each option, parents
should then select one or more of them and go with it. While we have
pointed out again and again the importance of collecting information,
of course this can be overdone. Parents must accept the fact that every
decision they make is a tentative one, based on the information they
have available at that time. Again, it is the "best *possible* choice." If
parents establish too high standards to judge options against, they
could reach a state of decision phobia and immobilization. Remember,
the decision not to decide is a decision, even if it is by default. So,
despite our highly recommended deliberative approach, we urge parents to implement with confidence the option that they have selected.
Nothing makes a family more insecure and uncomfortable than a wa-
vering decision maker as leader. Children are very sensitive to this, and
parental effectiveness can be severely damaged when insecurity is
present.

The basic principle of parental decision making is paradoxical: fathers and mothers should have the highest respect for the uncertain
and labyrinthine nature of the decision-making process in the family
but must carry out decisions with the boldness and alacrity of a ship's
captain on the high seas.

Several issues that arise in parental decision making may confound the
process for mothers and fathers: What happens when one has to
change a decision? What happens when the selected option doesn't
work as expected? What is the role of intuition?

First, because decisions are always tentative in the making, modifications should not be surprising. They are to be expected. Because the
family is constantly evolving and its environment is so dynamic, circumstances change. It is important that everybody in the family understand this, and the earlier the better. Changing plans is part of living,
and our ability to tolerate this human condition and still maintain a
confidence and commitment to goals is a sign of good mental health.

We recommend that parents use changes in decisions as opportunities to teach their children this important lesson. It is far better for them to experience "life's disappointments" while under parental guidance than later. Mothers and fathers can work through the emotional letdown of changed plans with their children. What one does in response to a modified decision is usually more important than the change. If parents use changed decisions as learning experiences, eventually the whole family will be able to function purposefully in the always tentative climate of the family. For instance, if a father, with all good intentions, decides to take his wife and children to the college football game on Saturday afternoon in response to their request, but because of a problem at work must cancel so he can take care of the job situation, what will the rest of the family do about it? The possibilities range from spending the whole day pouting about the missed game to using that day to do something even more exciting and rewarding. Much will depend on the family members' readiness for decision modifications and whether they view changes in plans as disappointments or opportunities. A key factor in this choice will be the family leader's example.

Sometimes the option selected in the decision process doesn't work. This could be the case for several reasons: it was the wrong choice to begin with; circumstances have changed to the point where this option is no longer viable; or it was implemented improperly. Whatever the reason, it is important for parents to discontinue executing the decision as soon as this is discovered. To attempt to force an erroneous decision can do tremendous harm to family relations. Even obedient, loving children are placed in a predicament if they are caught between their parents, who may be obviously dead wrong, and the evidence of reality and reason. Parents who insist on having their children and spouses condone their decision as the correct one, even though it is clearly not, threaten their own legitimacy as family leaders. They gain the respect and confidence of their children if they are willing to recognize that they are off course and work to get back on. The greatest obstacle to the process of effective redeciding are the parent's own self-confidence and ego needs, especially if he or she feels compelled to defend decisions as a means of protecting self-worth in the eyes of family members.

Lastly, what do parents do about intuition? While the parentship approach to decision making is fundamentally rational and systematic, we do not discount intuition. In fact, the distinction between the two is not related to the content of the decision information, but to how the information is taken in. Systematic, rational decision making is a sequential, more logical (step-by-step), and deliberative process, whereas intuition is more spontaneous, holistic, and therefore faster. Split-brain theorists would locate the more rational process in the left hemisphere of the brain and the more intuitive activity in the right hemisphere. The fully integrated person, of course, would attempt to develop both sides of the brain as much as possible. The result would be a decision maker who uses systematic logic as well as intuition . . . a truly capable thinker.

Parental intuition, often commingled with instinct, does then have a role in decision making. In the case of some mothers and fathers (those with right-brain dominance), intuition is the major avenue for taking in information. ("I can feel it in my bones; I just know that it is the right thing to do!") For others, particularly those dominated by the left hemisphere of the brain in their thinking style, concrete evidence is what counts. ("Seeing is believing. Time will tell!") These basic differences in how information is taken in can cause discrepancies in decision-making methods among family members. An intuitive wife might become impatient with a more deliberative husband who needs more time and information to mentally construct and conclude what she already knows almost instantaneously. The husband, in turn, may view his wife's decision as premature and even irresponsible because it is based on insufficient evidence. Children, too, differ in their way of taking in information. As a result, some children are sequential and deliberative in making decisions. Others are more intuitive.

Differences in decision-making styles can have a complementary value or can be a source of contention in the family. For example, a parent who is highly systematic and deliberative may be well served by a spouse who is exactly the opposite—i.e., highly intuitive—and vice versa. However, if the differences are not recognized as such, the consequences could be troublesome. *Daughter:* "Dad, I don't think that you really care about us anymore." *Father:* "Karen, how could you say such a thing? Look how much I do for this family. I work day and night." *Daughter:* "But, Dad, I don't feel your love anymore." *Father:* "What? I told you I loved you just last week, didn't I? What do I have to do, say it every day? Just look at the facts. You could never draw that conclusion." Who is right? Who is wrong in this case? In a sense, both are. Dad is taking the concrete facts (that he is working so hard, etc.), arranging them in a logical order, drawing the conclusion that he is a good father, and expecting his daughter to do the same. Karen, on the other hand, is attuned to other, less concrete information that is more powerful than the "facts" that her father is regarding. It might be that

Dad's first love is really his work and not the family, or that Dad buries himself in work to avoid the family, or that Dad finds people at work more enjoyable than his family, or that Dad is just plain selfish or egotistical. The "bad vibes" that Karen is getting are not consistent with the "good facts" that the father has constructed for himself. Unless this basic difference in information gathering is addressed and understood, decision making in the family will be of poor quality and even destructive.

While mothers and fathers are influenced by both brain hemispheres in decision making, there is most likely a dominance. Parents should determine the extent of their reliance on systematic logic (left brain) and/or on intuition (right brain) in the decision-making process. The following index will be helpful.

PARENTAL DECISION-MAKING STYLES INDEX

Instructions: Indicate to what extent each of the following statements describes you, using the scale provided below.

```
     1      2      3      4      5      6      7
                                                         ⟶
     Does not describe me fully     Describes me fully
```

1._____ I remember faces more than names.
2._____ I like to see things kept in order.
3._____ I love modern abstract art.
4._____ I like action more than thought.
5._____ I don't develop a positive or negative feeling toward people until I know them well.
6._____ I'm more concerned about atmosphere than service in a restaurant.
7._____ I like creative people.
8._____ I would rather listen than talk.
9._____ I like to write letters.
10._____ I enjoy solving practical household problems.
11._____ I like to listen to music and read at the same time.
12._____ I like to be in control of a situation at all times.

Scoring:
   Left hemisphere score (total of statements 2, 4, 5, 9, 10, 12) _____
   Right hemisphere score (total of statements 1, 3, 6, 7, 8, 11) _____

Interpretation:
    33–42: highly developed hemisphere
    20–32: moderately developed hemisphere
    13–19: mildly developed hemisphere
     6–12: minimally developed hemisphere

Interpretation: If both hemispheres are highly developed, then you most likely utilize maximum powers in gathering information for decision making: rational, systematic thought as well as intuition. If both hemispheres are minimally developed, then you are using low-intensity powers to gather information. Both of these situations are unlikely. What is more probable is a tendency to have one hemisphere developed more than the other. You should then be sensitive to what information you may be missing because of an underdeveloped left or right hemisphere. You can also work to develop that approach to information gathering to bring about a greater balance in your decision-making capabilities.

8

Financial Management and Budgeting

It is understandable that families with limited incomes feel the economic constraints of their resources. But it is surprising how often families with substantial incomes are poor financial managers. Mary and Wayne have a combined income of over seventy-five thousand dollars but they do not feel wealthy. At a recent party, they discovered in conversation that most of their friends have much more money invested than they do. They bought their house when interest rates were high, so they have a large mortgage payment, and private school education and child care costs are high for their three children, ages five to fourteen. They want to start saving more for a college fund for the children, and Wayne's brother recently proposed sharing the purchase of a vacation house on a nearby mountain. Wayne has dreamed of early retirement but they have not saved much because they often have to dip into their savings to cover bills. We advised them to try to get a picture of their spending by constructing a statement of income and outflows. By going back over their two checking accounts for the past year, they came up with this summary.

Income

Salaries (after taxes)	$51,750
Interest (credit union and money market account)	1,100
Dividends (Wayne's stock bought on company plan)	860
	$53,710

Outflows

Mortgage payments	$13,200
Automobile loans (2)	6,848
Life insurance premiums	1,020
Utilities and telephone	2,880
Food at home	6,000
Food away from home	3,000
Recreation/entertainment/vacation	5,000
Gasoline	1,400
Medical/dental	900
Clothing	3,000
Church/charity	800
Education/child care	4,800
Miscellaneous	4,862
	$53,710

It made them feel better to know where the money was going, but they also resolved to change some of their spending habits to reflect their values and goals. Next year, child care expenses will be lessened as the youngest starts school, and one car loan will be paid in full. This will give them almost three thousand dollars extra. They plan to save this for the children's education expenses. They can take advantage of the Uniform Gifts to Minors Act to transfer some tax obligations to the children. They also will both open an Individual Retirement Account (IRA) and will try to save the two-thousand-dollar annual maximum for each of them. They have a neighbor who is a CPA and he is going to show them how a budget can control their spending, especially in the miscellaneous category. They hope to save here, and cut back on "food away from home" and "entertainment" to fund the IRAs. The accountant will also look at their tax return from last year to make recommendations for other tax savings. They told Wayne's brother "no" to the vacation house, even though they were embarrassed by his surprise that they couldn't afford the venture.

Financial planning and budgeting have more to do with values and less to do with money, which is only a means to an end. Values influence daily living in many ways. The things a family considers good, important, or beautiful will guide how the family lives. If education is valued, the parents will see to it that children have a time and place for doing homework; they may decide to buy a family encyclopedia, or other learning aids; money will be saved for college education. If religion is valued, the family will belong to a church community, attend services regularly, contribute money to the congregation. If honesty is valued, the children will be taught not to lie or steal, and the parents will set an example of honesty for the children. Parents will not ask children to tell a caller "They're not home," will not call in sick to work when well, or cheat on income tax returns. For beliefs to be truly called "values," they must influence how one lives. In every situation involving a choice, values influence decision making. Values can be moral, social, aesthetic, or cultural; but they are perhaps most evident in economic decisions. Values influence how a family chooses to spend money, where the family will live, and the family's lifestyle.

It is important for parents to recognize this as a starting point in financial management. Values are not innate. They are learned from parents, friends, peers, church, and are the product of experiences. A man and a woman are likely to start a family with two different sets of values and have to compromise or negotiate in ranking them. Neither are values static. They change with experience and over time in the family life cycle. But the couple needs open communication and understanding of the basic role their values will play in decisions involving the spending of money.

Values likewise influence goals. What is considered important will determine where parents want the family to be financially. But before they can decide where they want it to go, it is important to take a look at the current financial picture.

FINANCIAL ASSESSMENT

Where does all the money go? Why do we never seem to get ahead? If we pay all the bills, how can we expect to save any money? If parents are asking questions like these, it may mean that it is time for a financial assessment. Mothers and fathers will need to take an inventory of resources, analyze current habits, project future needs, and make a plan to achieve financial goals. Many parents do not have an accurate idea of how much money they spend. If most bills are paid by check, a record can be constructed from the checkbook ledger. If many expenses are paid in cash, each parent will have to carry a notebook and record expenses over a period of time to get a record of expenditures. This is called a "cash flow statement." The parent can use a form similar to the one below. The cash flow statement shows the family's source of funds and allocation of money over a specific period, usually one year. It is a summary of expenditures by category.

CASH FLOW STATEMENT
For the year ending_____

REVENUES
Salaries (after taxes)   _____
Other earned income   _____
Interest received   _____
Dividends received in cash   _____
Bonus and commissions   _____

                        Total revenue   _____

EXPENDITURES

SAVINGS AND INVESTMENTS   _____

FIXED EXPENSES
Rent or mortgage payment   _____
Installment debts   _____
Auto loan   _____
Other bank loans   _____
Insurance
  Life   _____
  Auto   _____
  Homeowners   _____
  Health   _____
  Disability   _____
  Other   _____
Taxes not withheld from pay   _____
  Real estate   _____
  Other   _____

VARIABLE EXPENSES
Household operation   _____
  Fuel   _____
  Electric   _____
  Water   _____

Household maintenance
   Home furnishings/equipment   _____
   Repairs   _____
Food at home   _____
Food away from home   _____
Recreation/entertainment   _____
Telephone   _____
Credit cards*   _____
Transportation   _____
   Gasoline   _____
   Auto repairs and maintenance   _____
   Other (bus, etc.)   _____
Medical/dental   _____
Clothing   _____
Laundry   _____
Gifts   _____
Church/charity   _____
Education   _____
Personal allowances   _____
Miscellaneous   _____

Total expenditures

* Some families budget for credit card use as a separate item. Other families may use department store credit cards for clothing purchases, bank or entertainment credit cards for entertainment and recreation and travel, gasoline credit cards for auto upkeep costs. In that case the purchases may be in specific categories.

If records are not available to complete the cash flow statement for the past year, your first job is to start recording expenditures for the current year.

Another important item to consider in conducting a financial assessment is the amount of short-term debt carried, excluding a home mortgage. Below are some debt-management habits that may indicate a reevaluation is due:

· Paying only the minimum amount due each month on credit card accounts with the result that outstanding balances shrink very slowly.
· Making many new credit purchases so that the debt load rarely shrinks at all.
· Having to take out new loans to pay off old ones, or having to consolidate loans.
· Having to skip payments, adding to the interest charged.

• Relying on the "overdraft protection" feature of the checking account.

The amount of debt that can be managed by a family varies widely when other factors are considered. However, as a rule of thumb, if more than 20 percent of take-home pay each month is going to short-term debt, it is probably too much.

If too much debt is in the family's financial picture, parents definitely need to make a plan for spending. They also should carefully assess their use of credit cards. They could even seek professional consumer credit counseling, if their situation warrants it.

THE FAMILY'S FINANCIAL POSITION

In addition to understanding where the money goes, it is important to get a picture of the family's financial position at a given period in time. This is called the Net Worth Statement. It is a profile of what is owned (assets), what is owed (liabilities), and the family's net worth on a specific date. This could be done on the first day of January or first of July or on Mom's or Dad's birthday. If an individual is applying for a loan at the bank or estimating the value of an estate, this information will be needed. The statement of financial position is also used in personal financial planning—in making decisions about insurance and investments, in tax planning, and in retirement and estate planning. It is also useful for comparison with previous or subsequent statements. Through such a comparison over time, trends can be identified, and progress toward financial goals monitored. The net worth statement can be viewed as a snapshot of the family's financial situation. As new snapshots are taken, the picture changes. A form for determining net worth is presented here:

NET WORTH STATEMENT
(Statement of Financial Position)
Date_____

ASSETS

LIABILITIES

Cash and Equivalents
Cash _____
Checking account
  balance _____
Savings account
  balance _____
Credit union balance _____
Money market fund _____
Other liquid funds _____

Total cash assets _____

Investments
Bank CDs _____
Stocks _____
Bonds _____
Treasury bills, notes,
  etc. _____
Life insurance cash
  value _____
Vested portion of
  pension _____
Other investments _____

*Total investment
  assets* _____

Use Assets (current market value)
Home _____
Rental property/
  vacation home _____
Automobile _____
Household furnish-
  ings _____

Amount due on
  mortgage loan _____
Car loan _____
Other loans _____
Credit card(s)
  balance due _____
_____
_____
Unpaid bills _____
_____
_____
Taxes due _____
Other debts _____
_____
TOTAL LIABILITIES _____

ASSETS

    Clothing, jewelry, etc.   ‾‾‾‾‾
    Antiques, silver   ‾‾‾‾‾
    Boat, recreational
        vehicle   ‾‾‾‾‾
    Other use assets   ‾‾‾‾‾

    Total value of use
        assets   ‾‾‾‾‾

      TOTAL ASSETS   ‾‾‾‾‾

TOTAL ASSETS less TOTAL LIABILITIES equals NET WORTH

‾‾‾‾‾‾‾‾‾‾‾‾ − ‾‾‾‾‾‾‾‾‾‾‾‾‾‾ = ‾‾‾‾‾‾‾‾‾

FINANCIAL GOALS

Once parents have an idea of where they stand financially by completing the cash flow statement and net worth statement, it is then time to decide where they want to go. Both parents in a two-parent family need to discuss financial goals. Conflicts are likely to occur, but with open communication, goals can be ranked in hierarchy of importance. Older children should be involved in a discussion of the family's financial goals. It helps them to understand why they cannot have a new ten-speed bike or their own car at age sixteen, or go on a skiing trip to Vail.

Goals can be classified by how long it will take to achieve them and defined as either short-term or long-term. "Short-term" refers to financial objectives the family wishes to achieve within the next three years—for example, an annual vacation, purchase of a recreational vehicle or boat or second car, redecorating the living room, or buying a home computer. Every family's first short-range goal should be the establishment of an emergency fund, if it doesn't already have one. The size of the emergency fund will depend on many factors, including the net worth statement, amount of debt, and job security of the breadwinner(s). As a general rule of thumb, parents should have available an amount equal to three months' expenses from the cash flow statement. This money should be in an accessible, liquid form, such as a money market account at a local bank or credit union, or in a money market mutual fund with check-writing privileges. Also included on the list of goals are large expenditures the family is anticipating within the next three years. This might include replacing appliances or furnishings, Christmas or other gifts, additional insurance, dental braces, or child care and education costs.

Long-term goals, like short-term goals, vary widely from family to family. A young family may be saving for a down payment on a house. Families with older children may be saving for college education and/or the parents' retirement. Long-range goals should be listed by priority. Priority may be determined by time and/or amount of money needed, as well as values. For instance, retirement may be low on the priority list for a young family because there are other anticipated goals before that time. Having a will may not seem like a high priority for the same reason, but all parents should have one, no matter how small their assets, to answer potential questions of guardianship of the children.

It is helpful for the family to write down the goals with an anticipated target date to see if their expectations are realistic.

FINANCIAL GOALS OF THE HAMMOND FAMILY

	Target Date	Approximate Cost	Planned Monthly Saving
EMERGENCY FUND	July 1, 1988	$ 6,000	$166.66
Short-term goals in next 3 years			
1. Trip to Disney World	July 1, 1987	$ 1,800	$ 75.00
2. Braces for Jimmy	Dec. 1, 1987	$ 2,000	$ 68.96
3. New shrubs for yard	June 1, 1986	$ 500	$ 41.66
Large expenditures expected in next 3 years			
1. New automobile	Oct. 1, 1988	$ 15,000	$416.66
2. Living room carpet	Nov. 1, 1988	$ 3,000	$ 83.33
3. Air-conditioning system	Feb. 1, 1988	$ 2,500	$ 69.44
Long-range goals* (listed by priority)			
1. Children's college fund	Sept. 1, 1998	$ 50,000	$320.51*
2. Retirement accounts (IRA, etc.)	July 1, 2015	$180,000	$500.00*
3. Travel funds	July 1, 2000	$ 20,000	$111.00

* Excludes compounded interest, which will substantially increase totals, but which is also subject to fluctuations.

Margaret, a divorced mother of two in Minneapolis, earns close to $20,000 a year after taxes. Her job as a secretary is fairly secure, and she has comprehensive health insurance coverage with her employer, but she has little savings. Her major asset is the small home she received in the divorce settlement. She worries about what would happen if she lost her job or was injured, because she has low disability insurance. Also, she would like to take the children on a vacation to the beach next summer.

Her fixed expenses for the mortgage payment, car loan, auto and homeowner's insurance, are $617 per month. Utility bills, food, gasoline, church contributions, and baby-sitter fees add an average of about $650 a month to expenses. That leaves a little more than $4,000 per year for other household expenses, recreation, auto maintenance, medical and dental bills, clothing, gifts, and personal allowances, as well as for achieving her financial goals.

Goals	Target Date	Cost	Save per Month
1. Emergency fund	2½ years	$3800	$157
2. Summer vacation	1 year	$ 700	$ 58

Margaret can decide that if she is careful to limit flexible expenses, she may achieve these two goals. Once she has saved the targeted sum for the emergency fund, she can develop other goals for the money saved each month. For example, she could investigate better disability insurance coverage.

A PLAN FOR SPENDING

If parents find themselves in good financial shape after this assessment, they may decide no changes are necessary to stay on target for their declared goals. This financial assessment may reveal that the family is doing the best it can with available resources. If, on the other hand, they are not satisfied that they are going where they want to be financially, they will need to plan a budget. If additional goals are to be met, the family will either have to increase income or reduce expenses. Or, perhaps there is enough money, but it is slipping through the cracks. A budget will help fill in the cracks. A budget is a positive step for achieving financial goals. It is a rational plan for spending limited funds within an almost unlimited set of possibilities.

The categories on the budget form will look like the cash flow statement. The major difference is that the cash flow statement is a record of past expenses, and the budget is a plan for future expenses. Parents must be sure that lines are provided on the budget form for financial goals. "Savings and Investments" is listed first as a general heading. If the family is saving for many goals, that may need to be subdivided.

Under fixed expenses, payments that can be predicted but not changed should be listed. Flexible expenses will vary and the family has some control over the amount spent in these categories. This is the place for the parent to practice cost-cutting skills. There should be enough categories of expenses to get an idea of where money is to go, but not so many categories that bookkeeping becomes tedious.

One way to create a balance is to give each member of the family a personal allowance. The amount of the allowance, as well as which expenses it is expected to cover, can be negotiated in advance. A six-year-old may want to buy ice cream or soda as a treat occasionally, or a new toy or book. Seventy-five cents a week may cover such discretionary expenses and introduce money management skills to a first grader. An older child may, in addition, go to movies or sporting events. As long as it is clear between parent and child which expenses are to be covered and how often money is received, the amount is negotiable. Children need to receive enough allowance to have the opportunity to make choices.

Parents, too, need pocket money for which they do not have to account. Their allowance may cover necessary expenses such as lunch at work, bus fares or parking fees, or midweek milk and bread for the family; however, some of it should be for discretionary purchases. Adults may feel the budget is a straitjacket if they have to account for every magazine, paperback book, pack of cigarettes, or beer with a friend.

(SAMPLE FORM)
ANNUAL BUDGET
For the year_____

INCOME

Salaries (after taxes)   _____
Dividends, interest   _____
Other   _____

Yearly total _____   Monthly total income _____

EXPENDITURES	JANUARY		FEBRUARY		MARCH	
	Projected	Actual	Projected	Actual	Projected	Actual
Savings and investments	___	___	___	___	___	___
Rent or mortgage payment	___	___	___	___	___	___
Installment debts	___	___	___	___	___	___
Auto loan	___	___	___	___	___	___
Other bank loans	___	___	___	___	___	___
Insurance premiums	___	___	___	___	___	___
Household utilities	___	___	___	___	___	___
Fuel	___	___	___	___	___	___
Light	___	___	___	___	___	___
Water	___	___	___	___	___	___
Telephone	___	___	___	___	___	___
Household maintenance	___	___	___	___	___	___
Food at home	___	___	___	___	___	___
Food away from home	___	___	___	___	___	___
Recreation/entertainment/vacation	___	___	___	___	___	___
Credit cards	___	___	___	___	___	___
Transportation	___	___	___	___	___	___
Gasoline	___	___	___	___	___	___
Auto repairs and maintenance	___	___	___	___	___	___
Bus and other transportation	___	___	___	___	___	___
Medical/dental	___	___	___	___	___	___
Clothing/personal care	___	___	___	___	___	___

Laundry	——	——	——	——	——	——
Gifts	——	——	——	——	——	——
Church/charity	——	——	——	——	——	——
Education/child care	——	——	——	——	——	——
Personal allowance	——	——	——	——	——	——
Miscellaneous	——	——	——	——	——	——
TOTALS	——	——	——	——	——	——

The monthly columns allow for irregular payments, such as annual insurance premiums or school tuition. The best way to prepare for such irregular expenses is to set aside one twelfth of the anticipated bill per month. Savings and investments are listed first in order to make it easier to achieve financial goals. If savings are what happens last, after bills are paid, there often is nothing left. Therefore, parents need to use the "pay ourselves first" rule to build financial security. Then, flexible expenses can be trimmed as needed. Of course, if there is continually a battle to cover expenses, a reevaluation of the budget is in order. Perhaps the savings goals are unrealistically high or discretionary spending is out of control. Periodically, the plan needs reviewing anyway, to see if adjustments are necessary. That is why monthly columns are provided for projected and actual expenses. At the end of the first year, the cash flow statement will now be very easy to construct. Parents can simply add the actual expenses each month for an annual total.

Ed and Louise are planning a budget. Louise is going back to work after years of homemaking. Their combined income this year will be about $38,000 after taxes. They are accustomed to living on Ed's salary, and would like to allot the extra income to some long postponed purchases, including a sailboat, summer camp for the children, and a college fund. They also will buy a second car with an auto loan from the bank in order not to deplete the emergency fund below $5,000. Their budget looks like this:

Expenditures	Projected Monthly Amount
ED	
Mortgage payment	$634
Auto loan #1	156
Insurance—life and auto (homeowner's included in mortgage; health through Ed's employer)	117

Expenditures	Projected Monthly Amount
Utilities (electric, gas, water)	140
Food at home	400
Telephone	25
Gasoline and auto maintenance	150
Clothing and Apparel maintenance	100
Recreation/entertainment	50
Gifts	50
Church/charity	50
Personal allowances	120
Miscellaneous	150
LOUISE	
Saving for boat	300
Auto loan #2	237
Food away from home/entertainment	100
Set aside for summer camp	60
Additional clothing/gifts	80
Education fund for children	200
After-school sitter for children	50

They plan to monitor this for a few months, and reevaluate, but they are optimistic they may be able to save even more than they planned.

TEACHING CHILDREN HOW TO MANAGE MONEY

If the financial planning is going to work, both parents and children must be involved. Consumer education for children begins the first time they see a TV commercial for a toy or sugar-coated cereal, and beg their parents to buy it. Most preschoolers can walk down the cereal aisle of a supermarket and identify the products. They know which boxes contain a "prize" and can probably try to convince a parent that the cereal is "part of a nutritious breakfast."

So parents find that explaining "truth-in-advertising" may be the beginning of consumer education for their children. They should teach them to examine advertising claims, read ingredient labels, and talk with them about product safety. Some children "nickel-and-dime" their parents regularly with requests for money. Rather than respond to this nagging it is far better for parents to give children an allowance

—a set amount of money at regular intervals with no strings attached. Children learn how to make consumer decisions and achieve financial goals, if they have some money to control.

By the time children start school and can count, they can begin to receive an allowance. If parents are tempted to begin with a quarter, they shouldn't forget what a quarter can buy. Twenty-five cents is not enough in this day and age. The amount must be large enough to give the child a choice. Most six-year-olds like candy, gum, toys, soda, "stuff." Seventy-five cents is the minimum needed to buy two snacks or treats and have a few pennies left to save toward a larger goal.

If the child must carry money to school for lunch or bus fare, the management of these funds will be an important lesson too. But the allowance should also include some money for discretionary spending. It may take a six-year-old several months to adjust to making choices with money. If he or she spends it all on Saturday and then on Wednesday thinks of something else to buy, parents shouldn't bail the child out. One major lesson for the young child to learn is "When it's gone, it's gone."

A weekly allowance is a good frequency: by the time children start school they are beginning to understand how long a week lasts. If the allowance is to be given with no strings attached, it means the child must be free to choose on what it is to be spent. While buying two packs of bubble gum a week may seem like a waste of money to an adult, the six-year-old who's learning to blow bubbles with the gum will consider the purchase a wise decision. Next year, the passion may be for grape popsicles, or chocolate soda, or dime store makeup, or videogames.

Parents should consider the values they want to transmit to their children through the process of money management. It is important that money management practices be supportive of family values. Parents may want to teach their children that money itself is not very important compared to other aspects of life, but withholding allowances as a punishment will demonstrate that money is indeed very powerful. Likewise, the child may confuse money with love if money is withheld by an angry parent. If money is used as a reward, it is likely to put family relationships on shaky ground. A better approach is to reward good behavior by showing pride and affection and to discourage wrongdoing with a punishment that fits the crime. Children are expected to do household chores as part of "family work." If they fail to do their chores, a more appropriate punishment might be no TV or withdrawal of other privileges.

Sometimes parents may give children the opportunity to earn additional money by doing additional work (cleaning out the garage, helping to paint, etc.). This can be a good introduction to economic realities and help the child to achieve a desired financial goal—buying a new toy or a gift for someone. As the child grows older and more skilled in managing money, the amount can be increased to cover additional expenses: scout or club dues, movie tickets, posters, records. If a teenager is interested in managing a clothing budget, the amount can be increased to cover clothes too. Teenagers often can manage a monthly or bimonthly receipt of funds. If it has been determined which expenses are to be covered by their allowance, some teenagers like an envelope system. Envelopes are labeled "lunch," "bus fare," "clothes," "charity," "savings," "snacks," "recreation," or whatever. When they receive their allowance, they allocate the money by category into the appropriate envelope. This is to insure they still have lunch money or bus fare at the end of the month. Of course, if they have to take a peanut butter sandwich for lunch, or walk home from school, they've learned a valuable lesson. Parents must remember not to bail them out! Their allowance is a learning tool. If they continually run out of money, parents should counsel them and try to decide whether the allowances are too small or spending habits are undisciplined.

Older children should be included in family financial discussions so that they can see how the family has to trade off values and goals to make economic decisions. This will be a most valuable experience for them as they prepare for adulthood. Should the vacation be one week at the beach or two weeks visiting the grandparents? Should the family dog come from the pound or be a pedigreed pet with papers?

Parents should not wait until children are teenagers to begin their consumer education. American teenagers have a great deal of money to spend, and they are easily influenced by peers, advertising, and their strong desire for independence. If teenagers take jobs to earn extra money, their initiative shouldn't be thwarted by reducing their allowance, unless financial circumstances leave no choice. Teenagers should have a bank account for savings, not just a piggy bank. It is a good introduction to the services of financial institutions and mathematical principles such as compound interest. Lastly, teenagers should have enough familiarity with family finances to know if they must save for some of the college expenses or car transportation costs.

HOW PARENTS CAN MAKE MONEY WORK FOR THEM

As parents set money aside for short- and long-range goals, they may start to question: Where is the best place to keep the money? If the most the family has ever saved is a few hundred dollars, they probably have their savings in the local bank or credit union. A good way to establish the savings habit with the "pay ourselves first" philosophy is through automatic payroll deductions or bank savings plans. As the savings grow, the money can be put to work to earn more money. The emergency fund should be in an accessible, safe place. If the fund has been accumulating in the local bank or credit union, the family is probably comfortable with the safety and convenience of that location. But if it is in a share account at the credit union or passbook account at the bank, it is not earning as much interest as it could. Parents should ask about opening an insured money market account. Although a minimum deposit of $1,000–2,500 may be required, the emergency fund will most likely be more than that if its targeted sum is three months' expenses. The interest rate will fluctuate, but usually stays higher than in a regular account.

Some families have their emergency savings in a money market mutual fund with check-writing privileges. Most are not insured, but they invest depositors' funds in the same type of short-term debt instruments as the bank funds. Money will be invested in large denomination short-term money market instruments issued by the Treasury, government agencies, banks, and corporations. Most issue checks which depositors can write to access the money, but the check must be for at least $500. Many people feel this is an ideal constraint for the emergency fund. They will not tap the fund for a night on the town, but replacing the refrigerator or a major car repair is the type of emergency that is likely to cost more than the $500 minimum, and is a justified use of the fund.

Every working adult who has listed retirement as a financial goal will consider opening an Individual Retirement Account (IRA). Up to $2,000 of earned income can be deposited each year and is not subject to income tax. In addition, the interest earned is not taxable income, and the account grows and compounds tax-free until withdrawals are made during retirement. Spousal accounts are also available for nonemployed husbands or wives. IRA accounts can be opened at banks, credit unions, with insurance companies, mutual funds, and brokerage houses. Parents should compare safety, convenience, and rate of return in deciding on a vehicle for the IRA. They should also plan on not withdrawing the money before age fifty-nine and a half because penalties are charged for early withdrawals.

KEEPING FAMILY RECORDS

Records are essential for parentship, and the better they are kept, the more effectively the entire family functions. How often do parents turn the house upside down looking for important papers? The family needs to have a filing system based on the principle that every record must be placed, as soon as possible, in its "home." A basic plan that will suit most families' needs includes a safe-deposit box, a tax file or box, an action file, warranty file, check file, alphabetical file, and memory box.

Safe-Deposit Box

If the family does not have one, a safe-deposit box should be rented from the local full-service bank. A small box costs only a few dollars per year. All court-issued or government-issued documents or any papers that would be difficult or expensive to replace should be kept in it: original copies of birth certificates, marriage certificates, adoption papers, military discharge papers, lot survey of house showing boundary lines, auto title, passports. Other valuable items kept there might be insurance policies, stock and bond certificates (copies with your broker), broker statements showing price of holdings purchased, loan agreements, leases, and expensive or heirloom jewelry not worn often.

Tax Records

Parents should have a file or box where they keep all the statements and records used for preparing each year's income tax return; they should also keep copies of the federal and state forms filed. A separate folder should be kept for each year, and records should be kept for at least six years.

Action File

Unpaid bills, solicitations from organizations to which you intend to contribute, charge slips, credit slips for items returned to stores and not yet credited to the account, installment loan payment books, mortgage payment books, etc., should be kept together.

Warranty File

Every time parents purchase a large or small appliance, they should place the warranty, instruction booklet, purchase date and price, and bills for any major repairs in a warranty file. They might also keep a folder on the family car to keep track of major repairs.

Check File

Most families use a checking account. It provides a convenient method for paying bills, as well as a handy record of payment if the records are kept organized. If your bank returns checks, use a shoe box or deep drawer to keep each monthly batch of cancelled checks and deposit slips wrapped in the corresponding bank statement and secured with a rubber band. It is best to keep these for six years also.

Alphabetical File

Parents keep here anything that does not fit into the previous categories and a second copy of the items in the safe-deposit box to minimize trips to the bank: insurance policies, a list of all credit card numbers, a copy of the household inventory, diplomas, transcripts of school records, organization membership cards, social security numbers of family members, lists of investments, savings account booklets, a list of birthdays and anniversaries, a copy of each will, etc.

Memory Box

Some things are saved for purely sentimental reasons: these might include prom favors, photographs, award certificates, or blue ribbons from the fair. Unless they have real value, they need not be in the safe-deposit box. A drawer or box at home for each member of the family will do. It is nice to have the memory box easily accessible for nostalgic rainy afternoons.

Here is one last tip for parents: for the household inventory, consider taking photographs of everything valuable in the home. On the back of the photo, they should write the date and purchase price. Insurance companies like this type of inventory, and it is easy to keep up to date—just add a new picture!

Finally, it is important to remember that records have to be weeded from time to time. This can be done easily enough by periodically combing each file while adding something new.

Financial management and budgeting, then, serves three functions of effective parentship. First, family plans and goals are translated into meaningful operational statements: money is allocated according to plan. Second, the budget statement clearly indicates family values: What is top priority? Where is the money going? It also provides a framework for evaluating actual expenditures against proclaimed or supposed values. Are they compatible or contradictory? Third, the process can serve as an excellent learning experience for children, if parents appropriately involve them. Most adults who have sound money management skills learned them in childhood and young adulthood. This critical skill, then, serves the polar limits of the parentship spectrum. At one and the same time it fulfills the "nitty-gritty" dimensions of family management while serving as a catalyst for the most philosophical questions a family could ask: What's it all about? What's important for us?

9

Delegating: Sharing Parenthood in Home Management

Some family leaders, usually ineffective ones, believe that the best way to get a job done is to do it themselves. The reasons for not sharing their responsibilities and tasks with others in the family are many: perfectionism, lack of trust, fear of not being needed, or even more deeply rooted psychological barriers like paranoia. Whatever the barriers, they must be overcome if parents are going to develop a necessary system of delegation of tasks within the family. Fathers and mothers cannot do everything.

Delegation is not only an important logistical skill for maximizing family members' time and talent; it is also an effective tool for building family teamwork and *morale*. Likewise, children who participate in the accomplishment of family chores develop a sharper sensitivity to their parents' roles and more empathy for the difficulties of managing a household. An additional benefit of participation by children is a sort of "parenting apprenticeship" that will help them lead their own families when they grow older. In general, everybody in the family gains when there is a consciously coordinated plan for delegating.

You have to be particularly aware of the flip side of this, what we call delegation-in-reverse, whereby children get mothers and fathers to do for them what they could do themselves. When this happens, little good is likely to ensue for any family member. Precious parent time and energy is underutilized, and children develop a shallow sense of responsibility and a dependency that will most likely handicap them as they get older.

This happened to Jenny, the mother of two teenage daughters in a suburb of Washington, D.C. Ever since her girls were infants, Jenny "did" for them. She was jubilant in her motherhood, and she waited on her kids hand and foot. "I thought that was what a mother was supposed to do," she told us recently after decrying the fact that her two teenagers wouldn't "lift a finger . . . Their room is always a mess . . . They never help out with the dishes . . . I have to pick up after them continuously . . . I've had it. I am completely exhausted and have lost focus of what I'm supposed to do and not supposed to do." After sobbing profusely she continued: "God knows what they will be like when they become wives and mothers. I'm beginning to realize that I've really failed them by not having demanded more involvement around the house. It would have been better for me and them both." Jenny's resentment and guilt are shared by her husband, and it has been the source of much hostility in that family. Like many other good, caring parents they did not know how to delegate, nor do they know how to control the reverse delegation that is going on. As a result, their success in leading an internally and externally sound family has been seriously jeopardized.

Why should you delegate? What are the specific benefits? First of all, prudent delegating frees you to spend your time and energy on some of the important parentship tasks mentioned earlier (planning, decision making, communicating, etc.). Often parents are so tied up with the petty household tasks that they don't even get to the top priorities that only a parent can attend to.

You must remember that you have only a limited amount of time and energy. If you use it to accomplish tasks that could be done by a child who does not have as many top-priority responsibilities, you are underutilizing those resources. For example, if the father of an idle fifteen-year-old son uses three hours on a Saturday morning mowing the lawn and washing the family automobile, when he could be doing some financial planning for the family, he is most likely underutilizing his time. Of couse, if he finds that work beneficial in terms of exercise, that is a different story. Often, however, you may feel that you "have to" do things when, in fact, you really do not.

By listing all the key tasks that have to be done and assigning them to the person who can do them at the lowest cost (that is, who will have to give up the least important other task to do it), you can get much more done for the family's time, energy, money, enthusiasm, and interest. For example, if Mom does the vacuuming, she will not be able to sit down and balance the checkbook for the week and write out checks for bills that need to be paid. Eleven-year-old Louis is capable of vacuuming, but not of bookkeeping. These are some of the tasks that can be delegated to children in most households, with the suggested minimum age for performing the task in parentheses: grocery shopping (16); cooking (15); cleaning bathroom (12); vacuuming (11); dusting (10); washing clothes (14); washing cars (12); making the beds (10); sweeping (10); emptying the trash (9); organizing and cleaning bedrooms (10); setting the table (8); washing and drying dishes (10); getting the mail from the box (8); putting washed clothing away (8); helping younger children with homework (10). Of course, minimum ages for task readiness will vary among children and families. The key, then, is for parents to sit down and carefully examine what has to be done and who in the family can do it most efficiently (least cost). Coupled with this analysis must be the parent's self-assessment: Am I using my time and energy in the most rewarding way possible? Parents must remember that any time they spend doing one thing they cannot spend doing another. All good executives, including parents, are conscious of this principle. Letting another person do it is good home management!

A second reason for delegating is to teach children how to handle more responsibility. As parents delegate downward, children rise to the occasion. In a gradual but steady fashion they find themselves growing in maturity as they attempt to respond to their parents' confidence in them. As we have seen, an essential ingredient in motivation is growth. Children whose parents delegate responsibilities and tasks to them experience high levels of growth and the consequent motivation. They sometimes have to "stretch" themselves to accomplish the tasks, but that is what maturing is all about. On the other hand, the children of parents who do not delegate sufficiently often develop a lethargic, dependent, and even demanding attitude. They remain in a "no growth" posture, unmotivated because of this lack of personal development, and feeling bad about themselves. Ironically, often the parent who does everything for his or her children trying to make their lives enjoyable and carefree does the most damage. Those who delegate to their children bestow on them the greatest gifts: responsibility, initiative, and a sense of accomplishment which will guide them through adulthood.

Before engaging in the process of delegating, it is important for parents to consider several issues that could interfere with its success. First, parents should ask themselves why they are choosing a particular child. Is it a critical task and is the most qualified child being chosen? Is it a fun task and is the delegating a reward for prior performance? Is it because this particular child needs it for his or her own growth? A clear definition of purpose is important in evaluating the success of the delegating after it is done: Did it have the payoff intended?

A second important issue to be considered is whether the delegated task is appropriate in terms of children's ages, danger involved, knowledge needed, agility, etc. Sometimes there is a fine line separating capability and incapability. When in doubt, it is always best to test out the proficiency of the children involved by having them attempt the task in the presence of the parent. This can be a good opportunity for the parent to serve as teacher if the ability of the child is not quite up to where it should be.

Thirdly, parents should make clear to children why they are being asked to perform the task. What is their special talent? Why does Daddy or Mommy need their help? How does their participation help the family and its members? What will Dad or Mom now be able to do because of the help provided? How will this help everyone else in the family? Providing a reason for the delegating increases greatly the probability of compliance and emotional acceptance of the request. It is important for parents to be sensitive to the possible tendency to keep delegating to those children that do a good job. Sometimes the conscientious children get all the work. The reward for working hard becomes more work. While this may not bother children at first, after a while they begin to resent the inequity.

Lastly, it is important for parents to communicate clearly what is expected of the child to whom a task is delegated. After all, children have to have some sense of parents' expectations—for example, in terms of degree of completeness and precision, time frame, and manner of execution of a task. Sometimes parents feel that it takes so long to delegate, especially initially, that it is easier to do the task themselves. This is, of course, short-range thinking. While the time required may have no return immediately, it certainly will—for the child as well as the parent—over the long run. A popular proverb points this out quite well: "If I give a child a fish, he can eat today. If I teach him how to fish, he can eat for a lifetime."

How, then, can parents go about delegating? There are several steps in the process:

STEP 1. DECIDE WHAT TASKS ARE TO BE DELEGATED

Parents should use the "management by exception" rule here: if one of the children can perform a task safely and effectively without interfering with the accomplishment of any personal obligation (e.g., school work), let the child do it. By delegating, parents will preserve the time and energy needed for those tasks (exceptions) that only they can do.

STEP 2. DEFINE THE SPECIFIC END RESULTS OF THE ASSIGNED TASK

Parents need to define exactly what they would like done— the more specific, the better. For example, if they want the dishes washed, they ought to specify whether they want them dried, stacked, etc. If the lawn furniture is to be put out, do they want all of it or just a few chairs? Often parents' conception of what a completed task looks like and the children's conception are quite different. Parents should be sure that they and the children are in agreement on the nature of the final product or outcome. It is always risky to assume that there is mutual understanding between the parent delegating the task and the child assigned to do it. Remember, as we pointed out in Chapter 2, that discrepancies between what parents and children consider to be completed tasks are usually present. When in doubt, check it out. There is much room for miscommunication and misunderstanding in the early part of the delegation process.

STEP 3. SELECT THE CHILD TO WHOM YOU WILL DELEGATE

It is important that parents match a delegated task with the child who is suitable for the task. Parents must likewise decide which incentives will serve to motivate the child to accept and implement the delegated responsibility. They must also be careful to distribute delegated responsibilities equitably among children and in accordance with their ages. For example, to ask a younger child to do something that an older one could do might be insulting to the older child. An established hierarchy of assigned tasks should be respected, everything else being equal. The hierarchy may be based on various factors, including tradition, physical strength, and emotional stability and development.

STEP 4. PREPARE THE CHILD TO PERFORM THE TASK

It is often important to provide a context for the delegated tasks. This usually involves explaining to the child why he or she was chosen, the importance of the task, and what will be the consequences of doing it or not doing it correctly. All three of these and other explanations help in motivating the child to do the task well. Ample opportunities for asking questions, getting clarifications, and requesting demonstrations should be provided to the child. Patience is critical here. It must be remembered that the process of delegating has a relationship-building benefit as well as a work-sharing one.

STEP 5. TEACH THE CHILD HOW TO DO IT

This is an optional step. If the child does not know how to perform the task to the parent's level of satisfaction, then it is the responsibility of the parent to teach him or her what to do. The best method of instruction usually is "show and tell," demonstrating and verbally explaining what to do step by step. It is important that the child have at least as long a time to practice the newly learned skills as the time it took to teach them. Teaching quickly and skimping on practice time is a formula for disappointment and frustration. To modify a popular expression: "If a job is worth delegating, it's worth *teaching* right."

STEP 6. ENCOURAGE THE CHILD TO PERFORM THE TASK INDEPENDENTLY

As soon as there is reasonable assurance that children know what to do and how to do it, they should be encouraged to begin doing the delegated task on their own. Some children can't wait and will jump right in, feeling confident that they know what they are doing. Others, even though they know how to do it, are fearful of even the slightest risk involved, afraid that what could go wrong will go wrong: they want to check with parents every few minutes as they perform the task so they won't make any mistakes. This style of accepting and performing delegated tasks, of course, is counterproductive: the work is not really distributed away from the parent, and the child does not grow to the extent possible.

One way for parents to encourage independent action is to give children some extra practice time and then set limits on how often they can look to the parents for approval. Another approach is to assure them that they will gain parental approval if they do their *best* and not worry so much about possible failure: "Dad will only be disturbed by one thing: if you do not try to do this the best way you know how. If you make a mistake, which *can* happen, don't worry about it. I'll be here to help you out. But, right now I'm counting on *you* doing it." The energy that children could waste in "disaster fantasies," worrying about potential failure, must be directed toward the accomplishment of the tasks.

STEP 7. MAINTAIN CONTROL OVER THE TASK

The difference between delegation and just assigning a task to a child is that the delegated task is still considered to be the ultimate responsibility of the parent, while the assigned task is the responsibility of the child. In the previous step we were concerned with children who might have difficulty actually practicing their independence in task performance. Here, our concern is with just the opposite kind: the children who run wild with a task. This step is designed to put some controls on them to preclude their making any serious mistakes or errors in judgment for which the parents will be held responsible. Remember, responsibility without control leaves parents distressed and vulnerable. We certainly are not recommending that parents sit on top of a child through every step of a delegated task. What we are emphasizing is that parents maintain an appropriate degree of *final* control over what goes on. Assigning a twelve-year-old son to study about and recommend a home computer is one thing; giving him a blank check to go out and purchase the recommended one is something else.

Because parents may need to monitor the performance of delegated tasks, indicators of successful performance by children should be established. Methods of observation of these indicators can range from a simple glance out the kitchen window every twenty minutes as children are raking leaves in the backyard to a more elaborate, step-by-step work breakdown and evaluation for more complex tasks (e.g., assigning a fifteen-year-old daughter to plan and implement the entire redecoration of her bedroom). If parents are sensitive to the always necessary balance between their children's independent and controlled behavior, successful delegation is highly likely.

The importance of clearly defined family delegation policy and practice is no more evident than in the home management and maintenance function. The family's physical environment is a major factor in its functioning. It is at one and the same time a cause and a consequence of family goals, values, interpersonal relationships, and quality of life. This environment has a tendency to feed on itself. A vicious cycle develops. The more parents are overwhelmed by the tasks of home management, the more overwhelmed they are likely to become. The more they have the situation under control, the more they will be able to control the situation in the future. If home management, then, is approached haphazardly, long-term dire results are likely. If addressed efficiently, however, it can greatly enhance the odds of successful parentship. Often the nature and condition of the setting for parentship, the home, can establish the conditions for success or failure before the first word is uttered or the first behavior is attempted. Remember, parentship is a performing art. The stage setting is critical to the act.

HOME ORGANIZATION AND MANAGEMENT: SETTING THE STAGE FOR PARENTING

The family's physical environment has a tremendous influence on parent-child relationships. Since the physical environment or "plant" for the family is the home, parents need to plan, arrange, and maintain the home with the family and its interpersonal relationships in mind. Parents and children see home as a refuge from the outside world and want a comfortable, compatible environment. They want their home to be a reflection of their individual selves and the collective family's personality. A compatible environment makes people feel more fulfilled, and an interesting house sparks the imagination, makes a growing child brighter and more alert, and fosters rewarding family relationships. An organized home is less stressful for all family members and can contribute greatly to the success of the entire family and each member. Therefore, an important part of successful parenting is home management: the organization, operation, and maintenance of the family's physical environment. This leadership task, while certainly serving a practical, nuts-and-bolts purpose, can be much more than pure logistics. If approached with some careful thought, it can serve as a unifying force for the family through the need for cooperation and be an apprenticeship program for children who will some day be adults and parents themselves. After all, part of parentship is training future parent leaders!

What is an organized home? Standards vary widely, and family leaders must decide what level of organization is compatible with their lifestyle. Standards for home management cannot be imposed by others. Fathers and mothers set standards for themselves and should feel no guilt if their standards are different from other parents'. The family's own comfort level is of primary importance. Standards also change with stages in the family life cycle. Most brides and grooms enter marriage with no training in home management but with expectations based on their own respective family experiences. If both of them are employed, the time available for home management may be less than it was for their parents' generation, when many wives were full-time homemakers.

These time constraints, combined with changing roles, values, and expectations, as well as increasing technological advances, result in differing standards for today's parents. Furthermore, the standards of a family with young children may be very different from the standards of a family with teenagers or from an older adult family in an "empty nest." Standards also change as parents assume additional roles. The parent who returns to school or the homemaker who reenters the work force finds that decreasing time available for homemaking alters standards.

The goal in home management, then, is to provide an organized home environment, whatever that means by the family's own standards. The word "home" means not just the family's place of residence but also the social unit formed by the family living together in a congenial environment. Each family member contributes to making the family home. This means that housework is family work, not Mom's work. The role of the parent as home manager, then, involves dividing responsibilities, planning and scheduling tasks, supervising, and evaluating performance.

Resources of the Home Manager

The home manager has several resources to use in organizing and maintaining the home. First, and foremost, he or she can count on the interpersonal feelings of the family members as a resource in homemaking. Members of the family share feelings of loyalty, the need for cooperation, and intimacy. Because of these interpersonal feelings they have a vested interest in sharing homemaking tasks for the common good.

Secondly, parents generally have personal knowledge, abilities, and skills in homemaking through their own upbringing. Few people have any formal training in homemaking. Attitudes, values, standards, and role expectations are passed from parent to child. Some children learn a great deal about homemaking from their families. Others leave the nest and start a family and find that they have to learn as they go. Books are available at all public libraries that contain helpful hints or strategies to simplify tasks. Home management textbooks present theory as well as practical suggestions for improving efficiency.

The third resource of the home manager is his or her own time and energy. Most parents will understand why this is not at the top of the list in terms of availability. Working all day and then coming home to the needs and demands of children and house leaves many parents drained. The key is for them to utilize available time in an organized way to free more of it for leisure activities, including rest. Parents should remember the fundamental dilemma concerning time: none of us has enough time, but all of us have all there is. So the key variable is not amount of time, but *management* of time.

Finally, money is a resource that can be used by the home manager. Those who feel they can afford the expense may hire outside help for housekeeping, child care, lawn care, or home maintenance and decorating tasks. They may choose to use money as a resource to delegate tasks to others.

STEPS IN HOME MANAGEMENT

Once parents have recognized the need for an organized home, assigned responsibilities for it, and recognized the resources available, it is time to look at the steps involved in home management: planning, implementing, controlling, and evaluating.

The first step in any organized system is planning. This includes identifying tasks to be accomplished, analyzing the tasks, and setting realistic goals. For example, the parent should identify housekeeping tasks and decide who is going to complete the tasks, how often, and when.

The Home Management Checklist (Chart A) is useful for planning and can be used in a number of ways. This checklist classifies household tasks in three categories: food, clothing, and shelter. The list represents a sample of household tasks and is not meant to be all-inclusive. You can use it as is or adapt it to include other tasks you have identified.

The autocratic or bureaucratic parent will decide who should be assigned each task on the list. Cooperative or democratic parents may decide to give each family member a copy of the list and ask each to code the task according to preference:

1. Volunteer to do regularly.
2. Agree to do once in a while.
3. Would rather not do.

As discussed in Chapter 2, Parentship Styles, the approach that you take in home management should be a function of your own preferred style as well as the preferred follower style of your children and the nature of the task to be accomplished. Asking each person to complete the "how often" column and then discussing responses is an interesting exercise in negotiating standards for many parents. When children realize that clean sheets every week means they must strip and remake the bed, many opt for clean sheets less often. If the parent wants to organize the homemaking tasks and delegate to other family members, room must be allowed for modifying standards. It is important to set realistic goals when planning home management task assignments. Those who remember grandmothers turning the house inside out for "spring cleaning" and "fall cleaning" may be inclined to include that activity on the checklist. However, work schedules and other priorities may make the time commitment unrealistic.

CHART A
HOME MANAGEMENT CHECKLIST

	A. Who does it now?	How often?	B. Who could/ would do it?	How often?
FOOD				
Plan meals				
Shop for food				
Store food				
Prepare meals				

	A. Who does it now?	How often?	B. Who could/ would do it?	How often?
Serve meals				
Clean up after meals				
CLOTHING				
Purchase for parent(s)				
Purchase for child(ren)				
Sort/wash/dry				
Fold/store				
Mend/iron				
Dry-clean				
SHELTER				
Cleaning				
Picking up/putting away				
Sweep/vacuum/dust (family rooms)				
Garbage/trash—collection and disposal				
Mop/clean (bathroom, kitchen)				
Seasonal cleaning				
Maintaining				
Decorating/arranging/painting				
Shopping for furnishings				
Repairs: electrical, plumbing, etc.				
Exterior				
Mowing lawn				
Care of garden and plants				
Painting/repair				
Sweeping porch and walk				
Car care				
Strategic and Operational Planning				
Financial goals				
Recreation/vacation/entertainment				
Education/homework				
Housing decisions				
Calendar/scheduling system				

	A. Who does it now?	How often?	B. Who could/ would do it?	How often?
Personal Space				
Child(ren)'s room/space (bath/bed/work/play)				
Parent's room/space (bath/bed/work/hobbies/relaxation)				

Note: Column B may be used several ways, depending on the leadership style of the parents. Recognizing that tasks may be delegated, the autocratic or bureaucratic parent may decide who should be assigned each task on the checklist. The cooperative or democratic parent may ask each family member to code the task according to preference: (1) volunteer to do regularly, (2) agree to do once in a while, or (3) would rather not do. "How often" responses may lead to a discussion on compromising standards in a democratic household, etc.

Once parents analyze the tasks to be accomplished, they must match the worker to the task. A five-year-old may be able to help set the table by counting out and placing napkins and silverware, but may not be able to pour milk. To match the worker to the task may mean breaking each job into elements. The "Serve meals" item listed under "Food" might be further divided into:

- wipe off table
- set out plates
- set out silverware and napkins
- pour and serve beverages
- place salt, pepper, butter, salad dressing, etc., on table as needed
- place food on table

As many as six people then can help "serve meals."

If family members are to have some say in which tasks they assume, the parent still has the responsibility to delegate. If no one in the family volunteers to clean the oven, parents can assume, delegate, or rotate the task. They can make a list of tasks suitable for each child and then let the children express a preference. Such a list for ten-year-olds might include:

- set the table each night for dinner
- wipe off the table after dinner
- sweep under the kitchen table after dinner (using a dustpan and whisk-broom or portable battery-operated vacuum)
- put away the clean silverware

- help sort dirty laundry in piles by color
- dust books on shelves
- gather trash from wastebaskets around the house
- scrub ring around the bathtub while in the tub
- clean bathroom sink
- feed pet
- sweep sidewalk after grass is cut

From such a list, the child can choose three or four tasks to be done routinely as "family work." Children should remember, housework is not "Mom's work." The idea is to present homemaking as work to be shared by the family. This will be good not only for efficiency, but also for family unity and the children's sense of responsibility.

As children grow, the number and difficulty of assigned tasks will change. A twelve-year-old could assume all of the tasks on the ten-year-old's list and/or others that are more difficult, such as:

- wash car
- clean out refrigerator
- make salad (or the entire meal)
- wash windows
- polish shoes

The parent retains control by guiding and directing how each task is to be accomplished. The twelve-year-old in the above example needs to be shown what "set the table" means. What plates are to be used? Where are plates kept? Does each member of the family get a knife, fork, and spoon? Only adults get knives? Only small children get spoons? Where are napkins kept? Where are napkins placed on the table? A basic setting might be drawn on a card and posted for children to follow. One of the most effective controlling techniques a parent can use is praise. Praising a child for a job well done, or at least attempted in a spirit of positive cooperation, achieves much better results than negative criticism.

You need to remember to be flexible about delegated jobs. "Empty the dishwasher before you go out to play" or "Clean the bathroom each weekend" gives the child some control over time. Children are more likely to cooperate if their time and preferences are considered.

Once children are shown how to perform a task, you may realize some compromising of standards is necessary. Does the furniture have to be moved each time the living room is vacuumed? How often are windows washed? How often does each person want or need a fresh towel? Maybe the child who runs the vacuum, or washes the windows, or launders the towels, needs to negotiate with the parent for a mutually agreeable time schedule.

Most children respond positively to a posted chart outlining their household tasks to be completed. Some children like to receive stars or stickers in recognition of a task completed. The posted chart helps to cut down on nagging, which neither parent nor child likes. Parents need to decide what the consequences will be if the children do not complete their tasks. Depriving a child of a treat (TV, trip to the store, ice cream) may be chosen by autocratic parents. A family conference and renegotiating of expectations may work in cooperative or democratic homes. Children like knowing they are making a genuine contribution to the family's well-being. The system weakens, however, when children feel like servants being assigned unpleasant chores. It is important that each child have clear-cut responsibilities with minimal overt supervision.

Evaluating

One of the most important, but often overlooked, steps in any management system is evaluation. The parent evaluates by observation and the feedback of family members. Some families schedule problem-solving conferences on Sunday evenings or at the end of each month. Whether at a conference or in informal discussion, family members should be able to renegotiate task assignments. The twelve-year-old who volunteered to prepare Sunday breakfast for the family may find after a month or two that it's not a terrific way to spend Sunday morning. On the other hand, helping with the grocery shopping and storing food when it is brought home might suit a preteen's interest.

As children grow older, they should be able to assume additional homemaking responsibilities. As each birthday approaches, or each January, they might be presented with a new list of options. Adults, too, may need to assume different tasks. Variety alleviates boredom and also prepares more competent homemakers. Women who have never managed money, paid bills, or gathered family records for preparing an income tax return, can be true displaced homemakers if they become widowed or divorced. Men who have never been in a grocery store or prepared a meal or used the washing machine may feel helpless if their wife is hospitalized or goes to visit her mother in Florida. While each family member has preferred tasks, it is not bad for each member to have some idea of how to do the tasks of others in the family.

HOME MANAGEMENT SUGGESTIONS FOR PARENTS

Effective home management involves an understanding of the process at the broader level, which we have just discussed, as well as at the nuts-and-bolts level. Both dimensions are necessary for the development of a comprehensive approach to the task. Included here are some recommendations for the day-to-day management of the home.

Food

Planning meals is an important part of home management. Meals are planned around family preferences, food on hand, and weekly specials at the supermarket, as well as the cook's time and interests. Meal plans might be posted on a corkboard or the door of the refrigerator. If two or more persons share the cooking or someone has to "sub" as cook, food should be available to prepare the posted meals. Every family should also have some "shelf" meals on hand for emergencies (e.g., pasta and bottled sauce or tuna noodle casserole). Some families use a rotating fourteen-day meal plan to minimize time spent on meal planning and shopping.

Every family should have a market list posted. While a plain piece of paper will do, the ideal list is set up to correspond to the aisles in the supermarket or store most often used by the family. In that way, the food shopper can more quickly purchase the items on the list. Everyone can contribute to the market list. The five-year-old who likes bananas with lunch, the ten-year-old who notices the peanut butter running low, and the adult who gets a craving for sardines can enter their request on the list. If the market list is viewed as a shared responsibility, each member of the family will feel his or her preferences are being considered.

BREAKFAST

Few families eat breakfast together. Some families smooth the way by setting the table the night before, others have a selection of cold cereals on hand, some grab toast and juice on the run. To encourage children to eat breakfast and participate in its preparation, parents should make the meal as simple as possible. Cereal, milk, juice, and toast is a very adequate breakfast. No parent should feel guilt over not preparing a bacon-and-eggs breakfast. For variety, they may try assorted muffins or quick breads, toaster waffles, blender fruit shakes, peanut butter sandwiches.

LUNCH

Most children and some adults pack a lunch from home to eat at school or work. Some kinds of sandwiches can be made ahead of time and frozen. Lunches can be made the night before and taken from the refrigerator on the way out.

Some children like to be surprised at lunchtime by the meal sent from home, but most like to know what they are getting and have a say in the selection and preparation. Parents should encourage that interest as early as possible. The first grader who helps pack a lunch box is taking a step toward increased self-sufficiency. Of course, an occasional surprise treat in the lunch bag is always received with fondness by the child at school.

DINNER

Ideally, the family should eat dinner together as a social unit. It is a time to share the day's accomplishments, discuss current events, make plans for the future. If family members also share in the planning, preparation, and cleanup of dinner, they each have a vested interest in being present.

Dinnertime should be a pleasant time. However, expectations should be realistic and you must not panic if dinners are not characterized by perfect harmony. Sometimes children will demonstrate their happiness with the family's being together by animated behavior, giggling, and teasing. The family table does not have to resemble the mess at a military school!

Dinner preparation can be one person's task or it may be shared or rotated. For example:

- one child can make salad Monday, Wednesday, and Friday
- another child can prepare and serve dessert Tuesday, Thursday, and Saturday
- some husbands and wives like to cook together and use that time to share the highlights of their day with each other
- one child makes dinner every Saturday night (the menu may alternate between tacos and pizza!)
- a budding gourmet may be inspired by a meal in a magazine and put in an occasional request to cook

Each member of the family above the age of infancy can be responsible for clearing his or her place. Scraping a plate and putting it in the sink or dishwasher is one simple homemaking task that all can share. Other cleanup comes under the category of family work and can be delegated, shared, or rotated.

Clothing Maintenance

Many parents feel stressed by the never-ending stream of dirty clothes to be washed, dried, folded, ironed, mended, and stored. Some homemakers wash clothes daily and feel alternately chased by dirty laundry or on top of the situation. The family without an automatic washer and dryer can minimize trips to the laundromat by pooling laundry until several loads are accumulated. The family that has a washer and dryer in the home has more flexibility in scheduling the task.

A small family that owns an adequate quantity of clothing may prefer to schedule one day a week as laundry day. Each member of the family has a basket for dirty clothes that accumulate throughout the week. On laundry day, each person strips the bed, gathers towels, and carries the basket to the laundry room. One person (or two sharing the task) sorts, washes, dries, folds, and places laundry back into each person's laundry basket. At the end of the day, each basket is collected by its owner, the clothes are stored, and the empty baskets are ready for next week's soiled clothing. Larger families may need to wash clothing more often. An alternate system might be to have three laundry bags or baskets in a central location (hall, bathroom, or laundry area) labeled "white," "dark," and "colors." Everyone places dirty clothes in the appropriate bag. As each bag is full, someone washes that load, dries and folds it, and leaves it on top of the dryer to be collected by the owners. Or, to get the laundry returned to its owners and stored, the person emptying the dryer might place the clean laundry in front of the TV. The laundry's owners collect and fold their laundry while watching TV, and during commercial breaks they return the clean clothes to the appropriate storage place.

Parents should adopt two basic principles:

1. Try not to use the washing machine for one item of clothing. To economize on water, electricity, detergent, and time, wash full loads only.

2. Each family member should assume some responsibility for clothing care.

From the age of two, children can put their dirty clothes in an assigned
hamper and return clean clothes to a drawer. Children *like* to cooperate. Parents should start the habit early.

Boys and girls by about the age of twelve can be taught how to sew
on a button and use the iron. They should also learn how to use the
washer and dryer and read care labels in garments. If the family members vow to buy only clothes that will withstand machine washing and
drying, the job is simpler for all.

Housecleaning

Cleaning of rooms used by the entire family is "family work." This
includes living room, den, dining room, kitchen, bathroom, etc. Bedrooms will be discussed later under "personal space." Regular pickup
of out-of-place items is the most important habit for all family members to establish in an organized household. Some homemakers routinely go through the house with a basket each day, collecting misplaced items and depositing them in the proper room. An efficient
home manager encourages that routine in all family members. In a
two-story house, the family might keep a basket at the top of the stairs
and one at the bottom, for depositing objects that belong on the other
floor. If everyone in the family makes a habit of using the baskets, this
can minimize clutter. "Don't put it down, put it away" is a motto that
helps remind some families how clutter can get out of hand.

Clutter Components

Mail that comes into the home needs to be handled daily. Each
family should have a designated place where mail is always placed. If
mail is laid on the kitchen table or the living room sofa, someone will
have to pick it up later and move it; also, it is more likely to be
misplaced or lost completely. A centrally located desk is a good idea. It
could be at the Kitchen Control Center, in the hall, or the family room.
Bills and financial mail should have a designated place on the desk—a
folder or shoe box will do. Another folder or box might be labeled
"filing" for storing important papers for taxes, assessment, insurance,
etc. "Things to do" might include party invitations, magazine sub-
scription renewals, and reading material. Everything that is of no interest should be thrown away immediately: many people save mail that

they "might need someday" and have clutter that is useless and out of date as well as out of hand.

As a rule, newspapers should be discarded after two days, if not sooner, unless there is a reason to hold onto an issue. No one will read old news when newspapers come in daily. Likewise, weekly or monthly magazines should not be simply piled someplace unless there is a reason to keep them. If an article in a newspaper or magazine is worth saving, it should be clipped and put in the appropriate folder.

Toys create clutter in many homes, at least from the parents' perspective. Toddlers need to be encouraged from an early age to pick up one toy or set of toys before moving on to another. Toy chests should be banned! Children find it frustrating to dig to the bottom and tend to toss everything else aside. A toy chest might be the answer for a large collection of stuffed animals or balls, but low shelves create a better space for most toys.

Parents should line a cabinet or lower part of a closet with shelves. Board games, trucks, building sets, dolls, and books can be grouped in boxes or trays on the shelves. Toys of different sizes can go in different size or color containers. Plastic wash tubs work well. "Doll clothes in the green box," "rubber balls in the red box," "blocks on the yellow tray" make it much easier for children to control their toy storage. Remember that play is a child's work and toys are the child's tools. Children like knowing where their tools belong. Organizing their toys relieves what the parents view as clutter and satisfies the children's craving for boundaries. As children outgrow or wear out toys, parents ought to give them away or throw them out and only keep accessible the current favorites. If trucks are currently out of favor but the child is likely to come back to them, they can be packed in a box on a high shelf for a few months' rest. They will seem new when returned but will not add to clutter in the meantime.

Children's schoolwork has the potential for creating clutter. Homework should be done at an assigned spot, and all school supplies should be kept there. Children should be discouraged from dropping books on the floor by the front door when they come home. In fact, no one should drop anything by the door. If clutter is the first thing noticed when the door is opened, people entering the home are likely to feel the entire house is a mess and may even begin to behave accordingly. Clutter has a tendency to beget clutter!

The system for trash removal begins with a wastepaper basket in every room. This encourages family members to throw things away. Once or twice a week someone in the family should take a paper grocery bag or a plastic trash bag and walk around the house collecting the contents of all wastebaskets. Kitchen trash and garbage will be taken out more often, perhaps daily. Garbage should be stored in a can or plastic bag outside the house, but protected from animals, until it is collected or taken to the dump.

CLEANING

Rooms used by the family will need to be dusted and swept or vacuumed on a regular basis. Dusting is easy for children to do weekly. Sweeping the kitchen floor may need to be done daily in most homes. Vacuuming carpets and other areas can have a more flexible schedule. This type of regular cleaning can be broken into component parts and divided among family members. For instance, on Saturday morning, instead of watching cartoons, young children could dust the living room while older children vacuum for part of that time. Sweeping the kitchen floor could become a part of kitchen cleanup after dinner.

Other regular cleaning includes "wet cleaning" of bathrooms, kitchens, floors, and windows. In a two-bathroom house, adults can clean one and children the other. The job can be delegated, shared, or rotated among family members. It can also be subdivided into specific tasks. For instance, if each child scrubs the tub at bath time, it may never need a separate cleaning. One child can wash the floor one week, another the toilet, and the next week switch with each other. The kitchen floor can be washed with a wet mop as part of weekly cleaning. Windows may be washed seasonally, except perhaps sliding glass doors that are targets for fingerprints.

SCHEDULING

One of the most important systems in managing the home is a scheduling system. Central to the system is a family calendar and corkboard or chalkboard for messages. Some families use the door of the refrigerator for this purpose. They display school work, leave notes for each other, and post the school lunch menus and the market list on the refrigerator with tape or magnets. Adults who are busy with work, volunteer, recreational, or social engagements during the evenings and weekends will recognize the value of the calendar. It reminds them and others in the family of outside commitments and responsibilities. As children get older and their circle of activities widens, their social life may interfere with family plans, so it is important for them to use the calendar too.

172

PERSONAL SPACE

Children from an early age should take responsibility for their own personal space. Whether a child has a bed to share, or a room of his or her own; has two toys or two hundred; is a preschooler or in college—whatever the circumstances, he or she can assume some responsibility for belongings. A parent can make a chart for a three-year-old with pictures or words to illustrate daily responsibilities:

- get dressed
- put away pajamas
- brush teeth
- comb hair
- make bed (may need help)
- clear meal dishes
- pick up toys before bedtime
- hang up jacket
- put dirty clothes in hamper

As children start school, items to be added may be:

- do homework
- make lunch for school, etc.

Note: these personal responsibilities are not to be confused with family work. These are personal tasks to be performed by any independent person. Sometime around the age of two, when children start to assert their independence, is a natural time for parents to ease them into some of these things. It is easier on the children and on the family than letting the children expect someone to wait on them. Parents should teach the children how to keep their own bathroom clean, make their beds, and take care of their clothing.

There are times when all children get cranky and obstinate. You may decide to skip the task until tomorrow or cajole your young child by helping with pickup, but you should never feel "It's easier to do it myself." In the short run, it may be easier. But in the long run it is always preferable to see the youngster grow in self-sufficiency.

Having said earlier that each family must set its own standards, we offer one final suggestion: if the parent wants to get the family to agree on a set of standards for homemaking, they should be kept simple. The essentials might be:

- put things where they belong when you are through with them (or: "Don't put it down, put it away!")
- close closets, cupboard doors, and drawers before leaving a room
- turn off lights, radios, etc., when leaving a room
- wash dishes daily
- straighten beds daily
- serve well-balanced meals regularly
- take out garbage as often as needed
- clean and straighten bathrooms regularly
- keep up with the dirty laundry

To have cooperation from children, partners or spouses need cooperation in home management from each other. Couples who have been together for a while may have already established patterns for division of responsibility. The pattern may be based on preference, or habit, or role expectation.

The fact is, however, that gender does not determine ability to write checks, wash dishes, clean the house, carry out trash, shop for food, cook, mow grass, change a flat tire, bathe children, or choose home furnishings. An open mind and open communication are also important resources in home management.

In conclusion, an essential part of parentship, then, is the skill of delegating. Successful family managers universally have talent in this area. They are willing to share their leadership with the rest of the family. In so doing they allow their families to accomplish more and they give their children the opportunity to grow. They are not driven "to do it all" and do not feel the need to be viewed as indispensable. All the glamorous aspects of parentship will amount to little if the "nitty-gritty" tasks of home management are not systematically shared and accomplished by *all* the family members.

10

Discipline: Enforcing the Rules of the Family Game

Six-year-old Kevin had looked forward to his first sleep-over at his best friend Michael's house for weeks. His parents, Matt and Libby, were totally unprepared for his sobbing phone call half an hour after his usual bedtime. "Come get me," he pleaded. "I don't want to sleep here!" After a thirty-minute drive to Michael's house, Matt found the boys happily playing with their trucks on the floor of Michael's room. "Go on home, Dad," Kevin said. "I wanna stay here." Matt left without a word and drove home with gritted teeth and hands tightly gripping the steering wheel.

Who's in charge here? How often do we observe the behavior of our own or someone else's children and say, "What that kid needs is some good, old-fashioned discipline."

But what does the word discipline really mean? For many parents, discipline means punishment: spanking, reprimanding, taking away privileges—any of the negative consequences of misbehavior. However, discipline actually means "training to act in accordance with rules." The word itself was derived from the Latin word for instruction.

The purpose of children's discipline, then, is to train or enable them to act in accordance with family values and expectations as well as society's rules. Punishment can be a part of this process, but it is not the only part. The role of the parents as effective disciplinarians should involve two processes: first, setting children on the road to success by helping them develop self-discipline; and second, accepting responsibility for course correction when children behave inappropriately.

THE ROAD TO SUCCESS

George and Sandy had decidedly mixed feelings about two-year-old Erin's negative behavior. Her adamant NO in response to dinner time, bedtime, going to grandma's . . . just about anything her parents wanted . . . was very frustrating to these young parents. But mixed with the frequent irritation and occasional anger was an element of pride—"Erin was establishing herself as a separate, independent person whose unique feelings and opinions were not to be denied. Good for her."

And so it is with some discipline problems at every age: the preschooler and temper tantrums, the fourth grader who experiments with profanity, the teenager who dresses like a punk rocker. Sometimes problems like these are simply side effects of growing up, of becoming an independent, self-controlled (rather than parent-controlled) person. Every child—and parent—experiences them to some degree. After Erin passed through her negative stage, George and Sandy were relieved to see their child's behavior improve, and thankful they no longer needed to discipline her constantly. But they were also very proud of her: she was now controlling her own negative behavior without intervention from them. Erin was developing self-discipline.

Self-discipline—control over one's own behavior—is the ultimate goal of all parental discipline. When we say parents need to set their children on the road to success we mean that they must enable them to control their own behavior in accordance with family values and society's rules—even and especially when parents are not there.

Parents can determine if they are setting their children on the road to self-discipline by completing the following index:

SELF-DISCIPLINE INDEX

Instructions: Answer "yes" or "no" to the following questions.

_____ 1. Have you discussed family values (kindness, helpfulness, trying hard, etc.) with your children at a level that they can understand?

_____ 2. Have you discussed society's rules (school attendance, traffic, drug and alcohol laws) with your children at a level that they can understand?

_____ 3. Can your children explain family values and rules that have an impact on their behavior?

_____ 4. Do your children have the right to question or to challenge family values?

_____ 5. Are you aware of what problem behaviors are typical for your child's age level?

_____ 6. Are you aware of what problem behaviors are typical for your child's next age level?

_____ 7. Do your children know what specific behavior is expected of them?

_____ 8. Do you encourage your children to be proud of themselves for their own good behavior?

_____ 9. Do you give the right amount of praise—not too much or too little—for appropriate behavior?

_____10. Do you help your children develop positive behavior patterns before problems develop?

_____11. Do you address any behavior problems that do arise quickly, before the behavior is worsened?

_____12. Do you try to let your children know they are respected and loved as people, regardless of their behavior?

_____13. Do you encourage your children to make their own decisions about their behavior as soon as they are ready?

_____14. Do you feel confident of your children's ability to behave well most of the time?

_____15. Do you let your children know you feel they are capable of behaving well most of the time?

Scoring: Give yourself one point for each "yes" answer. A score of 12 or more means you are already doing a good job of setting your child up for success. A score of 7 or less means that you should spend much more time developing self-discipline in your child. Scores from 8 through 11 should be viewed as a warning sign that some modification, albeit moderate, is necessary in disciplining approach.

The first step in setting children on the road to successful self-discipline is to let them know exactly what is expected. This may seem to go without saying, but in reality many cases of misbehavior can be attributed to the parent neglecting to communicate expectations—or assuming the child already knew.

This can sometimes cause serious problems, as in the case of Robin, a fourteen-year-old girl distraught after her first sexual encounter with an older boy. "I didn't know what he was doing, Mom," she wailed to her mother who had discovered them on the couch minutes before. "I sort of felt it was wrong, but I didn't know!" "But I told you all about this a year ago," her exasperated mother replied. "You told me about periods and ovaries and stuff like that, but you never told me what to do when a boy did what he did."

Robin's mother assumed that her teenage daughter was able to make the appropriate inferences from limited information. However, her explanations as well as expectations were not explicit enough. Parents are not clear enough for several possible reasons. First, they may not know how to translate their vague and nebulous behavioral desires into concrete terms: a communication problem. Secondly, they may not be able to discuss certain delicate topics for fear of implanting "bad ideas in the kids' heads," especially in the areas of sex and drugs. Thirdly, they may falsely reach the conclusion that their children understand and accept what their parents want because they fail to question them, erroneously perceiving tacit consent when, in fact, the children are too afraid or confused to challenge their parents' implicit instructions.

Letting a child know what is expected, then, is not always easy. The process starts with defining and communicating family values. To a very small child, the family is his or her society. If children are to conform to society's expectations as adults, it is imperative that they learn to get in step with their family's values while they are still young. However, often parents themselves have to develop a clearer understanding of exactly what those family values are before they can transmit them on to their children. In a two-parent household both spouses will have to work together to develop a consensus on some commonly held values and/or reach an agreement on what differences in values each would be willing to accept.

Gus and Joan, a young couple in Boston, were like many parents who have only a vague idea what their values are. They began to clarify their values by listing what characteristics they wanted their newborn son, Jeffrey, to have as an adult. Then they decided how important each was in comparison with the others and ranked them by placing a 1 after the most important, 2 after the next most important, and so on. They spent time discussing the values over which they disagreed and tried to understand each other's reasoning. Then they either reached a consensus or compromise or one agreed to defer to the other. When they were finished, part of their list looked like this:

honest	3
healthy	1
sociable	7
sensitive	9
inquisitive	5
optimistic	10
realistic	6
considerate	8
hardworking	2
creative	4

They then put the list in a drawer and promised themselves they'd review it at least every year on Jeffrey's birthday and any other time they felt the need to revise or review the list.

Naturally, Gus's and Joan's list was different from the list that would be compiled by many other parents. Some parents might emphasize strength, courage, and determination; others may put a higher priority on caring and patience.

Here is a list of some common values that may help parents define their own family's set:

progressive	reserved	trusting	helpful
modern	suspicious	happy	kind
liberal	quiet	critical	respectful
independent	sensitive	observant	hardworking
conservative	inquisitive	verbal	obedient
natural	open	healthy	generous
youthful	friendly	thrifty	resourceful
religious	educated	chaste	assertive
delicate	honest	polite	tolerant
particular	traditional	neat	thick-skinned
different	conforming	clean	realistic
strict	strong	self-reliant	bold
hard	flexible	caring	cooperative
passionate	optimistic	loving	soft

It is also important that family values be reviewed periodically, for several reasons. First, parents and children often need a concrete reminder of where they want to go—just as they would check a map on a long trip to assure themselves that they are still on course. Also, values may change over time. For example, with differences in sex-appropriate behavior diminishing, parents are beginning to value caring and nurturing in their sons and strength and independence in their daughters. And sometimes we find that children simply do not have the innate capability to behave in a way their parents value. A child whose parents place a high priority on creativity, for example, may not always be imaginative.

Once family values have been established, the next step is to communicate them to the child. This is accomplished in two ways: by demonstrating the valued behavior in practice and by discussing values with the child. The demonstration can be a real-life situation ("See how Daddy was courteous to that man who was trying to cross the street in front of our car") or simulated ("Son, what do you think I would do if I was at a traffic light that was turning green and some person was halfway across the street?" [Child's answer . . .] "No, I wouldn't get angry and yell at him. I would give him a chance to get by. While he may be doing something dangerous, my screaming at him isn't really going to help matters. Two wrongs do not make a right").

If parents review and compare their list of valued behaviors, they will discover the way they would like to see themselves. By putting their beliefs into practice, they will be setting a positive example for their children. Of course, it is important for parents themselves to understand and help their children know the complexity of values. Every value issue or situation is not cut and dried. In fact, few are. However, within this framework of frequent ambiguity this exercise of defining and communicating family values will help in the alignment of family priorities.

Although Joan placed a high value on honesty for her son, she knew she sometimes tended to stretch the truth and tell small lies when it was convenient for her in dealing with her parents or her boss. Luckily, she realized that no amount of discussion or lecture on the value of honesty and the wrongness of lying could have as much impact as her example, so she made an attempt to become more honest and open in her dealings with others. The old adage "Do as I say, not as I do" will not work in developing the children's self-discipline.

Discussion of values can take many forms. When Monica, age three, shoved her little brother to demonstrate her displeasure that he had one of her toys, her father knelt in front of her, placed his hands on her shoulders, looked her in the eye, and said, "In this family, we do not hurt other people." "But I'm mad—he has my dolly!" Monica screamed. "It's o.k. to be mad, Monica," her father assured her, "but it's not o.k. to hurt."

We know a Maryland family with three lively teenagers which holds a family values discussion each Thursday night at dinnertime. A recent discussion of teenage drug use included frank questions such as: Why do some teenagers use drugs? Are there any benefits to using drugs? What are the short- and long-term side effects of drug use? How do these conflict with our other values? All family members were encouraged to speak. Even when the twelve-year-old daughter said she could see why sometimes it might be more important for a teenager to go along with her friends than to conform to her family's values, rather than criticize her, her family listened to her thoughts and encouraged her to figure out why she felt that way and to examine some of the consequences of giving in to peer pressure.

It is important to remember that telling or explaining is only part of the process of communicating values. It is equally important to listen to and respond to children's needs and feelings and to encourage their active participation in developing their own value system, just as Monica's father and the family described did.

Conforming to rules and laws is usually an extension of family values. The requirements that a toddler hold your hand while crossing the street and that a teenager obey the speed limit are easier to conform to when viewed as a means of staying healthy and avoiding hurting others. But letting children know what is expected is not quite enough. It is just as important for parents to know what behavior they can realistically expect from children at any given age. Just as it is impossible to expect a preschooler to memorize multiplication tables, it is futile to expect an adolescent to always conform to family values when they conflict with those of his or her peers.

Parents have many resources to learn what behaviors can be expected at certain ages. Friends and relatives who have or have had children are a useful source of information, though sometimes not totally objective or realistic. Books and magazine articles on child development and parenting abound, and courses and seminars are often available.

Whatever the source, it is important for parents to have an accurate understanding of child development as well as a sensitivity to the unique growth path of each boy or girl. It will be comforting to see that, at every age, potential behavior problems are accompanied by the capability for increasingly mature, self-controlled behavior, and that the periods of most difficult behavior (two, four, seven, nine, and early teens) are followed by relatively stable, calm periods. Although parental intervention is required in the difficult times, it is nice to know that many of the discipline problems we encounter are really the natural side effects of growing up.

The parent who takes a positive approach to discipline views training as a large part of the job of setting his or her children up for success. Through a four-step training process, parents can help their children develop positive behaviors and habits before behavior problems occur. The procedure works well in almost all discipline/training situations including toilet training, taking responsibility for one's own belongings, developing study habits, safe driving, and many others.

THE DISCIPLINING PROCESS

The first step is *preparation.* It is much easier for children to learn a new skill or behavior if they fully understand what is expected and why. They need to know—in their own terms—why the new behavior is important for them and for the parents. How does what parents want them to do relate to the family's values or rules? What's in it for the children? For parents? They also need to know what the "standards of performance" are. How will they know if they have done a good job? How often and how well do parents expect them to perform? It is important that the expected performance be realistic in terms of the child's age and physical and psychological maturity. The standards of performance will probably increase as the child develops, and the child needs to understand this.

The second step is *demonstration:* showing and telling what the parent's preferred behavior looks like. For example, during toilet training parents may have the child watch an older sibling or friend perform. Parents could take teenage children who are learning to drive for a ride in the car while they discuss what they are doing. It is probably best to demonstrate the whole job first, to give an overview, and then to break it down into small, more quickly achievable parts. For instance, after taking the child who is learning to drive for a ride and discussing the whole job of driving, the parent might then demonstrate the smaller job of starting the car; adjusting mirrors and seat; fastening seat belts; coordinating clutch, accelerator, and ignition key, etc. Books, television shows, movies, and videotapes can also be effective methods of demonstration when followed by a discussion. Pointing out role models the child can emulate can sometimes be helpful if the model is someone the child respects and wants to be like. It is essential, though, to avoid fostering resentment by making children feel they are being compared unfavorably: "Why can't you be like Jimmy!"

Allowing the child to *practice* is the third step. Whenever possible, this should follow the demonstration step immediately. At this stage, parents need to be sensitive to the child's need for privacy. Some children at some ages balk at complying too easily or are afraid of failing in front of their parents. Forcing such children to practice or perform a new skill with parents "looking over their shoulder" before they are ready can result in resistance and resentment rather than learning. Above all, parents must *be patient.* Though they are totally familiar with what they are trying to teach their children, they must remember that the children are not. Empathy with the child's uncertainty and lack of knowledge is critical here. After all, parents themselves didn't always know how to drive—or use the bathroom either, for that matter.

Feedback is the final step in the four-step process. The children must know what they have done well and what they have not. Without feedback, children can assume they are doing well when they are not—and vice versa. Positive feedback is often some form of praise: "That's it!" or "Good job!" or a hug and a warm smile. Some parents find tokens, stickers, and treats helpful in addition to praise. When children are just beginning to learn something new it is important that they receive much positive feedback about what they have done well. If the behavior is particularly difficult or complex for a child, it may be necessary—at the *beginning*—to reward any change toward the expected performance: while the behavior may not be perfect yet, progress *is* being made.

But, after this initial stage, negative feedback may be an essential part of learning: children must know when their behavior is not up to standard so they can correct it. Negative feedback is *not* punishment; it is simply pointing out what part of the task needs to be improved. Negative feedback is most effective when it addresses the behavior, not the child.

Both positive and negative feedback are most effective when they follow the behavior immediately. It is also important to begin to diminish the amount and frequency of praise as the child begins the all-important task of evaluating and praising or changing his or her own behavior. Parents can ease this transition by changing "I'm proud of you" to "I bet you're proud of yourself," or by asking "How do you think you did?" when the child comes for feedback.

Clarifying, communicating, and discussing family values, expectations, and rules; understanding what behaviors can be expected of children at certain ages; and using a training process to develop positive behaviors and habits can all be instrumental in setting children on the road to success. When children know they are respected as individuals and that their parents have confidence in their ability to perform well most of the time, positive appropriate behavior is encouraged. High expectations—realistic for the child's age level—often result in good performance.

PROBLEM BEHAVIOR AND DISCIPLINE

But behavior problems do arise—in all children. Even when problems are expected at certain stages in the growing up process, some kind of parental intervention is necessary to return the child to more appropriate behavior and to prevent more serious problems later. This systematic, seven-step problem-solving process can be very valuable to parents:

STEP 1

The process begins with *awareness of the problem*. A discipline problem exists any time the child's behavior is inconsistent with parental expectations. Sometimes mothers and fathers are immediately aware of a sudden problem behavior such as a temper tantrum, fighting, or staying out too late. But other discipline problems are harder to detect. Sometimes a child's behavior changes slowly over time; a child can gradually become careless about grooming, withdraw from family, or develop a lack of interest in school work. These behavior patterns sometimes go unnoticed until a crisis occurs—a poor report card, an emotional blowup, a concerned phone call from a coach.

No matter what the discipline problem is, immediate recognition and corrective action are essential. The longer any behavior goes uncorrected, the harder it will be to change it later. Relatively small behavior problems that are not dealt with at an early age can also multiply into serious problems later. Sometimes parents will deny problems exist, diminishing their importance, fearful of what they portend, or hoping that they will go away. The best time to solve a problem is on first detection: it is usually easier and less costly to solve in terms of time, money, energy, and relationships. Problems that go unrecognized or are left to fester can reach chronic stages, where they become insoluble.

Ted and Marian had always been rather permissive with their thirteen-year-old daughter, Jodi. When she was a preschooler, they never went out because Jodi didn't want to stay with a babysitter. A long-awaited family vacation to the seashore when Jodi was eight was cut short because she didn't like the ocean. They responded to her fifth-grade teacher's concerns about Jodi's lying by criticizing the teacher for persecuting their child. They were devastated when the phone call came from the police station: their daughter had been arrested for shoplifting: could they come to the station to pick her up?

Why is it so tempting for parents to look the other way when their children display behavior problems? First of all, discipline is a very hard job. Discipline in any situation—at school or on the job—is hard enough, but the task of disciplining one's own children can sometimes be overwhelming. As one discouraged businessman-father put it, "You can't fire your kids. They are yours, for better or worse." Some parents identify very strongly with their children and view any problem in their behavior as a reflection on themselves. To recognize a discipline problem in a child would be to admit some failure or deficiency on the parent's part. Other times, parents just hope the situation will get better by itself: "I'm just going to wait for a while to see if he grows out of it." Sometimes a child will grow out of a behavior problem without parental intervention. But there is always the danger that the problem will just get worse, as in Jodi's situation. Some parents are afraid of their children's reaction. They fear the children may begin to dislike them, react with more difficult behavior, or feel bad about themselves. And in today's hectic, fast-paced society, some families spend hardly any time together. Finally, parents and potential parents receive little or no training in methods of disciplining children. They just don't know how. But although there are few high school or college classes in how to discipline, and although the parents' own parents and role models are often miles away, it is important to remember that the ability to use effective discipline is not an inborn trait or characteristic. It is a skill any parent can learn.

How can parents become more adept at picking up problem signals from their children? First, they can be aware of the temptation to look away from problems. Trying to observe each child as if he or she were a stranger can help parents to be more objective: "Would I like my son if he were a neighbor's or a friend's?" Being aware of how other children their age behave can also be helpful. Perhaps most important, parents can really listen to their children and be alert to verbal and nonverbal messages from them. Most often children really want their parents' help in controlling their behavior.

It is important for parents to remember that each act of discipline is not an isolated act, but an investment in the future behavior of the child. Well thought out and properly executed, discipline can help the child develop increasing self-control and become a more valuable member of the family. But when discipline is avoided or administered inappropriately, it can result in greater problems in the future. The following chart gives some examples of how poor discipline at one age can lead to problems later. This is intended only to illustrate the possible consequences of failing to discipline properly, not to predict actual future performance.

Poor Discipline at an Early Age . . .	Leads to Problems Later
Giving in to a two-year-old's temper tantrums . . .	Continued outbursts when she wants something at age three.
Rewarding every positive behavior of a four-year-old . . .	The child expects or needs some kind of reward for every good behavior at age five—and won't behave without one.
Threatening a six-year-old with withdrawing love if he misbehaves . . .	Fearfulness, insecurity at age seven.
Severely punishing an eight-year-old for a poor report card . . .	Resentment of parent, lack of interest in school at age nine.
Nagging a twelve-year-old about his friends . . .	Stronger peer group attachment and less attachment to family at thirteen.
Inordinate pressure to achieve high grades in high school . . .	Having too much fun in college and letting studies slip to make up for lost time socializing.

STEP 2

Gathering information is the second step in the parental problem-solving process. Parents need to ask the same questions any investigator would: Who is doing what, when, where, why, and how? There are many ways to do this. Simply observing the child is the method many parents use. This can be effective when parents are consistently aware of what their children are doing, and if they strive to be objective. Often, parental observations can be tarnished by a "halo effect." Parents of a child who has always been compliant can often ignore signs of behavior problems because they are inconsistent with their perception of a "good" child. On the other hand, it is often hard for the parents of a "difficult" child to see signs of good behavior—the "pitchfork effect."

There are several things parents can do to increase the objectivity of their observations. First, they can consider talking it over with the child: "How do you feel about what happened?" Or they can ask themselves the questions listed on page 188. Bringing children into the problem-solving process as soon as possible—considering them partners in the business of developing positive behavior—is often very effective.

It may be helpful for parents to talk with someone else who may have more information—or who may be more objective. Teachers, clergy, and physicians are good resources, but the parents of children's peers should not be overlooked as a resource. Developing a network with the parents of children's friends pays off not only as an "information pipeline" but also as a source of information about typical behaviors as well as mutual support at problem times. Be aware, however, that these methods can backfire if the child feels you do not trust him or her or if the people you consult use the information against the child or convey sensitive information to his or her peers.

Parents must be very careful to separate facts from assumptions. When their son Bradley's grades dropped suddenly and he began to be disruptive in his second-grade class, Jim and Carol began to punish him for his misbehavior by not letting him play with his friends after school and by isolating him in his room after a bad day. It was only after his yearly physical exam that his parents learned that Bradley's hearing was seriously impaired. Physical problems, then, are one of the many possible causes of problem behavior. Sometimes, as we saw with Robin earlier in the chapter, a child is not fully aware of what is expected. We often assume children know what is expected if we've told them once. "How many times do I have to tell you to do your homework before you can watch TV?" The answer usually is, more often than Mom and Dad would like, especially at the beginning of the school year.

Parental expectations that are not in line with the child's abilities are another major cause of behavior problems. When parents expect too much of a child in terms of age and physical and psychological maturity, he or she is likely to react in some negative way because of frustration and fear of failure. On the other hand, expecting too little of a child can be even more troublesome. Tony and Cathy's seven-year-old son, Gregory, had had a terrible year in second grade. He had been moody and withdrawn but frequently burst into fits of rage when another child bothered him. Each day after school Cathy looked through his school bag for a note from his teacher. "Let's see what trouble you got yourself into today, Gregory." That summer on his first day of camp, Tony, his hand firmly on Gregory's shoulder, advised the camp director: "Watch out for Gregory. He was a real problem child all year at school. He just couldn't seem to get along with the other kids or listen to the teacher." When the camp director called four days later to say Gregory had been expelled from camp, Cathy and Tony were of course not surprised. As they drove to pick him up, Cathy sighed, "I wonder what kind of trouble he'll get himself into next." Because this couple continued to expect and demand of their son a social maturity that he did not yet have, the child continued to be a discipline problem at school and in his neighborhood. Most recently, after several more episodes involving severe emotional outbursts while Gregory was interacting with other children, the school counselor recommended a psychological assessment for the boy and consideration of the possibility of family counseling.

Sometimes an event or condition seemingly unrelated to an area of behavior can cause a discipline problem: a four-year-old with a new baby brother starts wetting the bed; a nine-year-old having trouble learning to multiply neglects his household responsibilities; a four-teen-year-old whose parents were recently divorced gets into a beer-drinking crowd. Such connections can be hard to pinpoint, especially when the causing factors are concerns to the parents themselves—as a new baby, a child's slipping school performance, or a divorce would naturally be. In our experience we have encountered many parents who totally overlook and often deny the connections between children's problems and seemingly unrelated events. For example, many mothers and fathers who are in a stepfamily situation because of recent divorces and remarriages often appear puzzled by the hostile behavior, sarcasm, apathy, or lack of interest in school demonstrated by their preadolescent sons and daughters.

Many discipline problems can be traced to some need in the child that is stronger than the need to please his or her parents. Children may fully understand what is expected, and part of them may want to comply; but if the problem behavior is satisfying some other, stronger need, they will probably misbehave anyway. The rules that sixteen-year-old Maria's parents had for her after school and on weekends were reasonable and well communicated. Although Maria had usually been quite obedient, she began staying up past her curfew on weekends and "hanging out" with the kids at the mall after school instead of attending her usual activities. Her need to control herself, to make her own rules, was stronger now than her previously strong need to please her parents.

Seeking the cause of a behavior problem is sometimes simple, sometimes difficult. Some problems may have multiple causes; it may be impossible to pinpoint the cause of others. When gathering information, it is helpful for parents to ask themselves the following questions:

1. What is happening?
2. When does it occur?
3. Where does it happen?
4. Who else is involved?
5. Could there be a physical cause for the problem?
6. Are my expectations too high for the child's abilities?
7. Are my expectations too low?
8. Am I assuming the child will misbehave now because of problems in the past?
9. Does my child thoroughly understand what I expect?
10. What else is going on at home that could be contributing to the problem?
11. What else is going on at school, with the child's friends, or elsewhere that could be contributing?
12. What other needs may the child have that could be stronger than the need to behave well?

STEP 3

Once the parents have gathered sufficient information about a potential problem, the next step is to *define the problem*. There are actually two major types of discipline problems. When a child does not have sufficient knowledge, skill, or ability to behave as expected, or is not totally aware of what behavior is expected, the problem is a developmental one. If the child does know what is expected and has previously demonstrated the ability to behave well but changes suddenly or over time, the problem is a regressive one. It is important to consider whether a problem is developmental or regressive, since the corrective course of action is different in each case.

It is very important at this stage—and throughout the problem-solving process—to avoid "crucializing," or blowing the problem out of proportion. With time and patience, a systematic problem-solving process can help alleviate almost all discipline problems. Becoming upset, frustrated, or angry about a problem can only cloud a parent's judgment and objectivity. A difficult situation becomes even worse.

Sometimes parents make the discovery during the information-gathering process that a perceived problem is merely a symptom of a larger one. They may discover that their teenage son's dropping grades are due to experimentation with drugs. To define and treat this problem as poor study habits would be missing the point—and wasting valuable time that should be spent on the real problem.

It is usually best to state discipline quandaries in solution-oriented rather than problem-oriented terms. For example, the parents of Maria (the girl who began defying her parents' rules at age sixteen) defined their problem by saying, "Our problem is that Maria has begun to defy our rules about curfew and after-school activities." A more solution-oriented problem definition would be "We need to do something to help Maria comply with our rules about curfew and after-school activities." Defining the problem in this way leads naturally to the next step in the problem-solving process.

STEP 4

After the problem has been defined it is time to *establish a goal statement:* to determine what behavior parents want. Often it is helpful to do this in writing. Of course, if a mother were to discover that her two-year-old has decided to use the wall to demonstrate his artistic ability, writing a goal statement on the spot would be ridiculous. However, it is still important to take a few seconds to consider, "What do I want to happen here?" before acting.

If this behavior becomes habitual, though, writing a goal statement will help clarify what the parent is looking for. An effective goal statement should include three components: the specific behavior expected (use action words like "clean," "perform," "practice," etc.); the quantity and quality of behavior expected (how many, how often, how well); and a time frame (when the goal is to be accomplished). "By the end of the month Sandy will complete all of her math homework by 7:30 P.M. each evening, with at least 90 percent accuracy" or "The number of fights Gregory has with his classmates will be reduced from an average of four per week to an average of two per week within two months" are examples of effective goal statements.

There are some key points to remember in developing goals for your children's behavior. First, goals must be reasonably attainable. If Gregory is upset over his parents' constant fighting or is suffering from untreated allergies, a two-month time frame for reducing fights may be unrealistic. Overestimating the time it might take to reach a goal is usually better than underestimating it. It is always more satisfying to accomplish objectives early than to be frustrated about not meeting a deadline, even a self-imposed one. It helps to remember that goal statements are not locked in stone; they can be modified later if the need arises. More information about previously hidden causes of behavior may come to light, or an outside factor contributing to the problem may change. Thinking in terms of behavior sought rather than attitudes and feelings will make it easier to tell if goals have been reached. The goal of "practicing piano from seven to seven-thirty each evening" is measurable; "developing a greater interest in music" is not. There should be a clear relationship between behavioral goals and family values.

Many parents wonder when the child should be brought into the discipline process. If children have not already been part of gathering information or defining the problem, making them part of the goal-setting process is very often appropriate. One stern father of four sons questioned, "Isn't that sort of like giving your game plan away to the other side?" His view of his children as opponents was probably doing far more to delay the solution of his discipline problems than any giving away of strategy would have done. Parents who see themselves as partners with their children in the joint venture of discipline are almost always ahead in the game. In all areas of activity—work, government, education, religion, the home—people support what they help create. If children have had a part in setting goals for their own behavior as well as helping devise a plan to achieve those goals, they are much more likely to be successful.

Maria (the sixteen-year-old who stayed out too late on weekends) and her parents first independently determined their goals for the situation. Her parents' goal statement read: "Maria will be home at her established curfew of 11 P.M. every weekend night beginning this Friday." Maria's goal was: "I will be in on time every weekend night starting immediately if my curfew is changed to midnight." As they discussed the differences in their goals, Maria explained that eleven o'clock was often too early; there was too little time for a hamburger after a movie, and many parties lasted until after midnight. Together, the family established a compromise goal and made an agreement to achieve it: "Effective this Friday, Maria will be home at the new curfew of 11:30 every weekend unless special arrangements are made to extend it to 12:00. Extensions will be made only if the 11:30 curfew has been met consistently for the previous two weeks." This was a goal they all could accept. It gave Maria the opportunity to earn extra privileges by good behavior as well as one other thing she really needed: a little more control over her own life. And it worked. Her in-on-time record under this agreement has been nearly perfect.

STEP 5

Once the goal has been established, the next step is to *examine several possible courses of action.* In every discipline problem, there are several alternatives that might work, with varying degrees of success and consequences of their own. The key is to look carefully at all the alternatives to find the one with the greatest chance of working without causing more problems. A common tendency of parents new to this process is to take the time and trouble to gather information, define the problem, and develop their goals, only to use the method that they would have used anyway! It is very important at this point, as it is throughout the disciplinary process, to suspend judgment and keep an open mind. In order to find the most effective solution, it is necessary to use imagination to generate as many alternatives as possible. Even ideas that sound outrageous at first may lead to an effective solution. When Cathy and Tony were brainstorming a list of alternatives to help their son Gregory reduce the number of fights he had with the other children in his class, Tony joked, "Well, we could give him away!" Cathy dutifully added it to their list of alternatives. Although they would never seriously consider giving Gregory away, this "crazy" idea led to "giving Gregory away" to his grandparents for a weekend to give the whole family a breather. That one ridiculous alternative probably did as much—or more—to bring about the eventual solution to their problems as any sensible idea on the list.

Parents have an infinite number of alternatives to choose from in helping their children develop control over their own behavior. We will describe several of them, but this does not represent all of the alternatives in any situation. Often, if the problem is a developmental one where children are not aware of what is expected or are not yet capable of behaving as expected, a four-step method can be effective: explaining, sometimes again and again, what is expected and why; letting a child see and hear what the desired behavior looks like; giving children the opportunity to practice or demonstrate their abilities; and giving lots of feedback—praise and reward as well as constructive correction of mistakes. The feedback phase may need to continue for a long time; if the results are not what is expected, you may need to return to the preparation, demonstration, or practice steps—or it may be time to consider a different alternative.

Letting the child face the natural consequences of his or her misbehavior can often be the most effective form of discipline. The three-year-old who spills his juice can wipe it up himself; the ten-year-old who breaks a window playing baseball can earn some of the money to pay for it. One mother of naturally messy three- and six-year-olds sets a timer for a ten-minute cleanup before bedtime. Any toys not in place when the buzzer sounds get put in a "trash bag" to be stored in the basement for several weeks. The "trash bag" is often empty now; even when it's brought back into use, at least the house is clean! Sometimes, though, the natural consequences of behavior are too dangerous, troublesome, or inconvenient. The four-year-old who crosses the street without an adult could be seriously injured or killed; the eleven-year-old who listened to records until one o'clock in the morning will not be able to concentrate on schoolwork and will be prone to other behavior problems because of fatigue.

Diverting the child's attention from the problem may sometimes work, especially with younger children who have a short attention span. Mothers of toddlers often attempt to get an inquisitive child interested in a toy or picture instead of Aunt Erma's china goldfinch. Friendly chatter with a preschooler during preparation for bed can minimize balkiness. It can be effective with older children too, *if* the alternative offered to divert attention from an unacceptable behavior is attractive to the child. A thirteen-year-old hooked on video games would rebel at the idea of joining the Boy Scouts, but might lose interest in the arcade if the alternative were an after-school computer course.

Verbal appeals range from a simple reminder of the rules ("It's eight-thirty—bedtime") to pleading and coaxing ("Please, honey, you need your sleep and I need some peace and quiet for a change"). The closer a verbal appeal gets to coaxing, the less likely it is to be effective: children can feel they are totally in charge and that here is a chance to see just how far they can stretch the limits. Reminders and encouragement such as "I know you can do it," given with the expectation that the child *will* behave, are often valuable components of any plan of action.

And finally there is punishment—the negative consequences of behavior, brought about by the parent and serving to inhibit further undesirable behavior. Many forms of punishment are used, including spanking, isolating, depriving children of something important to them, scolding, and ignoring. Although punishment itself can often cause problems, if used properly it can be a very effective tool in helping a child develop self-control.

A major problem with punishment is that it usually tells children what not to do, not what they are supposed to do. When Johnny, age six, was sent to his room for swearing in front of company, he understood that he had done something wrong, but had no idea what he needed to do to avoid punishment the next time. The resentment that occurs when children are not sure why they are being punished often surfaces in another type of problem behavior toward the parent that did the punishing. Johnny might retaliate against his parents by stubbornly refusing to get ready for school on time or by causing a scene in the grocery store over a new brand of breakfast cereal.

Using punishment when the behavior problem is developmental (the child is not fully aware of what is expected or lacks the physical or psychological maturity to comply) is almost always counterproductive. Spanking the two-year-old who spills her juice or grounding the fifteen-year-old who comes home from a basketball game at 8:30 P.M. not knowing you needed him to babysit at 7:30 P.M. will do nothing to help these children control their behavior. Instead, resentment and anger can cause further problems. Parents must always be sure not to substitute, even subtly, punishment for teaching a child. Saying to the two-year-old who has spilled her juice, "O.k., let's get some paper towels and clean this up," Mom may feel that she is using the natural consequences of the spilled juice in a positive way to teach the child that she is responsible for her behavior even when it is an accident. But the glaring look on Mom's face and her angry tone of voice may be understood as scolding (punishing) if the child interprets them as "You're bad when you spill juice. You should be able to handle the cup without spilling even when it's full. What's wrong with you? Why do you always have to cause problems?"

Punishment must never be used to humiliate or intimidate a child. Parents who need to "show off" by punishing their child in front of others can cause irreparable harm to their children and their relationship with them. The feelings of hurt, anger, and resentment brought about in the child by this type of punishment are never useful in improving children's behavior.

To use punishment more effectively and to minimize the resentment it can cause, parents can use the "Hot Stove Rule" developed by management expert Douglas McGregor to help job supervisors discipline their employees. When you touch a hot stove (undesirable behavior) you get burned (consequences of behavior). The result is not that you resent the stove and think of ways to get even with it; you learn not to touch it. Four things that happen when one touches a hot stove make getting burned an effective punishment; let's see how they apply to punishing children.

First, when you touch a hot stove, you get burned immediately; you don't touch it one morning without consequence and then wonder where that painful burn came from when your hand suddenly starts hurting the next afternoon. Likewise, punishment is much more effective when it comes right after the undesirable behavior. To reduce the possibility of a misbehavior occurring again, the child must associate the punishment directly with the misbehavior. The more time that elapses between the act and the punishment, the less likely it is that the association will be made. When eight-year-old Jason refused to go to bed on time one evening when his mother was at a meeting, his father sighed, "Your mother will deal with you in the morning." Any punishment she'd come up with by then would not be associated by Jason with disobeying his father, and so would be ineffective in helping him be more obedient next time. Another undesirable side effect in this situation is that, if this type of situation is repeated, Jason may learn not to respect his father because he sees him as a person who is unable to deal with his son's misbehavior. In turn, he will resent or fear his mother as the person responsible for all punishment.

The second characteristic of getting burned by a hot stove is that the stove gives prior warning that touching it will result in a burn. Heat radiates from it; the burner glows red. Only by ignoring the warning and touching the stove in spite of it will you get burned. Suzanne, the mother of five-year-old Jennifer, was wise to consider this when her daughter, soon after she began walking home from school with a group of older children, stopped at a friend's house instead of coming home immediately. Suzanne remembered mentioning that Jennifer was supposed to come directly home before stopping to play, but she realized that they had not made it a firm rule, nor had they determined what punishment would result from infractions. Instead of punishing her daughter that day, Suzanne initiated a two-way discussion about what was expected and why. The two of them decided that the next time Jennifer stopped to play before coming home she would not be permitted to play with anyone after school for three days. When Jennifer forgot the rule and came home late the next week she was unhappy with the promised punishment, but at least she knew it was coming.

The third characteristic of getting burned by a hot stove is that the consequences are consistent; you get burned every time you touch the stove. It is important that Jennifer, now that she's had sufficient warning, gets punished every time she breaks the rule. If her mother forgets, or decides to let it go once because she's busy with other things, Jennifer is likely to get confused about just what is expected, or may try to test her mother to see just how far she can go next time. Another element of consistency is that the amount of punishment (degree of burn) is related to the seriousness of the misbehavior: touch a fingertip to the burner for a split second—the burn will always be minor; place the palm of your hand on it for one second and you'll always end up with a serious, blistering burn.

Finally, the stove is nondiscriminatory—everyone who touches it will get burned. A stove cannot play favorites or exempt any individual from being burned. All children in the same family should receive equal punishment for similar misdeeds. Of course the rules children must follow will vary with age and maturity—Jennifer's thirteen-year-old sister will probably not have to check in at home immediately after school, but might be expected to be home by 5 P.M. to help prepare supper. When she breaks this rule, her parents need to punish her in a manner appropriate for her age. If she is permitted to break rules with impunity, Jennifer is sure to notice. Her reaction might be to resent her older sister as well as her parents and to demonstrate this through further misbehavior.

Let us take a look at several types of punishment and how they can be used effectively. Scolding—or verbally reprimanding—is often used by parents as punishment. An effective verbal reprimand leaves the children feeling bad enough about what they did so that they don't want to do it again, but good enough about themselves to enable them to behave well next time. To accomplish this, a scolding must address the child's behavior, not personality or self-concept. A child who is told "You are bad" often enough will believe it, and continue to misbehave since that's how bad children act. On the other hand, when children are told "Lying (or cheating, stealing, hitting, or whatever) is wrong," they feel it's their behavior that's being judged, not themselves. Even though their actions have been bad, they can still feel capable of choosing other ways to behave.

Verbal reprimands should address specific behavior. To scold a child for "acting up lately" or "causing a lot of problems" is not very effective. If parents really want to help the child to change, they need to know exactly what he or she has done wrong. It is much easier to do this if parents do not "gunnysack" or store up lots of small misdeeds until the sack gets so full they drop the whole thing on the child at once. Lois, busy juggling her new job with caring for the house and her three school-age sons, had noticed that her middle son, Ken, was becoming more difficult to manage. He avoided doing his homework, complained bitterly when Lois reminded him of his chores, and often simply refused to listen to his parents at all. One day when Lois came home from work to discover his room a mess, she unleashed a tirade listing every incident of misbehavior over the previous two months— most of which she had never even mentioned before. Overwhelmed by the magnitude of the scolding for what he perceived to be the one incident of a messy room, Ken shut himself in his room and refused to come out, even for dinner.

No scolding or reprimand is complete without a discussion of what the child needs to do to avoid punishment the next time. In fact, many verbal reprimands should have the tone of a discussion rather than a scolding. This discussion could take the form of a simple reminder of the rules, "Next time, remember to be home by 5 P.M. so you can set the table for dinner." Or a detailed discussion might be appropriate between child and parent about what happened and why, with the parent really *listening* to what the child thinks and feels could prevent future problems.

All scoldings should end on a positive note. No matter how unacceptable children's behavior may be, it is important to remember that they must feel good enough about themselves to try to do better next time. A simple reassurance of parental love and confidence in the child's ability to do better, in an understanding tone of voice, can make the difference between a simple opportunity for the parent to "blow off steam" and a real step toward bringing about a change in behavior.

The night after her blowup with Ken, Lois and her husband sat down together to discuss a more effective method for disciplining their son. The next week, when Ken brought home a note from his teacher that said Ken was in danger of failing English because he had not turned in another report on time, Lois paused for a moment after reading the note to consider the problem in terms of her goals and to review her plan for reprimanding her son. Finally she said, "Ken, this is very upsetting. This is the second English paper you failed to turn in on time this semester. You know our rule about spending enough time on homework to get it done well and on time. What's the problem here?" Ken's first reaction was to stare at his feet and shrug his shoulders, but Lois persisted, reminding Ken he was capable of good work in English and that failing because of factors within his control would be unacceptable. Through their discussion, Lois learned that Ken had been feeling neglected since his mother began working and that he needed more help in organizing his homework time. "How about if we sit down after dinner to go over all your upcoming assignments and come up with a new homework schedule, including when you'll need help from me." As Ken nodded agreement, Lois ruffled his hair and continued, "I bet your next English paper will be in on time."

Isolating a child—sending a boy to his room, for example, or having him sit in a corner for a period of time—is especially effective when a "cooling-off period" is needed on either or both sides. If the emotions of anger, fear, or guilt are too high to make discussion possible, a brief period of isolation can give both parent and child a better perspective on what has happened and what should happen next. For some children, the isolation experience is unhappy enough to be sufficient punishment for misbehavior, but isolation will be most effective if followed by a reminder or discussion of what was done wrong and what must be changed to avoid future punishment.

Actively ignoring misbehavior can work if the child is acting up in order to get attention. Sometimes when a toddler has a temper tantrum or when an older child is disruptive at mealtime, any type of punishment that gives the child attention could be seen as a reward for the misbehavior, and could increase rather than decrease the chances of it happening again. It may be necessary to remove the child from the situation—carrying the kicking, screaming toddler out of the grocery store or guiding an older daughter to her room so the rest of the family can eat in peace. This should be done calmly and without comment to avoid giving the reward of attention. But then in a quieter moment it is important for the parents to determine why the child needs to misbehave for attention; children may need more attention from their parents when they are behaving well.

With younger children who have not developed a concept of time, be sure to remember that five minutes can seem like hours. The period of isolation should be just long enough for some discomfort to be registered and associated with the misbehavior, or to allow both parent and child to calm down enough for discussion. Older children can be told "Stay in your room until you're ready to discuss this"—but be prepared for a child to camp out indefinitely—just to show who is in charge.

Depriving children of something that is important to them is another form of punishment that can be effective when used properly. Putting a toddler's blocks on a high shelf after he has thrown one at a playmate, or "grounding" a teenager for the next week when he gets in a fist fight after school, can reduce the likelihood that throwing blocks or fighting will be repeated. But not letting a child go to a soccer game next week for cheating on a test today will not be as effective—the length of time between misbehavior and punishment is just too long. There are some considerations to keep in mind when using this type of punishment. Once parents take something from a child as punishment, it is counter-productive to give it back prematurely. If a child discovers that pouting or begging will change Mom's or Dad's mind, that child learns to pout and beg, not to change whatever behavior initiated the punishment in the first place. So it is wise to consider the consequences for everyone concerned before taking something away. Also, parents should never threaten a punishment they may not be able to deliver. (What would be done with Sammy while Mom takes the other kids to the movies?) Before threatening a punishment, be sure to ask if there is a reasonable way to follow through with the punishment promised. Children learn very quickly not to believe the parent who "cries wolf."

Likewise, parents should not turn every privilege, possession, or event into a reward or punishment used to control the child. All children deserve some good things in their lives, regardless of what they do or how they behave. They all need to feel worthy of some of the things that are important to them, no matter what they do. And there is one thing no parent should ever withdraw from a child as punishment: love. The unloved child has little to motivate or encourage him or her to improve behavior.

And finally, there is spanking. The appropriateness of this form of punishment is quite controversial. Parents who firmly believe that when you spare the rod you spoil the child would have a hard time disciplining their children without it. On the other hand, parents who want to raise nonviolent children would have a hard time justifying hitting their children. Striking a child is probably the least effective means of punishment: children who are so punished learn only that parents are angry with them, not what they have done wrong and what they must do better in the future. Spanking a child in anger can be very dangerous. When a parent is out of control, he or she can seriously injure or even kill a child. If a parent feels that some type of physical punishment is necessary, some basic guidelines should be followed:

1. Confine spanking to younger children who would not understand other types of punishment.
2. Spank a child only when he or she is caught in the middle of misbehaving; even a brief delay between the undesirable behavior and spanking can be confusing to the child.
3. Use physical punishment only for very serious or dangerous misbehaviors.
4. *Never* strike a child in anger; if you feel out of control, separate yourself from the child until you have cooled off.
5. If physical punishment is used too often or if children are really hurt, you should seek help from a support group or mental health professional (see Chapter 15, Parentship Resources).

Probably the most important thing to remember about punishment, no matter what type is used, is to return to a positive relationship as soon as the punishment is over. Sometimes, when a particular child is prone to frequent misbehavior, punishment hangs like a dark cloud over the entire family even between misdeeds. The more parent and child can look for ways to enjoy each other and create a warm and loving atmosphere, the more the child will exert an effort to behave well in order to live in a harmonious home. Parents need to avoid unconsciously punishing continuously, making life miserable for everyone. It is often helpful for parents to take a look at how often they say no to their children and how often they are in conflict with them. If it is more often than they like, it is worth the effort for them to try to find ways to say yes so that parents and children can enjoy each other more often.

The following list of "do's" and "don'ts" can help parents make informed decisions about punishment:

1. DO   fit the amount and type of punishment to the seriousness of the misbehavior.
2. DO   punish immediately after the misbehavior.
3. DO   make sure the child knows what is expected and knows he or she will be punished for misbehaving.
4. DO   be consistent in punishing misbehavior.
5. DO   administer punishment so that children feel bad enough

about what they did wrong not to repeat it, but still feel good about themselves.

6. DO	try to end all punishments on a positive note.
7. DO	combine any form of punishment with a discussion of the problem and how to do better in the future.
8. DO	try to let children face the natural consequences of their behavior instead of punishing them whenever possible.
9. DON'T	deal with more than one misbehavior at a time.
10. DON'T	punish a child when he or she is not aware of what is expected or is physically or psychologically incapable of behaving well.
11. DON'T	use punishment to humiliate or intimidate a child.
12. DON'T	punish your children without being absolutely sure they know why they are being punished.
13. DON'T	play favorites with your children or be more lenient with one than with others.
14. DON'T	strike your child if you're afraid you'll lose control.
15. DON'T	continue to punish the child when the punishment should be over, even by unconsciously creating an unhappy atmosphere.
16. DON'T	instigate actions or create an overall negative family climate conducive to problem behavior.

In deciding on a course of action, a final alternative is to make a conscious decision to do nothing for the time being. Parents must learn to "choose their battles" in order to be successful. Sorting out which behavior problems to deal with is not an easy task; it often requires a great deal of introspection and objectivity. But it is a very important aspect of discipline: to ignore a problem behavior that should have been addressed allows a problem to continue and perhaps grow worse; to discipline a child for a misdeed that should have been ignored can create a climate of frustration and tension that could also lead to further problems. But how can parents tell the difference? When is it an appropriate decision to do nothing about a misbehavior?

There are stages in every child's life when rebellious, undisciplined behavior is common. Although parental discipline is essential in these periods, to deal with each and every incident would mean a constant battle between parent and child—not an atmosphere conducive to helping the child become more civilized overall. Since a lot of misbehavior in these periods stems from children's need to control themselves rather than to be controlled by their parents, it is a good idea to take a close look at the "house rules": Which ones have the highest priority and are nonnegotiable? Which ones are less important for the time being? If you stick to your usual discipline plan for the important rules and bend a little for the less important ones, your family can become less of a battleground.

Franny had just turned four when her new brother was born. She began to defy many requests and directions from her parents about getting dressed, caring for her room, picking up her toys. She also began wetting her bed at night. Her parents decided that having Franny stay dry at night and picking up her toys after play were their priority goals. They initiated a retraining program with stickers on a calendar as a reward for a dry bed and began putting all toys that were out of place at the end of cleanup time in a locked closet. They decided not to make an issue of Franny standing at the table to eat her lunch or not getting dressed until afternoon on nonschool days. In time, Franny's behavior improved in all areas. Her parents had struck the right balance between what they dealt with and what they decided not to address.

It is important in these times that parents select problems that are priorities but that also have a high probability of being solved. To choose a battle that they are not likely to win does no good for parent or child. Ron and Nora's son Richard had changed rather suddenly at age thirteen. He began running around with a group of boys known for their sloppy appearance and disruptive behavior and began refusing to do his chores and homework at home. Ron and Nora realized that they could do very little to directly control Richard's friendships at school, so they decided to concentrate on his homework and household responsibilities as well as to encourage his new interest in the swim team. By nagging him and making an issue over the boys they did not like, Ron and Nora could have pushed Richard closer to these friends and further from his family.

Of course, choosing not to deal with a behavior problem is often the wrong decision. There is always the risk that ignoring a misbehavior may teach the child that such behavior is o.k. When the decision to do nothing about a behavior problem has been made to increase the chances of improving behavior overall, it is usually worth that risk. But when a parent fails to address a problem because he or she is preoccupied with other matters, further problems can result. Parents' failure to act because they are unsure what to do or because of fear—fear that the child will not like the parent or that the situation will get worse—is never appropriate.

STEP 6

After parents have examined all the possible courses of action, it is time to *select and implement the best solution.* Any action undertaken will have consequences, good and bad. The positive and negative results of each alternative must be considered. Withholding driving privileges for a week may make a teenager think twice about driving with the oil light on next time, but would cause Mom the inconvenience of extra carpooling. Requiring preschoolers to eat their peas in order to get dessert may teach them to hate vegetables and crave sweets. Behavior has consequences for parents, too!

Next, parents must decide what outcomes are most important to them. Do they need to achieve the goal in the shortest possible time? Or is long-lasting effectiveness, convenience, or avoidance of new problems more important this time? They must choose the alternative that has positive consequences closely matched to parental goals and the fewest negative side effects. For many behavior problems, this entire process is performed mentally in a matter of seconds. But for serious problems, plotting the whole process with paper and pencil is more effective. When Bob and Maureen discovered their sixteen-year-old daughter Emily was taking drugs, their initial shock was followed by denials. However, with the help of their minister they quickly and firmly decided that their goal was for Emily to be entirely off the drugs within six months. They talked with Emily's teachers, their physician, and several mental health professionals to discover the maximum number of alternatives and recommendations for their courses of action since they felt inadequate to tackle the problem themselves. Then they made a chart, listing the possible positive and negative outcomes of each alternative. Simply looking at the chart, they identified two alternatives that had achieved excellent results and were highly recommended by people they respected. Bob and Maureen chose an established drug counseling program that offered a support group for parents, even though it was more expensive than the other alternatives.

STEP 7

Once parents have selected and implemented the best course of action, the final step is *evaluation.* Parents need to be alert to what is happening as a result of their disciplinary actions and to evaluate their effectiveness objectively. Sometimes it is tempting to assume that putting a great deal of effort into planning and implementing discipline will make it effective. Parents may want so much to succeed that they ignore any information that tells them they have failed. But wishing doesn't make it so—in discipline or in anything else.

In order to evaluate the effectiveness of any discipline, parents need to ask themselves several questions: Am I progressing toward my goal? Why or why not? Do I need to revise my goal? Gather more information? Have I generated any new problems? Do I need to change my plan of action? What is the child learning from this experience— intended and unintended—about himself or herself? About me? About how he or she should behave? And finally, what have I learned from this discipline experience that can help me in the future? Even the most miserable failure can teach a great deal about self, children, and how to avoid problems in the future—but only if minds are kept open.

If becoming more effective in disciplining children is one of a parent's current goals, the first step is an objective analysis of his or her current knowledge, skills, and attitudes. The following Discipline Skills Inventory can help.

DISCIPLINE SKILLS INVENTORY

Instructions: How satisfied are you with your discipline skills? For each of the skills or attitudes listed, place the number that represents your degree of satisfaction with the way you function now. Use a 4 if you are very satisfied, 3 if somewhat satisfied, 2 if somewhat dissatisfied, and 1 if very dissatisfied.

_____ 1. I can keep in mind that my role in disciplining my child is to help him or her develop self-discipline.

_____ 2. I am certain my child knows what behavior is expected.

_____ 3. Family values are discussed with my child.

_____ 4. Both parents are in agreement about family values and their priorities.

_____ 5. I set a positive example for my child through my actions, not just my instructions.

_____ 6. I can relate house rules, school rules, and society's laws to our family values.

_____ 7. I am aware of what positive behavior to expect from someone my child's age.

_____ 8. I am aware of what negative behavior to expect from someone my child's age.

_____ 9. I view training as a large part of discipline.

_____10. I demonstrate behaviors I want my child to learn effectively.

_____11. I don't expect perfection right away when my child is learning something new.

_____12. I give honest positive feedback when it is deserved.

_____13. I give honest negative feedback when it is deserved.

_____14. I encourage my child to reward himself or herself for positive behavior.

_____15. I become aware of behavior problems quickly before they become serious problems.

_____16. I know what is happening with my child outside our home.

_____17. I can view my child's discipline problems in perspective without becoming overly upset.

_____18. I have a goal in mind whenever I discipline my child.

_____19. I am solution-oriented rather than problem-oriented.

_____20. I look at several alternatives before deciding how to discipline my child.

_____21. Whenever possible, I let my child face the natural consequences of his or her behavior.

_____22. I avoid pleading with or coaxing my child.

_____23. When I punish my child, I make sure he or she knows the reason for the punishment.

_____24. I never punish in order to humiliate or intimidate my child.

_____25. I punish my child immediately after a misbehavior.

_____26. I give my child prior warning about which behaviors will result in punishment.

_____27. I am consistent in the way I punish my child.

_____28. I avoid playing favorites with my children.

_____29. When scolding my child, I address behavior, not personality.

_____30. I am specific about what behavior the child is being punished for.

_____31. I combine any form of punishment with a discussion of what the child must do to avoid punishment next time.

_____32. I consider my child a partner in the venture of establishing control over his or her behavior.

_____33. I select a type and intensity of punishment that suits the misbehavior.

_____34. I avoid turning every possession, privilege, or event into a reward or punishment to control my child's behavior.

_____35. I choose my battles carefully in order to address the most important behavior problems.

After indicating your level of satisfaction with your behavior on each aspect of discipline, select two or three items that you wish to improve right now and circle them. You can begin to develop a plan of action to help improve your own disciplining skills. After they are accomplished at a satisfactory level, select two or three more that you can then work on. If this systematic approach is followed, improvements in disciplining will become evident to you and your family. All the way through the growth process, be sure to consider the attitudinal and emotional as well as behavioral aspects of the recommended principles and procedures.

The disciplining skills of mothers and fathers, then, are a cornerstone of parentship. But, as we have seen, effective discipline is not something imposed on a family in an arbitrary fashion. Rather, it is developed from the inside out. The essence of parental discipline is the ability to teach and motivate children to manage themselves.

11

Beyond Discipline: Motivating the Family

"I try to catch them when they are doing something right," a Virginia father told us recently in describing his approach to motivating his children. "I use the carrot and the stick approach," explained another father at the same workshop. Motivation is by far one of the most difficult tasks for the parent. It is a sensitive area, and most mothers and fathers have a tendency to motivate the way they were motivated by their own parents. It is often the only way they know how, and besides they "didn't turn out so bad after all!" Many parents, like some leaders in other organizations, take this seat-of-the-pants approach to motivating. While they know that it could be their most important role, they often feel helpless and amateurish in performing this leadership function. Their confidence levels are generally low, and there is a lot of "hoping for the best." Parents must keep in mind that they are continuously motivating or reducing enthusiasm and interest. They cannot interact with their children in some kind of neutral fashion. Their words, actions, and responses will always have some effect. However, there are proven principles and practices for motivating children in the family setting. Here are fifteen of the most important ones.

1. USE APPROPRIATE METHODS TO REINFORCE BEHAVIOR, ATTITUDES, AND DISPOSITION

Children function in anticipation of rewards and punishments. All youngsters need some form of reinforcement that will let them know that they are either on or off track. Here are some key points which parents ought to keep in mind. First, they should not assume that what reinforced their own behavior as children will reinforce their children's behavior as well. Perhaps, when the parents were young, good school grades were a great motivator for them and kept them studying hard. For their children this tangible reinforcement may have less weight than more symbolic rewards in the form of "attaboy's" or "attagirl's" expressed by the parents themselves. In fact, more often than not, the reinforcers that worked for us as children do not work for our own children. These are different times. Our children are different people. Likewise, it is important to remember that what one child perceives as rewarding in the family may not work for another. Some children need to hear direct commentary in the form of verbal praise and they may need it at regular intervals. For others, a smile or pat on the head or the "o.k." sign may suffice. One suggestion that is universally applicable, though, is to bestow reinforcement as soon as possible after the desired action or expression of attitude. We certainly do not recommend a mechanistic approach whereby parents would carry a bag of goodies, dispensing them for every little act. This approach to behavior modification can and has been overdone. We do, however, recommend connecting the reward closely and directly with the desired outcome. Timing therefore is an important factor. The key is to know the children well and use the reinforcer that truly motivates each of them as individuals. It is important to be open-minded and tolerant of the possible desired reinforcers. Parents should make few assumptions without validating them.

2. Make Sure that All Children's Accomplishments Are Recognized Fully

Most children have a strong need to be approved by their parents and they dread the nightmare of being rejected by them. We have not met a child yet who does not respond well to even the slightest amount of parental praise. Sometimes parents focus too heavily on the big accomplishments and miss many of the smaller ones because the latter fall out of their purview of what accomplishment is or because they do not understand the difficulty of the task completed by the child. A mother who does not recognize or value vigor in training for a swimming meet may not fully appreciate what it means to win the butterfly stroke event. A father who is not musically inclined may fail to grasp the difficulty of learning to play the flute. As a result, he may recognize the accomplishment, but not at the level that would satisfy the child's emotional need for approval. One college student, in a state of total exasperation with his parents, put it this way: "I call home in excitement and tell my father that I passed organic chemistry with a B+ and all he does is say, 'Good. What else is going on? Did you get a chance to see the basketball game? That kid Jones is fantastic, isn't he?' He has no idea of how I'm busting my ass to get through chem so I'll have a shot at med school. It drives me crazy. Sometimes I feel like going out and screw around every night like all the other guys in my dorm. They're probably the smart ones!"

The key task here is for parents to make sure that their sense of what is accomplished is congruent with what value the children place on their accomplishments. Unfortunately, many children do not feel adequately recognized by their parents. Parents need not worry about praise overdosing. Most boys and girls can use a little more.

3. ENCOURAGE CHILDREN TO SET THEIR OWN GOALS

While parents often find this hard to believe, children tend to know their own capabilities and limitations better than anyone else, including their mothers and fathers. Accordingly, when parents ask their children to set their own goals, they pay them the highest compliment and many good things happen. First, there is the implicit recognition on the part of the parents that it is o.k. for children to have their own personal and distinct plans for themselves. This does wonders for children's self-concept: they are legitimized as unique, valuable human beings. It becomes clear to the child that family membership is not incompatible with strong individuality and that families are not suppressive, but rather supportive.

Secondly, when parents ask children to think about and develop goals, they teach the importance of a sense of direction as well as the value of planning. Children learn quickly that the goal-oriented person is generally more accomplished and that this carries with it a good feeling about oneself.

While the simple act of asking children what their goals are is an effective motivation technique in itself because of the psychological benefits the children receive, it is also beneficial to encourage the children to formalize their objectives, usually in writing, within a specific time. Parents should work with the children to be sure that the goals are realistic and attainable. Likewise, they must remember to allow the goals to emerge from the child and not impose them from above, even subtly. A goal that is developed by the child has a much greater chance of coming to fruition. When there is conflict between the individual child's goals and those of other members or of the family as a whole, the parent will have to explain this and together with the child forge a mutually satisfying objective. For example, twelve-year-old Kevin's goal to become a jazz drummer may mean long hours of loud practice in the basement at times when all the other children are doing homework. The pursuit of his goal could preclude the attainment of the other children's goals (not to mention parental peace and rest). Kevin and his parents will have to examine several options before deciding whether or not to establish this as a workable goal. He could defer to his siblings' needs and decide to pursue another musical instrument altogether—one less noisy. He could hold on to his goal but find another place to practice. He could strike a deal with his siblings whereby he could practice some nights when they would study elsewhere, and vice versa. He could restrict his practice to weekends only and slow down the pace of his musical development. Lastly, Kevin could request that his parents soundproof a small room in the basement where he could practice without interrupting everyone else. Whatever the choice, if mutual respect is established between the objectives of the family as a whole and Kevin as an individual, the conclusion will be healthy for all.

When children are encouraged to set their own goals within the framework of sensitivity to the needs of other family members, whom they view as their support group, much good will result.

4. CLARIFY EXPECTATIONS AND MAKE SURE THAT CHILDREN UNDERSTAND THEM

Often parents know what they mean when they say something but children do not know what their parents mean. Unclear expectations will generally lead to a decrease in motivation and even to frustration on the part of the children. Sometimes mothers and fathers intentionally or unintentionally will let their sons and daughters "discover" what is expected of them. This guessing game approach ("What will make Mommy and Daddy happy or disappoint them?") causes the children to burn off tremendous amounts of energy in wasted fashion. One father told us that he intentionally kept his children "somewhat in the dark" concerning his expectations of them. "It keeps them on their toes. They never know if I'm pleased. It's interesting to watch [the children] compete for my attention and approval." While these comments are indicative of someone bordering on the sadistic, there are many parents who play a similar game, only less cruelly.

As we have shown, communication in the family is very tricky business. Often parents assume that their children understand them when in fact they do not, and vice versa. Likewise, children and parents differ in what constitutes precision, accuracy, and completion. Children are often reluctant to ask parents to clarify expectations for them. They may feel that they will incur their parents' wrath or cause their parents to insult them: "How many times do I have to explain? Don't you understand English?" Therefore, the rule of thumb for stating expectations is for parents to be as concrete as possible. "Stuart, don't forget to go out and clean the station wagon" won't do. A preferable approach is: "Stuart, I would like you to clean the station wagon by 11 A.M. Don't forget to vacuum the floors, front, back, and storage area; go over the inside and outside of all the windows with the cleaning spray, and dust off the dashboard and steering wheel and post. Also, throw out any newspapers on any of the seats."

Children who do not know what their parents expect of them flounder, often aimlessly, in a state of high anxiety. Eventually, they turn their anger inward in the form of guilt or outward in the form of hostility expressed through withdrawal.

5. INCREASE THE LIKELIHOOD THAT CHILDREN WILL EXPERIENCE SUCCESS

With children the old adage could not be truer: nothing succeeds like success. What a child immediately feels and thinks, particularly after accomplishing a difficult task, is "I want to do it again." Imagine that your four-year-old daughter is going off a diving board for the first time. She would probably edge out carefully, hesitate, go back, and repeat this cycle several times, usually with a scared and dreadful expression on her face. Eventually, she would jump off the board. Trace the path of the successful little diver. Will she go sit down and gloat about her recent accomplishment? Will she spend the rest of the day reminiscing about her feat? No. More than likely she will swim to the edge of the pool, climb out, and run right back to the diving board, reveling in her success. When children succeed, it is instinctive for them to want more success. Success feeds on itself.

What are the implications? Parents must work hard to uncover avenues of success for their children. Too often the opportunity for children to experience success is much too limited: academics, sports, music, and maybe art. If children cannot find success within this framework, they may not experience it at all. Success, however, can be experienced in many other ways outside of this traditional mold. A critical part of the parent's job is to discover these avenues and make them available to each child. If need be, children must be steered toward them. This is one of the most crucial contributions that a parent can make in child rearing. What are some examples of the nontraditional, often unrecognized ways to succeed? An important one is personality: being a kind, pleasant person. Another might be in the area of citizenship: becoming a successful community member with a concern for neighbors and a strong desire to help them. Others might involve the child's physical, moral, or spiritual development. A mother or father who believes that all children have in them the seeds for success is more likely to draw them out by working hard to provide an opportunity for these seeds to come to fruition. If parents limit their children to the narrow concept of success, then they are less likely to experience it.

It is equally important that children be taught to use their own judgment as the criterion for judging their own success levels. They should be taught to establish their own criteria and compete against these and not anyone else's standards. They have the power in them to declare themselves successful and they should feel free to do so. They know themselves better than anyone and they are the best judges of their own progress. Parents need not worry about children being too lax in their self-judgment. Most will be just the opposite.

Parents set their children up for failure when they use narrow or stock criteria for judging their sons' and daughters' success. The "standard" criteria are hypothetical hybrids that rarely, if ever, exist in any one child. The scholar-athlete-musician-nice-kid (all rolled into one) exists nowhere but in the figments of the imagination and fantasies of parents. It is a perfection prototype that is generally not reachable. When children have this as their model, it is small wonder that they often develop a sense of failure.

We will often meet boys and girls in their middle and late teens who are exceptionally adept in school work or sports or music, but who still feel inadequate or feel like "failures." One high school senior, on his way to a prestigious Ivy League college, put it this way: "Big deal, so I got 1,410 [out of 1,600] on the college boards. But I didn't play one varsity sport." A fine young lady, a concert pianist at seventeen, likewise expressed her sense of failure: "Frankly, I find piano easy. For me it is not hard work. I'll tell you who I really admire . . . girls who have outgoing personalities, who can fit into any crowd, and are not afraid to express themselves in front of other people. I can't do that."

6. PROVIDE A MIXTURE OF EXTERNAL AS WELL AS INTERNAL REWARDS

The proportion of external and internal rewards in the family is established early. Children will quickly respond to the reward system used and grow accustomed to it. External rewards are those that are tangible and usually outside the children themselves. They can be seen, touched, eaten, felt, etc., and often include objects like candy, toys, clothes, and automobiles. Internal rewards are those that children experience within themselves: a sense of accomplishment, the joy of achievement, pleasure derived from the accomplishment itself, a feeling of growth and progress. Parents make a grave error when they limit their whole motivation system to one type or the other. Children who are motivated by extrinsic rewards alone generally reach a point where they will do very little unless they are duly compensated. Furthermore, the motivational value diminishes as the material rewards no longer contribute to the satisfaction of a need that has been fulfilled over and over again: "Another pint of ice cream, Dad? We already have two in the refrigerator!" Likewise, the need to raise the ante becomes more and more intense; finally it can reach a point at which parents just cannot keep up financially or, in total frustration at what it is costing them to get what they want, decide that the price is too high and opt out of the game. The motivational road that is paved with external rewards alone leads to sure disaster for both parents and children.

On the other hand, full reliance on internal rewards will also not work. The appeal to the internal titillations of success has its merits, but children often need some external compensation as well. Most children are not able to work toward goals for long periods of time and with great intensity without some tangible reward that is either enjoyable in itself (e.g., a candy bar) or symbolically pleasurable (e.g., having Mom or Dad write about their school success in a letter to the grandparents). It is important to remember that children are both mind and body. The internal rewards generally satisfy the former dimension, while the external rewards gratify the latter. Determining the correct equation between external and internal rewards is tedious. No major mathematical formulas can be applied, other than a sense of balance. Furthermore, the balance between these two types of rewards may vary from child to child and for the same child over time. There is no reliable way to measure the exact amount of each ingredient needed for any one child. What is important is the realization that if the need for either type is starved or overindulged, trouble is on its way.

7. ENCOURAGE CHILDREN TO PARTICIPATE IN DECISIONS THAT AFFECT THEM

Often children in families feel powerless to affect their own destiny. While reliance on one's mother and father is indeed necessary, particularly in the early stages of development, this dependency should diminish at a steady rate beginning as early as possible until full independence is achieved, usually in the child's early twenties. This progressive reduction in dependency is what self-motivation in children is all about. Nowhere is this independence as important as it is in decision making that affects the child's life. Other than during the period of infancy, parents should begin to see this kind of decision making as a partnership, a joint venture. The amount and weight of the child's input should increase with age, and the parent's should decrease correspondingly.

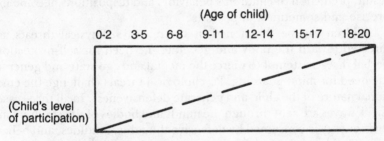

(Age of child)

| 0-2 | 3-5 | 6-8 | 9-11 | 12-14 | 15-17 | 18-20 |

(Child's level of participation)

The inclusion of children in decision making cannot begin too early, providing the *amount* of involvement is appropriate for this stage of chronological age and maturity. There are several benefits of involvement in decision making. First, children begin to develop the healthy notion that they can and must chart their own course and that they need not abdicate control or responsibility for themselves. Second, there is a strong tendency to want to carry out the decision if they participate in it. The children "own" the decision, it is personal property, and not simply something laid on them from above. Pride in the decision as well as its execution develops. Third, children feel complimented by their involvement and respond to this positive expectation on the part of parents. They are dignified by the parental confidence shown them and reflect this feeling by working harder to live up to parental expectations. The benefits of involvement in decision making are self-generative: the more children do it, the more they want to do it.

Before the children are invited or allowed to participate in decisions that affect them, three points should be understood by them: (1) they, with you, are responsible for the consequences of their decisions to the extent that they participated in making them; (2) the quality of their decisions will always be influenced by the quantity and quality of the information that they have at the time the decision is made; and (3) quality involvement requires much effort and energy; there are no real shortcuts.

Lastly, it should be kept in mind that children improve the quality of their involvement by getting involved, the sooner the better.

8. Avoid Use of Threats

Threats, even veiled ones, generally lead to nothing good. They bring about and encourage avoidance behavior in the family. More importantly, the effects of threats rarely disclose themselves fully. As a result, prediction of children's behaviors and dispositions become imprecise and sometimes impossible.

Children can be threatened in several ways. Physical threats are directed toward the body and generate the need for self-protection. Verbal threats attempt to pierce the mental and ego state and generate the need for mind guarding. Psychological threats challenge the emotional nature of the child and generate defensiveness. In all three cases shock waves are sent through the minds and bodies of the children and their energy is consumed by defensive thoughts, attitudes, and behaviors. Their agenda then focuses on strategies and tactics to deal with the threat that they are experiencing. This is a draining experience for them and leads to high childhood stress. As they burn off energy coping with this stress, their capacity to perform, to achieve, and to relate to others is severely diminished. It is important to keep in mind that whether or not the threat is real is not as important as the *perception* of threat by the children. What they perceive to be true is true for them.

Children will respond to threat in one of two ways: they will engage in active defense or passive defense. Remember, healthy people (children included) respond to threats by fighting back. Active defense involves outwardly responding to the threat: recognizing and rejecting it verbally or physically. It could be in the form of an argument, physical struggle, refusal to obey orders, tantrums, or even a deliberate and outward lack of response through the "silent treatment." Passive defense involves the withholding or retarding of action and/or lack of conformity to family values, rules, and desires. This can take many forms, either at the conscious or at the subconscious level. Examples include failing in school achievement, getting pregnant out of wedlock, shoplifting in a manner visible to security guards, saying or doing shocking things in front of parents' friends while feigning ignorance of the self-indictment (e.g., leaving a birth control pill container in the bathroom for all to see).

Active defense behavior is generally easier to deal with because it is in the open: what parents see is what they get, no more and no less. Passive warfare, however, is much more difficult. Children, in the terror of being threatened by their very own parents, weave an intricate web of severe hostility, denial of the reality of the situation (they don't *want* to believe it!) as well as denial of their own feelings of parent and/or self-hatred, remorse, attempts at coping and reconciliation and submission, and finally even greater feelings of threat and anger, deeper hostility, and a stronger need to protect themselves. So the cycle goes on and on. Once the chain of events begins it is most difficult to stop without some outside counseling. A parent who has several children in a passive defense state is in for a rough time. The sooner the corrective program is begun, the better for everyone. This problem will not go away on its own, but will get worse until it reaches the point where the family as a unit is destroyed. The seeds for annihilation are sown the day that the parent is perceived as a threat. Some of the most chronic cases of family discord we have witnessed involved children perceiving their own parents as the greatest threat to their physical, mental, or emotional well-being. Several teenagers shared with us the trembling that they experienced whenever their mothers or fathers just came into their presence. Adults themselves, now in their twenties and thirties, recount how they experience heart palpitations or stomach camps or stuttering whenever they encounter their parents, "even by telephone."

If parents who are in fact threatening were to be asked, "Do you want your children to perceive you as a threat?" two types of responses would ensue: (1) "Yes, I do. I don't mind it, if it keeps them in line. A little threat is good for everybody. It won't kill them. Besides, they know that I love them"; (2) "No, of course not. That's the last thing that I want. That would be terrible." Parents in the first category are in need of enlightenment. They are unaware of the counterproductive nature of their behavior and are functioning under some traditional but mistaken notion regarding what it takes to motivate children. Perhaps their own parents attempted to motivate them this way. They ought to seek counseling immediately or engage in a good parent-training program on the topic. Parents in the second category are likely to be insensitive to the discrepancy between their children's perception of their threatening behavior and their own perception of themselves. It would be in their best interest to do some self-examination on a regular basis, checking the congruence of their children's and their own perceptions through appropriate questioning and discussion. With arm on shoulder, or while hugging, or while having a nice quiet lunch, they might ask their children: "Does Dad ever frighten you or scare you? Do you fear that I would ever hurt you in any way?" If the answer were affirmative, the parent could discuss why the child feels that way and assure him or her that that would never happen. The nonverbal aspect of this communication (the setting, physical contact, etc.) could be a useful tool in this endeavor.

9. LISTEN TO AND RESPOND TO CHILDREN'S COMPLAINTS

Parents have a tendency to trivialize, discount, or rationalize away children's complaints. Adult criteria are often used to judge the validity or worthiness of the complaint. If it doesn't "make sense" to parents, it is dismissed. Usually the child, who sees things quite differently, is not privy to adult rules, and does not have the historical perspective of the parent, feels frustrated as his or her expressed needs are not only unmet, but not even considered. There is nothing more frustrating for a child than to have what he or she considers to be legitimate concerns pushed aside prematurely by a parent. The methods and motives used by mothers and fathers vary widely. Some ignore the child's emotional state altogether, and appeal strictly to "the facts." For example, a young high school girl may come home from school quite depressed because a boy with whom she is infatuated did not invite her to the school dance. She may be crying or sulking. A mother may challenge the justification of the daughter's complaint about her state in life by petitioning her in the following manner: "Look, honey, with all the problems in the world—people are starving in China, the world is on the brink of nuclear war—not getting invited to a dance is really not a major tragedy." Parents may dismiss complaints by comparing them to all the good things that are going on: "Look, things could be worse. You should be happy that you are healthy and have good, caring parents." Some try to outdo their children's complaints by referring to "war stories" of their own: "You think this is bad. Believe me, nothing will compare to what I went through when I was a kid. I would have traded places with you anytime. I survived, and I think you will too." All of these responses to children's complaints do nothing but exasperate sons and daughters. They are symptoms of low empathy and they demotivate and demoralize. Eventually children who are treated in this manner "disconnect" from their parents. When this happens, family relationships tend toward the stormy or, for the sake of peace, they become superficial.

How many times will a child go to his or her parents for help, understanding, and empathy, if they respond by pushing aside the complaint or diminishing its intensity? Two? Three? Four times? No more, that's for sure. To ignore these complaints is one of the surest ways to break the emotional bond between parent and child. Parents themselves know how they feel when another adult does not pay attention to their complaints, say, at work or in a department store, or judge them unjustifed. There is probably nothing that will get them angrier and more frustrated! Yet they often forget this when they treat their children's complaints with contempt. Parents must remember one thing: every complaint of a child is legitimate, at least for the child.

10. MAKE SURE THAT CHILDREN KNOW HOW THEIR ATTITUDES, VALUES, AND BEHAVIORS AFFECT THE WHOLE FAMILY

The family chain is only as strong as its weakest link. Children ought to know that if the family is going to be healthy and successful, every member must contribute. Each parent, son, and daughter counts, and all are necessary for the family's smooth functioning. The sooner children learn this, the better. Their level of motivation is dramatically increased when children feel that what they do or do not do really makes a difference. Conversely, it is discouraging for them to reach the conclusion that what they are doing makes little difference, has no impact. Think about this for a minute:

Suppose your church or synagogue was involved in a fund-raising effort and the pastor or rabbi called you and asked you to donate one hundred dollars. Let's look at two approaches that he might take: (a) "Hello, Mr. Sils, we are attempting to raise a hundred and fifty thousand dollars to refurbish the facilities. Could you donate a hundred dollars?" or (b) "Hello, Mr. Sils, we are attempting to raise a hundred and fifty thousand dollars to refurbish the facilities, part of which will be a new conference room. We would like to have two table lamps in that room. They cost approximately fifty dollars each. If you donate a hundred dollars, we will be able to have the lamps." Which approach do you think will be more successful? The answer is clear. In approach (b), the request has been concretized and the potential donor has the feeling that he can really make a difference: "If I contribute the one hundred dollars, they will have the lamps. If I don't, they won't have them." Of course, we all know that if the money had been obtained through approach (a), it could have been used to buy the lamps anyway. However, the chance of getting the donation would have dropped significantly because the potential donor would have felt that he was simply throwing his one hundred dollars into a big pot, his influence and impact being minimal. Just as successful fund-raisers are as concrete as possible to let potential donors feel that they are making a difference, so parents, too, must make it clear how their children's behavior and disposition affect the entire family. There are very few children who will not want to contribute action and energy if they feel that they are truly making a difference. As a matter of fact, they usually feel proud that they could actually influence a family outcome. Tell your children at almost any age what family good their actions or words are bringing about and watch them just radiate contentment. Certainly very few children will willingly refrain from responding to a request for help from parents if they understand that their involvement is critical to the accomplishment of a family goal or responsibility.

One of the greatest motivators for children is the feeling that they are doing something that will benefit all the other members of the family. Parents often have to explicitly translate the importance of a child's contribution because in itself the act may not be overly glamorous. One Baltimore mother has her nine-year-old son telephone the weather number every morning as soon as the family wakes up. He promptly announces the weather report to the rest of the family, who then dress accordingly, remember to take their umbrellas, etc. The child witnesses how the family benefits from his contribution and, of course, all the family members thank him for the information. Another child in the same family goes out to the newspaper tube at the end of the driveway and takes in the paper, serving as a lookout for the arrival of the newspaper delivery boy.

Parents who view their children's behavior with indifference or view it as insignificant generally lower motivation. Children, particularly in the adolescent and teenage years, develop a feeling of futility, boredom, and passivity. Apathy and disinterest in family affairs are heightened as the children seek other areas where they think they can make a difference.

11. Provide Children With Flexibility and Choice

Whenever possible parents should provide children with choices and flexibility in their lives. Children who do not have a chance to choose for themselves have a tendency to become lethargic and dependent. The art of choosing among alternatives is a critical skill for adults. The best way for children to develop this skill is to practice it as much as possible during childhood, their apprenticeship for adulthood. Parents, therefore, do their children a serious disservice when they narrow the choices available to them and/or diminish the opportunities for flexibility in their lives. The variance in decision-making ability among adults is very wide. Those who can make decisions skillfully and confidently are much more successful than those who cannot. The quality of their personal lives is much higher as well. Differential ability in decision-making acumen often stems back to childhood family decision experiences.

Well-meaning mothers and fathers, fearful that their children may choose wrong, often make choices for them: schools, clothing, food, pastimes, friends, and sometimes even dates. Other parents make choices for their child and limit flexibility because of a fear of the child's independence and consequent lack of dependence on them. Parents who have built their whole lives around "living for their children" are particularly vulnerable to this error. There is nothing sadder than witnessing a son or daughter who will not or does not know how to make choices in the presence of a parent.

We remember encountering a young college freshman who could not decide what flavor ice cream he would like to have without the assistance of his mother, who kept countermanding his expressed choices. Comments like the following kept coming forth: "Why do you want that? You know that you really don't like exotic flavors." This went on and on until the son finally relented and let his mother choose the flavor for him. Among the mothers and fathers that we have counseled, several decide on and purchase most of the clothing for their high school sons and daughters. They insist on doing this and see it as an integral part of their roles as parents. And these examples, while dramatic, are not isolated. Many other well-meaning parents are involved in the same kind of handicapping process.

Fathers and mothers who, on the other hand, allow and encourage their children to make their own choices—and to bear responsibility for the consequences—rear boys and girls who have a zest for life and feel comfortable in a world which they do not fear.

12. Provide Immediate, Relevant, and Continual Feedback That Will Help Children Improve Themselves

Effective parents take the time to provide feedback to their children as close as possible to the behavior that is to be reinforced or modified. To wait six months before saying anything or to dig up old skeletons from the closet, especially when angry at the child, is counterproductive for mothers and fathers. Timeliness is critical in the motivation of children, and the window of opportunity for success in this task is only open so long. The relative impact of feedback diminishes over time and at an exponential rate. Kids have short memories! They are more focused on what is happening now.

It is also important that parental feedback provided to children be relevant and concrete. Often parents develop feedback within the framework of their own personal experiences, values, needs, and wisdom. Children may not relate to it at all. For instance, a mother letting her daughter know her concerns about the girl's new boyfriend may use judgmental criteria that were appropriate for her day or her value system, but are not valid today or do not quite fit into her daughter's values. The daughter may truly not know what she is talking about. Whatever feedback is presented to children, it should have a constructive purpose. It should lead to either some improvement or some solidification of a currently held value.

There can be a tendency among some parents to neglect to point out improvements in attitude and behavior, no matter how small. This is particularly important when children are beginning to work on recommendations and suggestions. They need regular and continuous encouragement. Remember, it is not sufficient to simply initiate motivation. It is necessary to guide the child in the motivation process until the desired goal is achieved. Too many parents unwittingly abandon the child when he or she is 80 percent of the way there. Many accomplishments of children (academic, athletic, attitude, interests, etc.) are cumulative in nature. Some of the early development may not fully disclose itself. Parents may witness no visible signs of success and reach the conclusion that little is going on or that progress is not up to expectations. Maybe a child takes ten guitar lessons, but can hardly strum one tune. A father who is spending twenty dollars for each lesson might conclude, "What a waste of time and money. Two hundred dollars for that!" The danger is that he might express these feelings to the son, thereby discouraging him from taking further lessons. Perhaps what the son has learned in the area of coordination, instrumentation, reading music, theory, even self-confidence, may not be immediately apparent but will pay off eventually. If he had continued, he would have no doubt received the benefits of that early investment. Parents must remember that all tall buildings have foundations deep beneath the ground, out of sight.

Lastly, it is important for parents to remember to criticize children's behavior and not the children themselves. When parents criticize their sons and daughters they chip away at their dignity. The children's perception of their own value diminishes, giving rise to a strong feeling of self-consciousness which leads to anxiety, defensiveness, poor performance, and even more parental criticism. This downward spiral feeds on itself, causing the child to plummet on the motivation scale and to move faster and faster toward a state of total disillusionment. Teenage suicide, no doubt, is often triggered by adolescents' perception of parental rejection or devaluing of their personhood. It is the discounting of them as people, not of their behavior, that is the trigger of their despair.

While parent's attitudes are important on this issue, words are equally critical. The terminology used by mothers and fathers, including even subtle distinctions, can shift the focus from the child to the behavior or vice versa. For instance, "you" statements should be avoided when criticizing. When children hear this word, they generally become defensive and have difficulty really taking in any constructive comments. "I" statements are much less threatening and effective because the parent shifts the burden to himself or herself.

Consider the following two approaches that a parent might use in presenting negative feedback to a twelve-year-old who has a habit of not brushing his teeth before bedtime:

A. "You didn't brush your teeth, did you? You wait and see how many cavities you have when you go to the dentist next. You'll never learn, will you?"

B. "Gee, I was under the impression that everyone realized how not brushing your teeth every night will cause cavities for sure. I thought that every smart little boy knew that, but I guess that I was wrong."

In the first case there was a direct parental assault on the youngster. This will most likely cause him to either lie and say that he did brush his teeth, or was just about to, or simply become defiant and angry not so much because of the brushing, but because of the diminishment by his father. This approach will extend the conflict further and add on a new infraction (lying or defiance).

In the second approach, the father does not in any way diminish the worth or challenge the integrity of the child. He talks only about himself and *his* possible shortcomings ("I guess that I was wrong"), not his son's. In this approach the child then is more likely to direct his energies toward correcting his behavior than to use it in dealing with the stress of the situation. The last thing that he will want to hear is his father saying the same thing again the next evening. In short, the father, rather than painting him into a corner, has given the child an "out." And he, like most children, is likely to take it.

13. Appropriate Amounts of Stress Are Necessary for Motivation of Children

There is a common misconception that all anxiety and stress is bad. This is not true. As a matter of fact, the absence of stress leads to a lethargic, no-growth state for most children. Stress is the result of anything outside of us that causes us to change in some way. Stressors, then, are objects, goals, ideals, virtues, people, or any other factors in the environment that trigger a response in children. That is precisely what motivation is all about. A useful motivator will bring about appropriate levels of stress, thereby initiating some type of change (often in the form of growth). The key is for parents as motivators to be aware of and sensitive to the degree of stress introduced or allowed in relation to the child's physical, emotional, and mental energy at any one time. Sufficient stress will ultimately lead a child to peak mental, physical, and emotional performance. Too much stress, though, will detract from the quality of life of the family and become debilitating because of the eventual demotivation of the individual members. Parents should know the ideal stress load of each of their children. They should also be sensitive to the fact that tolerance for stress can vary widely depending, for example, on energy available, physical condition, emotional state, nutrition, or other stressors present.

14. Provide Children with Responsibility Along with Their Accountability

Nothing motivates children more than being given appropriate levels of responsibility: not too much but not too little. When their parents hold them accountable for what happens but do not allow them to have sufficient control over the situation, the children are placed in a position that is not only unfair, but also most trying for them. Responsibility without control is one of the major causes of distress not only for adults but for children as well. Often parents do to children what they would not think of doing to fellow adults in the business world or in social relationships. Adults wouldn't allow an impossible condition and would express themselves accordingly. Children, however, will accept it unknowingly or out of deference to their parents' judgment or out of fear of recrimination. Children in this state eventually feel powerless and confused, and their motivation is sure to be reduced. They often feel that they cannot win. Generally, they can't.

We often meet fathers and mothers who hold their sons and daughters responsible for high scholastic achievement, but then schedule so many extra activities for them (athletic events, social visits, outings, family trips, etc.) that the children have little control over the time, energy, and enthusiasm needed to study sufficiently. Others encourage their children to be creative and select an exciting career in a profitable industry, but then limit their educational opportunities because they will not allow them to go out of town for college.

What parents need to do is sit down and outline their goals for their children. Next to each goal, they should list the resources that will be needed to accomplish the goals. Then they should determine those resources over which they have allowed the children total control; some control; and no control. The following chart will be useful for this task.

RESPONSIBILITY-ACCOUNTABILITY ASSESSMENT

Goals for Children	Resources Needed	Children's Control Level		
		Total	Some	No
(Sample:)				
1. Proficiency in	a. lessons		X	
piano for	b. piano			X
ten-year-old	c. time to practice		X	
daughter Joan	d. interest	X		
2. Increased speed	a. reading instruction			X
and comprehen-	b. books		X	
sion in reading	c. time to read		X	
skills for twelve-	d. appropriate set-		X	
year-old son Louis	ting conducive to			
	reading			
	e. desire to improve	X		
(etc.)				

If parents find that generally their children have little or no control over most resources, they should be aware of the negative effect this situation will have for their sons and daughters, both externally and internally. First, children in this predicament will most likely experience less success. The odds are stacked against them right from the start. The means to accomplish goals are not in their hands; and no matter how close they are to their parents, there is no way that the resources will be there when and as they need them. Secondly, children in this state learn to develop an external *locus* of control—that is, they look outside themselves for the direction of their own destiny. Dependence on others is nurtured, and self-confidence and self-security are diminished, even abdicated in the case of many.

While the age of the child in comparison to the goal sought is a key consideration, parents who allow their children to have some or total control over resources needed will witness much more successful, happier, and secure children. Their children will feel more confident and will behave in a much more responsible fashion. They will show pride in their work and develop maturity at a pace that will be pleasing to their parents.

The two major obstacles to the development of compatibility between responsibility and control for children are their parents' fear that their sons and daughters will not know how to manage the resources and the fear that if their children take control, then Mom or Dad will no longer be needed. The first fear is founded on some legitimate grounds, and it would be prudent to be sure that the children are indeed capable of managing their resources. Once assured, however, parents should set this fear aside. The second fear, of being considered indispensable, is entirely in the head of the parents themselves. It is generally a counterproductive need and should be abandoned. In both cases it is a matter of putting the sure beneficial consequences of allowing the children some control above the remotely possible damage to the parent.

15. Parents Must Individualize Their Approaches to Motivating Children

Children within the same family require differing approaches to be motivated. If mothers and fathers develop a parent-centered framework for thinking about motivating their sons and daughters, they most likely will use their own styles, likes and dislikes, needs, expectations, values, and outlook as the key criteria for developing strategies and techniques. They will have a tendency not to distinguish among children and to expect each of them to respond in the same way and with the same degree of intensity. We often meet mothers and fathers who are perplexed because one of their children has refused to follow the pattern of an older brother who was interested in the rewards of academic achievement. "He's nothing like his brother," is not a rare statement heard in our counseling of parents. What they are really saying is something like this: "We have developed a pattern of motivation that has worked for *us*. We are confused and puzzled because it is not working for us *this* time."

On the other hand, parents who develop a child-centered approach to motivation recognize and accept the fact that each son or daughter is a unique and distinct individual. If motivation is going to work, it must not be placed on the child from outside, but must be developed from within the child himself or herself. These parents do not expect each child to respond uniformly to the same rewards and punishments. They therefore work to understand just what it is that will work with each child. They do not necessarily use what has worked in the past nor what is working now with other children. In motivation, more than in any other area, individualization is critical if success is to be achieved. The possibilities of what will work are virtually limitless: some children respond very well to material rewards (toys, clothes, etc.) and others respond to symbolic rewards (such as praise or pats on the back). As in all other relationships, stereotyping will not work. Respect for the uniqueness of the individual child will be the deciding factor.

Motivating children is a perpetual task in the parenting role. The job is never really finished and there is no "down time." In a sense, mothers and fathers are always "on," either increasing or decreasing interest and enthusiasm. Because the task is so pervasive, parents often feel that it is an impossible one or find themselves walking a tightrope: one false move and they are in trouble. This need not be the case, and parents ought not to become phobic concerning their motivational ability. No one act or comment is likely to do that much damage (or good, for that matter). Rather, a consistent sensitivity to the importance of understanding motivation and a respect for its complexity are what count. The recommendations presented above are a sound starting point and can serve as a framework for examining motivation difficulties.

The following checklist will help you review the major principles of parental motivation and reflect upon your own approach in this most important parentship function.

PARENTAL MOTIVATION CHECKLIST

Instructions: Answer "Yes" or "No" to the following questions by placing a check mark (✓) in the appropriate space.

Yes   No

_____ _____ 1. Do I attempt to reinforce my children's appropriate behaviors, attitudes, and dispositions with methods that are appropriate for *them,* not me?

_____ _____ 2. Do I regularly recognize my children's accomplishments, no matter how small?

_____ _____ 3. Do I encourage my children to establish and pursue their own goals?

_____ _____ 4. Do I clarify my expectations so that my children understand them fully?

_____ _____ 5. Do I try hard to increase the chances that my children will experience some form of success?

_____ _____ 6. Do I use a healthy balance of rewards, tangible (e.g., gifts) and internal ones (e.g., children's feelings of accomplishment), for my children when attempting to motivate them?

_____ _____ 7. Do I encourage my children to participate in decisions that affect them?

_____ _____ 8. Do I refrain from using threats, either open or veiled?

_____ _____ 9. Do I listen to, respect, and respond to my children's complaints?

_____ _____ 10. Do I explain and illustrate for my children how their attitudes, values, and behaviors can affect the entire family?

_____ _____ 11. Do I try to provide my children with as much flexibility and choices in their lives as possible?

_____ _____ 12. Do I let my children know how I think they are doing in a timely way so that they can improve their behavior?

_____ _____ 13. Do I recognize that a certain amount of stress in the family is necessary for my children's growth?

_____ _____ 14. Do I see to it that my children have levels of responsibility commensurate with that for which I hold them accountable?

_____ _____ 15. Do I personalize my motivation methods for each of my children?

Scoring and Interpretation: Number of "Yes" answers:
   13–15: superb motivation
   10–12: effective motivation
    7–9: average motivation
    4–6: ineffective motivation
    0–3: poor motivation

Motivation skills can be improved and progress can be observed rather quickly. If you need improvement, begin to work on each of the problem areas identified by your "No" answers on the checklist. You can either work on them one at a time in sequential fashion over several months or try to improve in several areas at the same time. The key is to begin to make improvements immediately and not to put off attempts to improve because you feel overwhelmed. The success that you will doubtless begin to experience in this area will encourage you to grow in this ability even more.

12

Family Information Systems

One of the greatest challenges to the family in the 1980s and 1990s will be represented by how it handles information. The family as a whole, as well as each individual member, is bombarded with literally tons of information on a daily basis. With the ascendance of cable television and its vast number of channels, more twenty-four-hours-a-day television and radio programming, and specialized magazines, this is sure to increase at an even more intense rate. Information is the oxygen of behavior. In many ways parents and children are what they take in. In a real sense, they are *formed* by information. The quality of the lives of family members will reflect the quality of the information that they receive and accept. When the impact of this information on the attitudes, values, and behaviors of family members is considered, the need for a *system* of control over information becomes clear. Not having a system results in a defenseless immersion into information, and the family's consequent loss of control over its destiny. If parents do not address the information issue, if they throw their hands up in defeat, or if their approach to information management is haphazard, they can be sure that trouble will be on its way. In terms of probabilities, there is just too much potentially unhealthy information in the family's environment for it not to have some negative impact. Effective parentship requires a set of principles and practices to be established for a sound family information management system. Developing appropriate guidelines in this area can be a most sensitive task and will require the judicious balancing of the need to monitor information with the children's rights to have access to sources of knowledge and to be inquisitive and curious. *The last thing that we would want to recommend or imply is that parents totally control information to which their children might have access.* First of all, we do not think that this is possible; secondly, it would be psychologically, educationally, and socially detrimental. However, *some* monitoring must be done.

Consider the case of Ted. His teenage children watched television incessantly, as soon as they came home from school and a good part of the weekend. Ted was concerned, but not overly, and used to shrug his shoulders saying, "What am I going to do? You know teenagers." What Ted and his children did not realize was that the real content of commercial television is advertising. The programming is actually filler to keep viewers' attention between ads. Something else that Ted and his children did not know was that all successful television advertising is characterized by three asssmptions: (1) you (the viewer) are not perfect —that is, you are missing something; (2) The image (the person, object, or scene demonstrating the product) *is* perfect; and (3) you (the viewer) get *some* perfection by buying the product. This exposure to television resulted in two false messages to Ted's children: first, that the world is filled with perfection—it is all around them—look at those young, beautiful, handsome surfers with perfect figures doing all those soft drink commercials, and those ecstatic teenagers romping in their designer jeans; and second, that they themselves are really pretty miserable creatures, deprived of what everyone else has. After being told over and over again that they were not as perfect as their counterparts on the television screen, they began to believe it. Because this level of perfection was absent in their lives (and only their lives, or so they thought), deep depression set in. If Ted's children continue on this course, they will sink deeper and deeper into a state of undeserved self-pity. Reversing this trend will be an uphill battle. Ted will feel that he is on a treadmill and is failing in his leadership role as a father.

Other parents have experienced similar situations. Many mothers have told us that their children, particularly daughters, are obsessed with weight control. A terribly worried mother of a sixteen-year-old girl in Wilmington, Delaware, relayed to us that her daughter who weighs 105 pounds at 5'6" is absolutely convinced that she is too fat, and therefore seldom eats. "Do you believe it? She hardly eats. And when she does eat even the smallest amount of food, she worries all day and keeps checking herself in the mirror. It doesn't make any sense to me. I am starting to think that she is anorexic or something! We are really worried about her."

These words are most probably familiar to parents of teenage daughters. We would estimate a full 80 percent of teenage girls "feel" overweight when in fact many are not. Why this obsession with weight? The answer becomes clear when one leafs through fashion magazines or looks at other advertising. The models are all size five! Any youngster on a regular diet of this information has a clear definition of beauty: "Thin is in. And the thinner the more beautiful." Teenage boys likewise are affected by this definition of beauty and seek the thinner girls as dates. This just intensifies the rush to even more thinness, creating a vicious cycle. The "thinness epidemic" is so widespread and so devastating to the physical and mental health of youngsters that many health and social agencies are inquiring what can be done to arrest this accelerating obsession.

Some parents are equally concerned about the impact of contemporary music on their children's values. One mother vividly described her shudders when she heard her ten-year-old daughter singing a popular song that glorified sexual promiscuity as she got ready for school one morning. "I had to wonder whether she really understood what those words implied. The thought that she might scared me. I was afraid to ask her," she continued.

What can the family do? Parents and children can only take in and accept so much information, really a minuscule amount compared to all there is. The quality of that information will be affected by its source, its accuracy and reliability, and its meaningfulness to the family members. Parents must recognize that while the amount of possible information available to children is almost infinite, the amount of time for receiving information is finite. To leave to chance what information will be taken in during those relatively brief time periods would be irresponsible. Of course, the age of the children will be a variable: generally, the younger the children, the more the need for parental involvement. Methods for accessing the highest quality of information and judging its worth must be an integral part of family life. What each family member reads in magazines, hears on the radio, and watches on television will affect the whole family. Just as communication is the lifeline inside the family, so it links the family with the environment. What passes through that external lifeline has a wide range of quality and depends very heavily on the information source to which it is connected. The approach to information management in the family should include three dimensions: (1) monitoring; (2) selecting discriminately from available sources of information; and (3) designing and developing a curriculum for the home. These are the building blocks of a parental management information system, a function necessary to increase the availability of beneficial information and limit access to the detrimental.

MONITORING

Fathers and mothers have the right and obligation to reduce the accessibility of information that they feel will be harmful to their children physically, emotionally, mentally, or spiritually. This may sound like a medieval concept in the 1980s. But to do otherwise would be a dereliction of duty. *While the ultimate goal of all parental information management is to teach children how to develop their own internal information monitoring system, mothers and fathers do have to intervene and use external influence, especially in the children's early years.* Of course, reason and prudence must always be the guides.

There is no escaping the fact that each family's approach to this task will differ in form and content—necessarily so, since family values will play a major role. Therefore, it would not be very beneficial for one family to use another family's judgment criteria, or attempt to impose its own on other families, or judge others according to its own standards.

In attempting to reduce accessibility of information to their children, families will always run some risk of going too far or not far enough. It is by no means an exact science, but calls for artful decision making and judgment. The control-versus-growth dilemma of parentship is very obvious here. While factors like children's ages, maturity levels, time of day (no scary home videotapes before bedtime!), and emotional stability often help parents determine what they should allow or should preclude, there are many gray areas. The purpose of monitoring information in the family is not to eradicate information forever. It is really a matter of *postponement* of information until the child is ready to receive it in a way that will not be harmful. If the children really want and need the information, they will, no doubt, get it at a later date. What monitoring does is to keep the flow of information and kind of information as compatible as possible with the all-around readiness of the recipient child. This *will not* occur naturally or automatically for every child. A superimposed management system may be necessary to make it happen. While parents can by no means control *all* the information or sources of information (media, books,

movies, records, peers, other adults, etc.) that might influence their
children, they can regulate some. That "some" could make all the
difference in the world. It is important for parents to understand the
actual degree of influence that they have over these sources. The
following grid will be helpful.

In analyzing this sample grid, parents will notice that degrees of
influence vary depending on sources of information. Likewise, they
can influence information more or less at various ages of their children. Let us examine each source of information in regard to parental
influence.

1. *Children's friends.* In most circumstances, parents are able to determine who will be their children's friends up to about age five
   because they can regulate physical location and proximity. Soon
   after this age, total influence becomes difficult as children begin to
   attend school and feel the need to play with other children. Parents
   continue to have some influence: they may be able to select their
   children's school and thereby influence their children's friendships and associations, but this is general in nature: they won't
   know *every* child. Likewise, during the period of age five through
   age fifteen, parents can forbid friendships with certain children.
   Fathers and mothers have this right and obligation and should
   exercise it fully.

   Defining the correct balance between parental influence and
   freedom for the child to choose friends is no easy task, especially in
   the early teenage years. Because of this pain of not knowing the
   right formula, parents can be tempted to abandon trying to find
   the right balance and either attempt total control or allow their
   children complete freedom to choose. In either case trouble will
   be on the way. When parents do deny requests for relationships
   with certain boys and girls, it is important for them to explain the
   reason, patiently and clearly, to their own sons and daughters.
   Most children will not understand it at first (and some perhaps
   never will, for that matter). Either they were attracted to these
   children for some reason or they were the object of the other
   children's interest and attention. Friendship bonds are quite nonrational; they often do not make sense to others. Children will
   likewise feel vicariously hurt and insulted by their parents' rejection of their friends: their judgment is being overruled and their
   social needs are being frustrated. Parents must understand this
   and have empathy. Communication, especially listening to the
   child, is important. However, parents must not relent and give in

SAMPLE PARENTAL INFLUENCE GRID

AGE OF CHILD

SOURCE OF INFORMATION	0-1	1-3	3-5	5-7	7-9	9-11	11-13	13-15	15-17	17-19
Children's Friends	T	T	T	S	S	S	S	S	S	N
Family Friends	T	T	T	T	T	T	T	T	T	T
Relatives (grandparents, aunts, etc.)	S	S	S	S	S	S	S	S	S	S
Other Adults (coaches, teachers, etc.)	T	T	S	S	S	S	S	S	S	S
Children's Books and Magazines (nonschool)	T	T	T	T	S	S	S	S	N	N
Family Magazines	T	T	T	T	T	T	T	T	T	T
Newspapers	T	T	T	T	T	T	S	S	N	N
Radio & Television	T	T	T	S	S	S	S	S	N	N
Movies in Theater	T	T	T	T	T	T	T	S	S	N
Movies at Home	T	T	T	T	T	T	T	T	T	T
Records & Tapes	T	T	T	T	S	S	S	S	N	N
Neighbors	T	T	S	S	S	S	S	S	N	N
Churches	T	T	T	T	T	T	T	S	S	N
Schools	T	S	S	S	S	S	S	S	N	N

Degree of Parental Influence:
T = Total Influence   S = Some Influence   N = No Influence

to their children in order to avoid the emotional trauma they may cause by forbidding or even breaking up a friendship. To avoid inflicting pain, parents may deny the potential damage that all their instincts flag and convince themselves that everything will most likely be fine: "Who am I to judge?" Caring, sensitive, and loving parents are the ones most vulnerable to this temptation. They want their children to be and *look* happy above all else. To avoid this pitfall, parents have to remind themselves that the long-term gains will far outweigh the short-term: the head must dominate the heart in this case. The emotional difficulty of these decisions for parents was expressed well by Lisa, a mother in Dearborn, Michigan: "My thirteen-year-old son is caught between a rock and a hard place, and so am I. He has always been a good student. But this year he has been accepted by the 'in group' at school . . . you know, all the jocks and the kids that have a lot of friends. While he's doing well socially, his grades are dropping because he's spending more time playing and talking on the phone, and less time studying. I don't think that his priorities are correct and his new friends are not helping matters. I feel that I must intervene somehow and have some more direct influence over his choice of friends. But I know in doing so I am going to hurt his feelings badly and most likely cause some family turmoil. I do the best I can to explain why I feel that his friends may be having some negative influence on him, but I can't get a guarantee that I will be successful. I don't look forward to this task. But I must do it."

In the case of older children (from age fifteen on), parents have an extremely limited control over their friendships. Of course, the child's early values developed in the home will have a lasting effect and will, no doubt, influence the selection of friends.

2. *Family friends.* The friends with whom parents themselves associate are chosen freely. Friendships can be begun and terminated at will. Parents should consider their children when establishing family friendships. Some adults may have a very positive influence over children and may, in fact, be good role models, not only for what they do but also in terms of who they are. Others could have an adverse effect—for example, because of their attitudes, values, behavior, or foul language. A person who was an acceptable friend when the children were young may no longer be so as the children get older. Parents often have difficulty dealing with such problems: they usually approach solutions awkwardly or overlook a friend's

offensive conduct, but boil inside. A mother in Hollywood, Florida, explained the problem well: "You know, I really don't like to hear my friend Julie tell me about her most recent romantic exploits, often with all the details . . . who she spent the weekend with, what they did, etc. Since her divorce that's all she talks about. The problem is that my fourteen-year-old daughter Ginny is often within earshot and hears the whole thing. Julie has less and less discretion, and Ginny has come to think that her lifestyle is just grand: candlelight dinners, trips to the Bahamas . . . all with sexy, handsome lovers. I don't think hearing all this is good for her, but I don't want to hurt Julie, especially when she is so happy finally after a terrible marriage and wrenching divorce. I don't want to break up our friendship." It does not always have to come down to a parting of ways. Often, if parents simply explain to their friends that their words or behavior are not in the best interest of their children, corrections may be attempted by the offending party . . . but not always. Some friends are seriously insulted, feel ashamed and even rejected, and withdraw from the relationship. Parents must remember that while they can be diplomatic in handling such a situation, there is no easy out. They are often choosing between two valuable things: the welfare of their friends and that of their children. Simply put, it is a matter of priorities; and the children, of course, must win out. We find a surprising number of fathers and mothers whose friends are having a questionable impact on their children, but who choose to minimize or ignore the problem altogether. They may well be inviting into their own household the planters of seeds of their own children's debilitation and destruction.

3. *Relatives.* Of course, parents can select their friends, but they can hardly do the same when it comes to relatives. In many circumstances, depending on the proximity of the extended family, relatives have a chance to influence children right from birth. Although the numbers are decreasing, some relatives live within the same block or immediate neighborhood. Like family friends, relatives as sources of information for the child present a special problem: there is generally an emotional bond with them; they are most often loved. In many cases the information that children receive from relatives is beneficial and supportive of parental values and goals. But this is not always the case: grandparents, aunts, uncles, or cousins may actually transmit information that is not compatible with what the parents are trying to instill. The discrep-

ancies could be in the area of religion, moral conduct, honesty,
styles of interpersonal relationships, nutrition and eating habits,
the value of school, art appreciation, or any other. Children are
put in a very difficult position by contradictory messages: they are
often confused and stressed because of the ambiguity. Whether
they ultimately tend to lean toward their parents' or their relatives'
point of view will be a factor of age, among other things. Younger
children (ages five to twelve) tend to give preference to their own
parents' teachings, while older children (age thirteen on) might be
more attracted to the dissenting perspective. These preferences
have more to do with the emotional state of the parent-child relationship than with the actual validity of the varying points of view.
In the earlier years children feel closely aligned with parents and
tend to see them as all-knowing, all-powerful protectors: whatever
they say is truth. At about age twelve this fantasized image of Mom
and Dad begins to vanish quickly as the reality of the situation
becomes evident: "My parents are not perfect." Sometimes the
disappointment and trauma of this discovery causes an inordinate
focus of attention on parental flaws. The hurt associated with the
discovery that one does not have perfect parents often causes the
child to angrily delegitimize everything that Mom or Dad says or
stands for: if they don't know one thing, they don't know anything;
if they make one error, they must always be wrong. In contrast, the
appeal of the grandfather, uncle, or aunt who has not let them
down is enticing. Besides, there is not the emotional strain that
they experience with their own parents and they may see these
relatives mostly during good times, such as holidays, birthdays, or
social events. Association with them carries pleasant memories.

Again, the balance between appropriate control and the children's freedom to associate is a difficult one to ascertain when it
comes to relatives. When in doubt, it is always best to opt for the
safe side: control. As with family friends, some very difficult and
sensitive decisions will have to be made. It is not an easy thing to
let relatives know that they are having a negative influence over a
child or to reduce the number or length of visits. They will often
not understand and feel offended. The relationship between children and family relatives can be a true double-edged sword: much
good can come from it, but also tremendous damage. The key
criterion, however, should always be clear: the long-term welfare
of the children.

4. *Other adults.* The other adults that are sources of information are

generally under the influence of parents while the children are under age three. After that, parents lose total control but retain some ability to monitor influence. Many four-year-olds are enrolled in preschools; they are involved in recreational activities, talk with neighbors, etc. This interaction, of course, continues to increase rapidly all the way through the late teens and beyond. The first signal that total control is gone comes on the day the child begins talking about or quoting a person that the parent has not met (e.g., a teacher's aide at nursery school, or a substitute swimming instructor at the community pool's Tiny Tots Program, or a visitor at the next-door neighbor's house). From that point on parents can maintain some influence by directly interviewing these adults if they are aware of some potential damage, or they can indirectly regulate the influence of adults and control access by manipulating the situation: seeing to it that contact with certain people is reduced (for negative influences) or enhanced (for positive influences). This becomes more and more difficult as the children get older and parental awareness of adult contacts diminishes. However, whenever possible and for as long as possible, parents should do their best to meet the adults who relate to their children in any way. Without becoming overly cautious, mothers and fathers need to follow their instincts with regard to the potential influence these adults may have on their children. It is always more prudent to learn more about a person who for some reason arouses negative feelings. Children will often resist parents who raise questions or doubts about people to whom the children have been drawn or whom they speak of fondly. Once again, the parents have to understand why the children will balk, but must proceed to validate or invalidate their misgivings or uneasiness.

5. *Children's books and magazines.* "What am I supposed to do? Check through their books, school notebooks, drawers every night? Look under their beds for dirty magazines? That would be insulting to them and show a lack of trust. I know my kids and they would *never* read anything that doesn't fit in with what we've taught them!" While this mother may be correct in her assessment, she may also be naïve in denying the *potential* damaging impact of information conflicting with family objectives and values. Parents have total influence over what books and magazines children have access to up to about age six. They generally do all the purchasing of such materials and therefore can regulate what comes in the house. Starting soon after this age, children begin to get more exposure

to public places and sometimes spend unescorted time at the homes of friends where parental control of information is minimal. By the time sons and daughters are fifteen years old it is almost impossible to maintain any semblance of control over information flow, except for dramatic violations of family codes (e.g., bringing pornographic material into the home). Whenever possible, however, parents should flip through books and magazines that children are reading and sample a page or two to be aware of content and implied values transmitted—with regard to moral perspectives, ideology, ethics, relationships, and attitudes. Parents may find that what children are reading is quite compatible with family values or may discover material that contradicts much of what they have been attempting to instill for many years.

While being exposed to information that challenges their position may ultimately be a strengthening experience for children, they must be mature enough and prepared to handle it. Allowing and even encouraging boys and girls to read material that *disagrees* with family values may be most beneficial for the development of mature and thinking children. However, timing and readiness are critical factors for success in this area. Striking a balance between too much control and not enough control may not be easy. Parents must not be tempted to avoid the internal anguish that accompanies not knowing the correct formula by adopting a policy of stringent censorship or completely abandoning any attempt to regulate what children read.

6. *Family magazines.* This source of information is entirely within the influence of parents. They can decide what magzines will be taken into the house and which will not. The publishers of most weekly news magazines are aware of parental concern for guarding their children from potentially harmful material. Their words, pictures, and advertising generally reflect this sensitivity. Of course, there are exceptions. Likewise, sports journals and domestic-oriented periodicals are often family-sensitive. The messages conveyed in other magazines, however, may either explicitly or implicitly preach a hedonism or amorality that contradicts family values and is ultimately detrimental to children. One has only to peruse the covers of some of the popular magazines to get a good sampling of possibilities. The subject matter included in a particular issue is boldly advertised across the cover: "How to get the most out of one-night stands" or "The ultimate orgasm" or "How to develop a seductive behind in 14 days!" This kind of material, while hardly considered pornographic, can do harm if left lying around and

available to young adolescents and teenagers. It is not to be taken lightly. The values and lifestyles promoted are vividly presented. Of course, parental control over this source of influence will begin to diminish as the child begins to move into the teen years and is exposed to it in public places and other people's homes. But parents do have much influence over what magazines come into the household, and they should exercise it.

7. *Newspapers.* Children can receive information from newspapers. Parents generally have total influence over this source until children reach approximately age ten. Most children can't or are not interested in reading newspapers until that time, although they may be exposed to pictures, advertising, or the comics. All of these can be sources of beneficial or detrimental information. Some newspapers sensationalize events and present gory material. Some of the supermarket type "scandal sheets" flash banner headlines or include pictures that may distort reality or present material that could be very harmful to an immature mind: e.g., "Lose ten pounds in five days on new grapefruit diet" in the hands of an adolescent or teenager could be very hazardous to his or her health! Likewise, the lives of famous people (actors, sports figures, etc.) are often glamorized in a most seductive way. They become models of really "making it." The image portrayed (usually materialistic opulence) makes it clear what really counts in life! Learning for learning's sake, art and music appreciation, ethics, courtesy, even contributions to medical science have a hard time competing with the payoffs of life among the Hollywood and jet sets. While aspiring for material gain is fine in itself, the glorification of this aspect of life beyond all others is counterproductive. Parents must also periodically review comic strips that children are reading. While most are generally harmless, they have the potential to inculcate incompatible values. After all, most comics are not just pure entertainment, but have an ideological, moral, or political message as well.

Parents begin to lose influence over newspapers as a source of information influence as children begin to enter the early teenage years, and they lose almost all control as their sons and daughters approach the late teens. Newspapers are all over the place and are accessible to children, although they are generally less attractive than magazines.

Finally, the accessibility of "underground" newspapers to youngsters is an issue that parents should address, particularly when living in large metropolitan areas. These papers are primarily marketed to young adults and much of the material, but not all, encourages permissive attitudes and behavior in the areas of drugs and sex. In discriminating and prudent hands these papers are not harmful. However, children who are impressionable may be unduly influenced by this ethic of the counterculture and be led astray.

8. *Radio and television.* Parents are capable of regulating what children watch on television or listen to on the radio up through age five. They can literally turn on and turn off the sets any time that they wish. At about age six, total influence becomes difficult as children begin to visit the homes of friends, neighbors, and relatives. This loss of control increases rapidly as the children move into the early teenage years, and parental influence dissipates almost entirely during the late teens. Parents must be aware of the major content of radio and television: advertising. There are very few families, if any, that can escape the impact of advertisements on the development of values. In many ways, advertising has become the literature of the 1980s. It is a major source of information for many children and it does indeed affect attitudes, dispositions, and priorites—in short, lifestyle. While parents are generally concerned about the nutrition levels of the food that their children eat and the quality of the air that they breathe, they are often not as concerned about the information ingested by their children through advertising. To truly understand the impact of the radio and television media, therefore, parents have to analyze the ads as much as the programs. Every ad has a value dimension, because—to be successful—it must get consumers to choose to spend money on one product above others; they have to see "value" in it. Sometimes the value that is being sold supports family principles, but sometimes it does not. Therefore, not exercising control can be a high-risk game for parents, especially if young children are inundated with advertising. Tremendous amounts of money are poured into advertising on a regular basis, and most ads are very effective.

In analyzing the advertising that their children are exposed to, parents must question what is really being sold. Clothing is rarely sold as a mechanism for keeping the body warm or covered or protected. What is sold instead is fun (jean ads), prestige (alligators, foxes, polo players), attractiveness, adventure, and even violence or horror. As a matter of fact, it is the rare product that is sold for its own sake. What counts is the connection between the product portrayed in the advertising and its symbolism. A Boston mother shared this observation with other parents at one of our workshops: "Can you believe the jeans ads that they have been showing on television lately? They are so suggestive and the kids modeling the clothing are so seductive. In one ad a young teenage girl and boy were practically doing it right on the TV screen! My kids sit and watch this stuff and are becoming totally desensitized to it. They're beginning to think that this is par for the course. I'm worried about it. I feel that I have an invincible competitor that is infiltrating my household spreading moral corruption. It's like germ warfare. The problem is that *we* have to pay the price of the havoc, not those television commercial writers and developers. They are making their money off the libidos of our children!"

Radio and television are, no doubt, the major suppliers of information for most children in our society. Other sources, including family members and schools, do not even come close to competing. Parents have to work exceptionally hard and go against the grain to limit the impact, but every effort must be made. By the time children reach their late teens it is hoped that they will be able to do some self-censoring if a strong enough value base has been established when they were younger.

9. *Movies in theaters.* Parents can have total influence over what movies their children go to see in theaters until about age fifteen, if they choose to exercise it. Children are dependent on their parents for transportation to the theater as well as the money needed to be admitted. If children are invited by the parents of their friends, parents still have the ability to get all the information needed concerning the nature of the film, ratings, etc. If in doubt, they may even elect to preview a film themselves before deciding whether to allow their children to attend. In many ways, movies are much more controllable than television and radio. Exposure can be easily regulated and there is no advertising interspersed throughout to exploit the attentive viewer. Likewise, the movie industry has been more sensitive (often because of external pressure) to the general "family standards," and its rating system forewarns parents that certain material may not be in the best interests of some or all children. Theater movies, then, should pose one of the least serious threats to family information systems, *if* parents want to exercise the minimal effort needed to heed the warning signals.

10. *Movies in the home.* During the past few years movies shown in the home through the use of videocassette recorders (VCR) have be-

come a growth industry. Families can literally obtain for home showing almost every film presented in theaters within a short time of release. Likewise, with the increased availability of cable television, all-movie channels are becoming more and more popular. Some of these channels offer an array of films, while others are more specialized. There are channels that offer special-interest programming, which includes films of only a certain type (e.g., the Playboy channel). Movies used with a VCR are entirely under the control of parents because they have to be rented and physically carried into the house and inserted in a machine that is tied into the television set. If need be, parents can even lock up the cassette so that children will not have access to it. Movies that are transmitted into the home through cable television are not as easy to regulate. Parents cannot be standing guard over the television set at every moment. Sometimes, too, teenagers are home alone, or they may be entertaining friends in the family room and need privacy. Parents also have an obligation to consider the impact of detrimental information on the friends of their children who visit and whose parents implicitly entrust them to their care and protection. Decisions to connect into cable offerings must be made with this control difficulty in mind. Parents must also remember that movies transmitted through videocassettes or cable are usually uncut and uncensored, unlike their commercial television versions.

11. *Records and tapes.* Music that children are exposed to through records and tapes can have a significant influence on their values, attitudes, and behavior. In most contemporary music that is appealing to adolescents and teenagers, the lyrics center on one or both of the following themes: sex and drugs.

If children are constantly bombarded by these themes, the results are often challenging to family values. Parents can totally influence what records and tapes children listen to up to about age eight because they control the money needed for the purchase and they also regulate time spent at other children's houses to a high degree. But after this age parental influence begins to evaporate quickly as children have more freedom to associate with other children outside their parents' supervision and also have some discretionary use of money to purchase these items. By age sixteen, parental influence over this source of information is almost completely gone.

Lastly, a serious difficulty for parents in controlling records and tapes is their inability to really understand what the words and the rhythm are conveying. Often the lyrics border on the unintelligible, have double meanings, or are heavily symbolic. The children may be getting the message because of their knowledge of and sensitivity to the culture (e.g., the teenage drug scene), but the parents may miss it altogether: it may be like a foreign language for them. Likewise, the beat of the music may communicate certain images, desires, and urges to the child that may not connect with parents because of their differing emotional state. The best that parents can do in this situation is to go with their instincts. If they suspect that the music is conveying a certain message, then it most probably is. They ought to verify their instinctive conclusions by discussing the matter with the children involved in a sensitive and caring fashion: "Dear, I wonder what 'let's get physical' means. What do you think it means?" might be an appropriate question posed to a ten-year-old girl while showing openness, and certainly without any threat of punishment for the "wrong answer."

Again, records and tapes are another avenue of information that parents have much difficulty monitoring, except for the early years. The amount of music available to children is staggering. With the increased popularity of earphones children can even literally block out access to the sounds that they are hearing. They can sit there or strut along shaking their heads to the rhythm of the beat in total audio privacy and seclusion. Parents can be tempted into throwing their hands up in surrender to this seemingly overwhelming force closing in on every front. This is the worst thing that they could ever do. On the contrary, we must recognize the battle is ongoing and seek rewards in winning small and medium-size victories. Sometimes the difference between a child abusing or not abusing sex and/or drugs could lie in the exercise of parental judgment and control in this area.

12. *Neighbors.* Where parents choose to live can have a significant impact on the information that children take in from neighbors. Family members do adapt to their environment. The predominant values, attitudes, and customs of certain neighborhoods can be either supportive of or contrary to parental goals for their children. For example, a neighborhood may be characterized by materialism (affluence is flaunted); anti-intellectualism (school and study are frowned upon); illicit drug culture; heavy alcohol drinking; and so forth. It is very difficult for children not to be influenced by what is going on around them. They face a dilemma if

they find themselves in an environment that is incompatible with their family's expectations: either blend in with the neighborhood children, thereby creating conflicts at home, or reject the neighborhood in favor of the family, suffering socially and perhaps risking ostracism. Parents reduce the chance of this dilemma arising if they seek neighborhoods that are supportive.

One point should be kept in mind: the best neighborhoods (in socioeconomic terms) are not always the "best" in terms of other criteria (such as attitudes, values, or customs). Physical property values are only one dimension of the quality of life in a community. Everett, an attorney in his early forties, learned that lesson: "I thought that moving to my neighborhood would be just grand for everyone. Living on Chesapeake Bay would be healthy and fun for all of us. My kids would associate with kids from a good socioeconomic class, the schools in the area have a fine reputation, and the community is safe. What I didn't realize was that half the families include at least one parent with an alcohol or tranquilizer dependency problem, a good 25 percent are having affairs with their neighbors, and almost all of them are totally status-conscious to the point of being complete snobs . . . all habits and characteristics totally foreign to my way of life. I find my kids defending our neighbors . . . they think that all of this is perfectly o.k. My wife and I really didn't realize the values of the neighborhood were seeping into our own family's values. It kind of crept up on us . . . We were too busy focusing on the psychological and social benefits of having the right zip code! I guess we foolishly thought that somehow we were immune from the influence of our milieu."

13. *Churches and synagogues.* Parents have total control over the influence that churches and synagogues have on their children until about age thirteen. They are able to regulate access to the church and synagogue through admission: children generally do not join alone, but through family membership. Likewise, children are dependent on parents for transportation to and from services and activities. Most parents carefully select churches and synagogues with an eye to compatible theological, philosophical, and moral teachings. They see these institutions as having a beneficial influence on their families and often as assisting agencies in the spiritual and educational dimensions of child rearing. Parents also recognize that the impact of early exposure to such teaching can last a lifetime. It is for this very reason, however, that parents must choose carefully the church or synagogue to which they do expose

their children. There is quite a variance not only in religious dogma, worship styles, and social and behavioral principles espoused, but also in attitudes toward the self-worth of the individual. On occasion, we have encountered parents whose churches or synagogues were contradicting what they were attempting to instill in the home. When this situation exists, needless to say, the children become confused. Rather than remain in this state for too long, they choose to favor one side or the other and develop a cynical attitude toward the rejected one, which is usually the church or synagogue. They then either learn to live without the influence of a religious organization, become nominal members or agnostics, or seek one that offers complete compatibility between home values and theology. In some cases they may seek a home in the church itself. This is one reason why many young adults are attracted to cults, even though they may already be members of an organized religion. The attraction of the cult is not so much theological as psychological. The internal dissonance and emotional strain of choosing between family and church is gone; the two are one and the same.

Through the early to late teens parents continue to have some direct control over church influence. In addition to the purely religious dimension, there are certain ceremonial rites of passage that young boys and girls fulfill as a part of their maturation process (e.g., confirmation, bar mitzvah). They are public statements and commitments that they will abide by a set of principles.

By the late teens most direct parental control over the church or synagogue as a source of influence has dissipated. Children usually remain members of the religious domination of their childhood, but not always, of course. They do this for theological, social, and ethnic as well as cultural reasons. In this sense parental influence is long-lasting. Parents must remember that children, especially adolescents and teenagers, often have difficulty with religious institutions. It is another dimension of the control/growth conflict. *Any* institution that attempts to place controls on attitudes, behavior, or thinking is often viewed as counterproductive by children who are growing mentally, socially, and emotionally. When children do react negatively to the influence of churches and synagogues, they are generally rejecting not the religious message *per se* but rather the process by which it is transmitted. What parents consider "teachings" are viewed as "impositions" by children. This is particularly the case in religious denominations that have a high degree of structure, organization, and bureaucracy. Parents who are members of less organized religious denominations may find less resistance by their children, since the constraints of the structural dimension have been diminished or removed. Parents need to have empathy with the ambivalent state of the youngster who is torn between the driving need to grow and the desire to be open to the good teachings of his or her parents' religious institution.

14. *Schools.* Parents have the least control over schools as a source of influence on their children. For this reason, parental decisions regarding schools must be made very carefully. The actual amount of control that parents have over schools varies widely, depending on several factors. First, whether the school is public or private can make a difference. Generally, parents have more influence in the private schools; they can simply withdraw their sons and daughters if they do not like what is going on. Most private schools need children's tuition for their survival. Therefore, they are responsive to the concerns of fathers and mothers. Sometimes, however parental influence in the private school is limited because the school offers something that the parent and/or child may want badly (e.g., a high chance of admission to a good college). In this case parents will have to tolerate some undesirable influences in order to gain their primary objective. For example, a family may not like the "preppy attitude" toward social drinking and parties, but may be willing to risk it for the sake of the sound academic preparation the prep school provides. Other parents might decide exactly the opposite and forego the superior preparation for college in order to lower the risk of their children developing what they consider to be a detrimental lifestyle.

Parents whose children attend public school can have varying degrees of control as well. It is important for parents to make a realistic assessment of precisely what power they have and where the leverage points are when it comes to schools. Some public school systems have a long tradition of responsiveness to parents' interests and concerns. Others are less sensitive. Some districts are operated by elected school boards and can be influenced through the political process. Others have appointed boards and may not have to be concerned about political pressures. The size of the district can make a difference as well: usually the smaller, the more responsive. Parents in states like New Hampshire, where school departments are rather small, are likely to have much more say over what is taught, how, and by whom than parents in the Los Angeles public schools.

Another important factor affecting degrees of parental influence is the actual location of the school. It is well known in educational circles that certain schools get better treatment because they are located in communities that either have clout (political, financial, social, etc.) or will respond aggressively if they don't get what they want. While educational establishment officials will deny responding differentially because of these factors, parents would be naïve to believe them. It is certainly in the parents' best interest to either have their children attend schools in the communities that have power, if they can, or initiate a power base with other parents in their own school community.

A second factor regulating parental influence levels in the schools is the grade level affected. Generally, the lower the grade level, the more control by parents. This is true for several reasons. In the early years parents usually have to interact with one, two, or perhaps three teachers—a controllable number. The material covered in school is understandable to most parents; therefore, they feel more confident in expressing their opinion. Likewise, their children may not have yet experienced many, if any, failures; parents are still filled with hope for their "budding geniuses." Teachers and school administrators expect and encourage this involvement by parents as they attempt to build a home-school partnership. However, as children move into the fifth and sixth grades the amount of parental influence begins to diminish rapidly: there are usually more teachers and school staff members (counselors, librarians, art and music teachers, physical education instructors, etc.) participating in the educative process; the subject matter is not as familiar to parents (new math!); and children no longer view parental involvement as socially attractive. It is not by accident or coincidence that most PTA officers and activists are parents of children in grades 1 through 4. Likewise, attendance at PTA meetings declines drastically from elementary school to middle or junior high school to high school, where principals are pleasantly surprised if twenty parents attend a meeting.

A final factor that will affect the level of parental influence on schools is the amount of time that parents will be able to devote to this activity. Many fathers and mothers have full-time jobs that preclude frequent visits to the school, whether it be public or private; they may also be committed to work-related, civic, social, or self-development schedules that limit attendance at such school functions as parents' nights. A parent who wants to have control over what goes on in the school will have to expend time, energy, and money. As a result, this need and the extent to which the parent can satisfy it will always have to be measured against other competing needs.

Are there any signals, then, to warn a parent that the school as a source of information may be detrimental and that intervention is necessary? The following can serve as a good checklist:

_____1. Is my child finding excuses not to go to school (feigning illness, intentionally bringing on minor accidents, etc.)?

_____2. Does my child cry or appear frightened when going off to school?

_____3. Does my child refrain from talking about or answering questions relating to school?

_____4. Does my child tell everybody, including strangers, how much he or she dislikes school?

_____5. Have my child's grades slipped drastically?

_____6. Does my child have to be reminded constantly to do his or her homework?

_____7. Does my child express hostility (e.g., throwing school books on the floor, or ripping up returned homework and tests) after returning from school?

_____8. Does my child regularly express fantasies about the day that he or she will no longer have to go to school?

If parents answer "Yes" to any of these questions, they ought to investigate the potential damage by discussing the issue with the child, the teachers, school counselors, and appropriate school officials.

SELECTING FROM AVAILABLE INFORMATION

While monitoring information is necessary for effective parentship, it is not sufficient by any means. While it is obviously impossible and undesirable for parents to control completely the information flow to their children, they *can* take steps to improve its quality. Rather than only attempting to block out low-quality information—a defensive strategy—parents must take the initiative to fill the limited time with quality information. This is a much higher obligation than simply filtering out detrimental information. If done well, it will preclude much of the need to monitor discussed earlier. To the parent who complains, "I don't know what I am going to do. My son is hooked into his radio earphones incessantly. I literally can't get through to him," we respond: "What have you done to provide an alternative? What *specific* initiative have you taken to provide your son with more valuable information?" There are several things that parents *can* do.

The whole family can sit down together on a Sunday night and the parents can put stars or check marks in the weekly TV guide to indicate what can be watched during the whole week. This is a more sensible and planned approach than having the children frantically switching stations to search for programs any time they want or need to have a visual tranquilizer. Guided choice is the alternative. With the advent and ascendancy of cable television in many geographical areas, this is even more important because of the enormous choice of offerings. The exercise of predetermining programs for the week can serve as an effective forum for family discussions on such issues as values, interests, morality, or violence. Healthy discussions, especially when there are disagreements over what should be allowed, can preempt emotional conflicts later in the week, at the actual time of the debated program, and reduce long-lasting hostility. After a while, children get to know where their parents stand on certain issues and why they do.

Likewise, parents can *help* children select the magazines, books, newspapers, records, etc., that are appropriate and beneficial for them. They can take the initiative and be providers of quality resources. Of course, it is important that the interests and readiness of the *child,* not the parent, be a major consideration. The following is an example of a resource discovery and planning program for use by parents.

Resources for: _____   Week: _____
           (child's name)   (date)

Interests	Books	Magazines	Radio/TV	Records/Tapes
e.g., base-ball	*The Lou Gehrig Story*	*Sports Illus-trated*	N.Y. Mets games	"Greatest Plays in Baseball" videotape
(etc.)				

This approach uses a *system* for a process that is most likely to be random and haphazard, thereby increasing the probability of exposing one's children to material that will be beneficial to them.

CURRICULUM FOR THE HOME

Information that is transmitted within the home environment has a major impact on the development of children. Experts in the social and behavioral sciences and professional educators recognize more and more the importance of the home in the shaping of children's attitudes, values, behaviors, and dispositions. Furthermore, the effects can be virtually irreversible. Therefore, what information the children breathe in at home is too important to be left to chance, especially when the window of opportunity for parental influence is open for truly a short period. Before parents know it, time goes by and whether they like it or not, their children have acquired a set of beliefs, values, and attitudes. In schools the curriculum exists only because there is limited time. The curriculum is to time what the budget is to money: both are statements of value for the use of limited resources; they only make sense because there isn't an infinite supply of time or money.

Curriculum planners in the schools must ask this basic question: of all the possible things that children could learn in the limited time of approximately 180 school days each year for 12 years, what should they learn? The answer will always involve choice among options, value judgments. But judgment, in the form of systematic planning and decision making, is necessary if the curriculum is to serve the children well. To leave what the children learn to chance would be irresponsible and harmful. However, parents often do precisely that as they fail to establish a planned "course of learning" for their children, a curriculum for the home. Parents must ask a question similar to the one that the school curriculum developers ask: "*What* do I want my child to learn, *when*, and *how?*" As the partner with the school, and with other agencies in the development of the whole child, the home must take seriously its essential role in this area, not just in word, but in action. Where does a parent begin in the development of the home curriculum? A series of steps should be followed:

Step 1: Develop a Definition of the End Result

Parents should define just what it is they would like their children to learn that they feel they are not learning elsewhere (school, church, sports organizations, etc.). In other words, how can the home complement what is already being learned? What are these other sources of learning leaving out? This could include cognitive areas, such as a subject not offered by the school (e.g., a foreign language, or astronomy, or some aspect of science, literature, or drama). It could also include skills: driving a tractor; woodworking; money management; household or auto maintenance; or certain sports that are not offered at school or through recreation centers (e.g., squash).

Furthermore, a solid home curriculum must include the affective dimensions of child development. It is here that the curriculum of the home should truly define childhood as an apprenticeship for adulthood: parents should work out a systematic plan to develop strong emotional systems in children so that they will be able to function and cope effectively in the even more complex and challenging world in which they will emerge as adults. For example, the information base in the United States is increasing at a rapid pace, a true knowledge explosion, doubling every five years and increasing exponentially. With increased knowledge comes change, often sending shock waves through individuals, families, once stable institutions, even the culture itself. Any adult who has difficulty dealing with change is sure to be emotionally handicapped in the years immediately ahead. The best time to develop an emotional tolerance for rapid change is when one is young. Part of the home curriculum, then, could be exposure to change (even if it is contrived on the part of the parent) and discussion with the children about the feelings that such changes arouse—for example, disappointment, concern, or anxiety. For instance, as a learning experience, a parent might deliberately change the family's plans to go to a baseball game. How do children react? How do they feel? How do they cope with disappointment? What do they do during the time that they would have been at the game? Can they learn to be productive in spite of adversity? Can they be taught to look for the potential opportunities in this apparent letdown?

Often a good starting point for parents to use in determining what they would like to include in their home curriculum is to think about what they wish they had learned as children: "If I'd learned then what I know now." Often adults have a good grasp of what they learned the "hard way" or "through the school of hard knocks." Examples of deficiencies which left them ill-prepared for adulthood usually center on issues relating to their own emotionality or interpersonal relations: assertiveness, anxiety, anger and frustration, guilt, dealing with difficult people, etc. They must be able to distinguish between the skills that, while useful in their lives, are no longer critical for their children and those that will be perpetually beneficial. Other good sources of information for the formulation of home curriculum objectives include discussions with older parents who have already raised their children as well as contemporary peer parents. We highly encourage schools, churches, and other such organizations to take the initiative to sponsor forums where parents can exchange home curriculum ideas and cooperate with each other in the development of learning experiences for their children.

Another source for home curriculum suggestions are young adults who are just leaving their teenage years. They might be asked: "As you leave childhood and approach adulthood, is there anything that you wish you had learned?" This information could be very useful for the parents of children who are just about to enter adolescence. One high school that we know of asks members of its graduating class this question each year. The students respond anonymously in writing and the principal reads sample selections to the parents who gather for an assembly just before graduation day. Most parents find this is an eye-opening experience. We highly recommended that parents of the middle school students in that school system be given an opportunity to hear or read the contents of those letters as well. There will be some very useful information for them as they prepare the home curriculum for their own pre-high school children.

This multisource approach to the definition of home curriculum goals will lead to a more realistic set of learning experiences for the children.

STEP 2: DESIGN A LEARNING PROGRAM FOR THE CHILDREN

At this point, parents must ask how the children will learn. What are the means of delivery? Several important factors will go into the design: (a) *Timing: when* will children learn in terms of their readiness and in terms of parents' schedules? When the parent is ready to teach, the child may not be ready to learn and vice versa. As much synchronization as possible is necessary here. (b) *Delivery methods: how* will the children learn? There are several possibilities: explication and exhortation by parents; parental example; discussion; reading materials; films; videotapes; exposure to other adults or children who can teach them; contrived or simulated experiences, including role-playing exercises ("Billy, what would you do if you were in the shoes of the surgeon who had to decide between the two patients . . . ?"), and games. A management matrix connecting home curriculum objectives and methods of delivery (books, parental explanation, etc.) can be helpful:

Methods of Delivery

		1	2	3	4	5	6
	A		X		X		
	B						
Home Curriculum Objectives	C						
	D						
	E						
	F						

This is a sample use of the matrix:

Objective A = developing courage in children to persevere in the face of difficulty

Method of Delivery 2 = a book describing the plight of the frontier settlers

Method of Delivery 4 = a discussion with a neighbor who overcame a physical handicap and started a successful business

If the children's learning experiences occur through Methods of Delivery 2 and 4, then Objective A is likely to be achieved. The parent's role is to design the relationship between objectives and delivery methods. The time invested in developing such a matrix will yield high dividends in terms of successful learning experiences for the children. (c) *Indicators of success:* the home curriculum must include preestablished indicators of success all the way along the learning path: How will I know that my children are developing as planned and are heading for the goals that have been set? Establishing signposts for the cognitive and skills areas may not be too difficult: the child can express his knowledge of Spanish or astronomy by words or in writing; the teenager can repair the broken tool; the young daughter is able to sew the buttons on the blouse; etc. Establishing indicators in the affective areas may be more difficult, but it can be done. For example, the road to the objective "to have my children appreciate classical music" may be monitored by observing how often children listen to such music on the radio and the stereo system; how often they take out library books on the subject; and whether or not they initiate discussions on the topic with family members, relatives, or friends. Progress toward the attainment of the home curriculum objective "to have my children develop good eating habits" might be reflected by the children's choice of desserts when given an option: Will it be candy or a piece of fruit? For breakfast, will it be toast and juice or a piece of cake?

Indicators of success are important because they will let parents know that their children are on or off course. If there is a problem, the sooner they know it the higher the degree of probability for correction.

Step 3: Implement the Program

Once the curriculum is planned and designed, parents will be able to put it into operation. This is best accomplished in phases: implement, observe, iron out wrinkles, correct, reimplement. If there is no home curriculum already in place, the initial implementation may be more difficult, but eventually parents and children alike will grow accustomed to it and perfect it as well. During the implementation, as in the planning and design stages, the focus should be on the children and their behavior—the home curriculum is only a tool to help the parents complement their children's education; it is not an end in itself, nor is it to be enforced rigidly if it obviously conflicts with what is ultimately good for the children. The curriculum should be a living document, not so firm that it cannot be modified if the need arises and not so pliant that it cannot withstand the environmental pressure to collapse. Like a skyscraper, the home curriculum should have a deep foundation and a strong infrastructure, but be pliable enough to sway safely with the wind currents which change in force and direction.

STEP 4: EVALUATE REGULARLY

Assessment of the ongoing home curriculum is important for two reasons: modify weaknesses and/or maintain strengths. Parents need to know what is working and what is not. The indicators of success that were established in Step 2 should be used as the focal point of the evaluation by parents. The primary skill here will be observation: Have the pursued goals been achieved by the children? Several answers are possible and the nature of the response will dictate the next step. If the answer is affirmative, the mission has been accomplished. If the response is "Absolutely not," which is highly unlikely if the indicators of success were achieved all along the way, then a review of the whole home curriculum-building process may have to be done: Were the goals realistic? Was the method used to teach the children appropriate and effective? Was the timing right?

If the response is a qualified "Yes," then whatever has to be done to correct the deficiencies in the curriculum will have to be done: it could be fine-tuning or something more serious. The sooner parents correct it, the better for everybody.

HOME CURRICULUM CONTENT

While the curriculum for each family will, no doubt, be unique, there are certain subjects that emerge as priorities for many families. Parents whom we have counseled and trained in workshops have indicated key areas for their own home curriculums:

1. *First aid.* Children should learn at least the basics: how to treat cuts, burns, bruises, etc. Learning how to administer the Heimlich maneuver for choking victims and CPR (cardiopulmonary resuscitation) for heart attacks is also considered important by some parents. Most bookstores and public libraries carry first-aid manuals. First-aid and CPR training is offered periodically by organizations such as the Red Cross and YMCA. Some parents elect to develop

their own learning materials in this area and use posters and other similar devices to teach children skills.

2. *Health care.* Children must learn the fundamental principles of sound personal health care, such as importance of diet, exercise, and rest. Some parents feel that more effort should be put into teaching children preventive techniques and "wellness" principles and practices. Methods and materials include published booklets, pictures, records, etc.

3. *Self-care.* Children should learn how to take care of themselves: cooking, cleaning, ironing, etc. As they prepare for a world where sex roles have become less rigid and where more and more individuals will live alone for at least a part of their adult life, learning self-maintenance is becoming a higher priority for both boys and girls. The major method of instruction is parental demonstration, illustration, and example.

4. *Self-defense.* As children become less reliant on other people and institutions to protect them, the need for self-defense increases. The ability to ward off attack or aggressive behavior by others is gaining in popularity. This includes the desire to protect oneself both verbally and physically. Children across the country are enrolled in martial arts programs and practice their skills under the watchful eye of their parents. Assertiveness training programs as well as karate, judo, and similar programs for children are offered in many communities.

5. *How to study.* Learning how to study can be the development of a skill with lifelong benefits. Schools do not teach children *how* to study. Teaching the techniques of this critical task is often a function of the home. Parents who have the necessary understanding and patience can be the best resource for success in this area. The next best are programs offered in local agencies or in self-help booklets.

6. *Creativity.* Ironically, the first day of formal education often spells the beginning of the killing of creativity; schools have a tendency to stifle imagination and encourage conformity. Creativity, the willingness and ability to rearrange the world around us into something more valuable, can be encouraged in the home more than any other place. Creativity is a spirit and outlook, a state of mind, not a skill. It is a learned attitude and can be developed and encouraged by the milieu more than by anything else.

7. *Stress management.* Children can be taught the nature, causes, and symptoms of stress and how to control it. Parental example, cou-

pled with explanation and discussion of the stress response, can be very beneficial for children as they experience it in the teen years and in adulthood. Periodic discussions on the topic among family members can be a useful means of reducing and preventing distress.

8. *Time management.* One of the most beneficial skills that children can develop is the ability to manage their own time effectively, to invest it where it will have the greatest return. The earlier this competence is developed, the better. It will have long-lasting results for the children involved. Children should be encouraged to develop their own written time management plan under the guidance of parents and on a regular basis.

9. *Money management.* Children should learn how to manage money as early as possible. They should be sensitized to the limited nature of total family revenues as well as basic principles of budgeting. As soon as they are old enough, children ought to be taught about investing, banking, and money management. The most effective method for such instruction is the issuance of a fixed allowance that will cause children to make financial choices.

10. *Developing self-confidence.* Children should begin as early as possible to develop a sense of self-worth and confidence in themselves and their own capability. Parents need to find areas of strength in the children and nurture their growth rather than focus on shortcomings or weaknesses. Success will breed success, as self-confident children generally become productive and happy adults. Finding the correct level of achievement for each child is a key factor in this learning experience.

11. *Problem solving.* Knowing how to solve problems is an essential part of a high-quality adult life. The earlier individuals learn problem-solving skills, the better for them. Parents who expose their children to this area of competence, either by having them observe their own problem-solving strategies or by explaining the process, bestow on them a rich gift. Simulated problem-solving activities in which children's analytical approaches and emotional states can be developed and observed are the most effective learning techniques.

12. *Strategic thinking.* Children should be given the opportunity to develop strategic thinking capabilities. Planning and analytical abilities are a necessary part of a successful adult life, both in the workplace and in personal affairs. If this outlook is ingrained early and practiced regularly through adolescence and the teenage

years, it will reach refinement in adulthood. Appropriate case study situations, designed for the age of the child, are effective learning tools in this area.

13. *Sociopolitical savvy.* Children must be given the opportunity to develop a "street wisdom" that will help them survive and flourish within complex organization and a dynamic society. Being able to "learn the ropes," the informal aspect of life, is an important part of growing up. There is no better place to learn this important skill than in the home under the tutelage of an insightful, trustworthy, and caring parent. Adults who do well in this area often credit their fathers or mothers for the inculcation of these skills. Parents who discuss or share their own experiences with their children in a way that is appropriate for their level of sophistication are often successful in this area of the curriculum.

14. *How to be self-reliant.* Children should be taught to be independent of other individuals or outside organizations and agencies. They must learn that if good things are going to happen to them, then they themselves must make them happen. If they truly need help, they should certainly seek it. But dependency on others, a form of parasitism, should be avoided at all costs.

15. *How to take and handle risks.* Children should develop the emotional courage to be able to take risks as well as the mental acumen to determine what the risk probabilities are. Fears of failure, inadequacy, rejection, etc., should be prevented from developing or controlled as early as possible.

16. *How to handle the full range of emotions.* Children ought to be given the opportunity to learn about, experience, and discuss a wide range of emotions—from love and joy to anger and mourning. The sooner the benefits and difficulties associated with these feelings are explored, the better. The legitimacy of expressing emotions must be learned as well. Regular family discussions on this issue should take place.

17. *The meaning of friendship.* Children ought to develop a reasonable set of expectations relating to friendship: What is it? What is a good friend? What are the difficulties associated with friendship? When is it detrimental? When should we break off a friendship? Parent-initiated discussions can prove a useful tool. However, timing and the child's readiness to discuss such issues are critical.

18. *Male-female relations.* Children ought to get to understand the dynamics of relationships with the opposite sex early. Sex-role stereotyping; emotional and cognitive similarities and differences

between boys and girls; the role of sexual attraction; awkward situations—all these subjects should be discussed in accordance with the child's level of maturity. One effective method for reducing this kind of stereotyping is involvement of children in co-ed athletic teams, where boys and girls can view each other performing in addition to developing camaraderie. Likewise, written material (often fiction) which explicitly or implicitly breaks down such stereotypes can be useful.

19. *Life isn't always fair.* Children sometimes develop a fantasized and mythological image of what life *should* be like. They are often emotionally wounded when they discover that this image does not always hold. A more beneficial approach would be to have them develop a sensitivity to the imperfect nature of relationships, policies, and practices. Reading fiction, accompanied by family discussions on the characters, theme, etc., is an effective learning tool.

20. *How to be a parent.* Childhood, and especially the adolescent and teenage years, can be an apprenticeship for motherhood and fatherhood. Parents will do their children a great service if they keep this in mind and share appropriate experiences and insights with them. Of course, they will teach best through their own example. As children enter adolescence and the teenage years, they can also participate in the actual rearing of younger siblings.

The potential amount of information which would influence the family and its members, then, borders on the infinite. However, the time the family has to take in information is infinitely small in comparison. If left to chance, the probability of taking in the best information is very low. Management of the information flow, therefore, is critical and is an essential parentship task.

13

Are We Getting There? Evaluation in the Family

"Sometimes I feel like I'm on a treadmill. Working harder and harder. Doing more and more. I wonder where it's really getting me. What's it all leading to?" These words, spoken by a Cincinnati father recently, are shared by many other parents. Often they have no system or clear signals to let them know whether they are really succeeding in leading their families. Parents, like all other leaders, must establish a system for assessing and evaluating family activities. The more comprehensive the system, the better. Without evaluation machinery, organizations founder, are unlikely to reach goals fully, and sometimes engender a spirit of futility.

Likewise, individual family members, both parents and children, need to know their successes and shortcomings on a regular basis. This feedback is critical if effective behavior is going to be reinforced and errors are going to be corrected. Feedback, especially positive information, also serves as a motivator for further achievement. If parents perceive that all their hard work and sacrifices pay off, they will want to continue on the same path. If they feel that they may be wasting their time, then they will be less likely to want to contribute action. Therefore, an important part of parentship is the establishment of family evaluation methods. This is not to imply that there should be a rigid and formal evaluation as might be found in a corporation. However, some predetermined set of observable outcomes for both the family unit as a whole and the individual family members will prove useful, serving as concrete indicators or cues of success.

To be of the greatest value, a family evaluation system should be thorough, comprehensive, and ongoing. Contrary to conventional wisdom, effective family evaluation does not come after an event or an activity, but actually begins before any action occurs. Its purpose is not solely to determine whether or not outcomes were achieved, but also to help shape those objectives. Useful family evaluation involves four phases: (a) situational analysis, (b) resource assessment, (c) operation monitoring, and (d) completion. Each of these evaluation phases provides significant information for parental decision making: situational analysis results are used in the establishment of family goals and objectives; resource assessment helps parents decide whether or not they have the sufficient means to reach those objectives; operation monitoring allows parents to regularly observe family or individual activities on the course toward the achievement of family goals; and completion encourages parents to decide whether or not the goals have been achieved. Evaluation in the family is not done for its own sake, but to service the process of parentship. The major purpose of evaluation is to provide *useful* and *timely* information to the parent as decision maker. Every phase is necessary, if evaluation is to be beneficial.

SITUATIONAL ANALYSIS

This is the first step in the family management process, and it is necessary if effective parental planning is to occur. Before they can even begin to think about family or individual goals or objectives, parents must know as much as they can about the environment (both on the global and on the local level) within which the family will function when the objectives are to be achieved. Economic, ideological, social, political, and cultural factors could have an important bearing on the appropriateness and/or probability of attainment of those goals. Projected employment opportunities in certain fields could be an important consideration in helping to shape educational goals for children: if there is a projected glut of dentists or engineers or teachers, this information could prove useful. Parents' financial decisons (investments, priorities, etc.) could likewise be greatly assisted by an understanding of the context within which the family will function in the years ahead. These are examples of the larger environment, but the more immediate situation can have an influence on parental decision making as well: "Is neighborhood X the place to raise my children in light of the long history of drug abuse there?" "Are my family goals, policies, and practices going against the grain of this materialistic community which is very much "thing-oriented?" "How long can we hold on against the pressure to conform?"

Dan, an Omaha accountant who recently accepted a higher position in St. Louis, spent as much time talking with residents of neighborhoods which he and his family might move into as he did meeting with people in his new workplace. He was very explicit about his reason for doing so: "My wife and I place a very high premium on education. We have always tried to instill strong study habits in our three young children. We know that while parents have a lot of influence on children, neighbors do too. If most of the children in a community value studying, then it is most likely going to rub off on my children. Of course, the opposite is also true." Dan, like many other parents, recognizes the importance of evaluating the context of his family situation. No matter how noble, worthwhile, or well-meaning the family goals are, if the context is not supportive they are unlikely to be achieved fully. On the other hand, if the situation is conducive to the attainment of the goals, much of the work is already done. To plan family objectives without evaluating the specific situation could be an exercise in futility.

The situational analysis offers two possible services: (1) it helps parents develop goals that are congruent with the broad and immediate contexts of the family; and (2) it forces a careful scrutiny of both the context of the family itself and the appropriateness of the family objectives and practices. As a result, it may trigger a change in situation (the family may decide to move away or to a new, more supportive context) or it may realign its objectives so that they are more compatible with the environment. Without the information gleaned from this situational analysis, parents may unknowingly be allowing the tail to wag the dog (i.e., the situation dictating family goals and practices) or putting their families between a rock and a hard place: if they do not adjust to the environment, they become social outcasts; if they conform, they develop values and pursue a course of behavior that is not in their best interests.

This first step, then, is a critical part of the continual process of evaluation in the family. Through it parents are able to crystallize collective and individual goals, recognize supports and blockers in the greater and immediate environments, and make beneficial adjustments.

RESOURCE ASSESSMENT

Once the situation surrounding the family has been evaluated and appropriate goals and operating principles reflecting this information have been established, parents must turn their attention toward the inside of the family and critically assess whether or not they have the resources to reach those goals, such as money, time, space, energy, interest, knowledge, social/political contacts, self-discipline, mutual support, or creativity. Realism and objectivity are important here. If there is a projected need for accountants, but a high school son or daughter has a very low aptitude in mathematics, then it must be recognized that while the goal of becoming an accountant may be fine in itself, it is not appropriate for this particular child. For this evaluation phase to be successful it is important that parents understand just what it takes to reach the goals established as the result of the situational analysis. To wish for an immediate infusion of self-discipline when a family has had a ten-year track record of abandoning projects soon after they begin them is foolhardy. Parents may hope to change old habits, but they must expect improvement to be gradual and be pleased with small gains at first.

Gene, a middle-aged father, pointed out the importance of this type of evaluation at a recent workshop: "Ellen [his wife] and I used to always have these grandiose plans for our kids and ourselves. This was going to happen, that was going to happen, on and on. Rarely did any of it happen, that is, at the level that we intended. Often our goals were just too high, too unrealistic. We meant well and certainly didn't mean any harm, although, looking back now, I think that our kids were probably often frustrated and felt a strong sense of failure. If we had only realistically examined our resources honestly and stopped trying to kid ourselves, our family would have been much more successful and we certainly would have felt a lot happier."

The ultimate question, then, in resource assessment is this: do we as a family have the means to accomplish our stated goals? If the answer is affirmative, the family should move ahead with implementation of the means to accomplish the objectives. If the response is negative, parents must secure (more money, time, space, etc.) and/or develop the resources (better attitudes; more structure; higher degree of interest); modify the goals by delaying them ("We will buy the summer cottage in 1988, not 1986"); redefine them to a more moderate level of attainment ("We will have a two-bedroom cottage, not a four-bedroom"); or abandon the goals altogether ("There is no way that we can afford a summer cottage in the foreseeable future").

Again, this evaluation phase serves two purposes for the parent-leader: (1) it provides a framework for aligning stated goals with resources available; and (2) it calls for a critical look at family resources. As a result of the evaluation, parents may conclude that their goals are too ambitious for their resources or are even too modest, that they could in fact grow to a higher degree and accomplish much more. They may also become vividly aware of the fact that their resources are just not enough, that they need to increase them if they ever want to improve their current state. This may lead the parents to a search for new jobs that pay more, a new disciplining procedure that will improve study habits of children so that they will become more knowledgeable, or a revised reward and punishment approach to increase motivation in the child. When parents realize specifically why they cannot reach the goals that they would like to, they then have a more clear-cut path for improvement: they know what they have to do to make it happen! If they perform this kind of assessment regularly, the quality of family life will no doubt improve.

OPERATION MONITORING

This phase of the family evaluation process involves observing what is going on and judging whether or not what was planned and intended is actually happening. There should be few surprises if the objectives were carefully designed (situation analysis) and the resources assessed accurately. Sometimes, however, despite good intentions, something gets lost in the transition from what is intended and what is performed. Children may mean well—they may desire to study and have the wherewithal to do well in school—but not be able to translate the good intentions into a daily schedule, or have a tendency to get distracted by television, or now be friendly with teenagers who were not in the picture during the first two evaluation phases. New situational factors can arise (the emergence of a boyfriend or girlfriend; a traumatic event in the community; even a drastic change in the weather—Indian summer—or an outbreak of the flu) that seriously affect the planned course of events. Likewise, unexpected uses of family resources might be given a higher priority than the intended use—for example, because of emergencies (illness or accident), necessities (new automobile), job responsibilities (new schedule or geographical location), or newly developed interests (children are now into skiing, a consumption of money and time).

The purpose of the operation monitoring, then, is twofold: in addition to assessing whether or not intended behaviors are on course, parents can reevaluate whether or not the original objectives and allocation of resources are appropriate or need updating. This phase closes any possible information gaps between statement of objectives, assessment of resources, and implementation. A key factor that requires caution here is the tendency to overlook or minimize facts indicating that the plan is off course or that things are not going quite as expected. Frieda fell victim to this temptation when her thirteen-year-old daughter was "obviously miserable" at the prep school that she was attending. As a single parent who was getting very little financial support from her ex-husband, she was struggling to make ends meet and pay the expensive tuition bills for her daughter. Her nurse's salary never seemed to provide enough money. She explained her difficulty in evaluating the reality of her family situation: "I just could not believe that my daughter was not happy at the school that many kids would just beg to attend, especially after all the sacrifices I was making to send her there. I simply blocked out all the facts supporting my daughter's claims of unhappiness and kept magnifying all the reasons why she should like the place, how it was good for her to be at that school. I would not accept anything but that conclusion. The only way that I could justify the struggle to come up with tuition each semester was to believe that what I was doing was the supreme sacrifice that was good for my daughter and for which she should be eternally grateful. I pushed and pushed my little girl to like that school to the point where she began to experience severe headaches, vomiting in the morning before school, and eventually at least one or two absences from school per week due to 'illness.' My family physician, who has known my daughter Kim since birth, was quick to detect that emotional factors were involved. After following his recommendation that my daughter and I discuss this situation with the school counselor as well as a private psychologist, we reached the decision that, at least for the time being, Kim and that prep school were not the best possible match. A more academically relaxed and less demanding environment would, no doubt, be more appropriate." Frieda fortunately was assisted in recognizing and assessing the invalidity of her plan to reach her objective—namely, the best possible education for her child. While the goal was certainly wonderful, the means of getting there was counterproductive. If she had continued on, unaware of or not accepting the problems her daughter was having, chances were high that the goal would not have been reached and that some form of emotional difficulty would have befallen her daughter.

COMPLETION

The last phase of the family evaluation process involves deciding whether or not the intended goals have been achieved as planned. Again, there should not be major surprises here. If the evaluation process has been carefully implemented all the way through, the end result should be as intended. However, because families are dynamic and because the task of leading a family is by no means an exact science, the possibility of error is always present. Things can, and often do, go wrong. The purpose of evaluation in the family is to decrease the chance of error; it cannot be eliminated entirely. This phase of the evaluation could have one of several possible results: total success and completion (son John graduates from high school in the college preparatory program); or partial completion (son John graduates from high school, but changes to general education program); or total failure (son John drops out of high school in senior year). The result of evaluation in another family situation might be: total completion (the family has been able to save twelve thousand dollars in a three-year period); partial completion (the family has been able to save eight thousand dollars in the three-year period); or total failure (the family was unable to save anything in that period). Thus completion evaluation can be directed toward one individual family member or the whole family itself.

Whenever the results of this evaluation phase demonstrate complete success for the one-time objectives, parents can then declare that an accomplished fact and go on to other concerns. If there is partial completion, then the task is to determine the cause of the discrepancy between intended objectives and results and make the appropriate corrections: modify objectives, resource use, family operations, or all three. In the case of total failure, a serious analysis of what went wrong must be made, as well as a critical review of how the family evaluates itself: Are parents missing vital information? Is the information that they receive untimely—too early, too late? Are parents insensitive to the subtle cues that children may be transmitting concerning academic, social, or emotional difficulties? In the case of ongoing family activities (e.g., saving money), parents have several options based on the results of the evaluation: if the savings plan was successfully implemented, then it can be "institutionalized" and replicated over and over again; if it was partially successful, the appropriate modifications must be made; if it did not work out, major surgery in family operations may be necessary. The completion phase of the evaluation, then, allows parents to either validate the success of some family activities and incorporate them permanently or decide to modify or even abandon others because they may not be attainable.

This four-phase process of evaluation in the family can be most beneficial for effective parentship. If implemented on a regular basis, and not just at a point of family crisis, family goals and operations will be refined and the success rate of the individual family members as well as the family as a whole will be enhanced significantly. However, effective evaluation by parents is not easy: several critical barriers must be overcome.

BARRIERS TO EVALUATION IN THE FAMILY

In our experience of training and counseling mothers and fathers in the evaluation process, several key roadblocks to parental effectiveness in the performance of this function have emerged: problem denial; avoidance; inability to extract the critical data from the plethora of information; "family think"; and selective perception.

Problem Denial

Often during the process of evaluation parents become aware of facts which can be threatening to them, their children, family values, customs, habits, and practices. Some of the facts may be mildly disturbing; others may send shock waves through the spirit. For example, to reduce anxiety in the home the parent may have to modify career or financial ambitions. Denying the ill effects of a change in lifestyle on the children's behavior allows the parent to continue on in the same pattern.

A West Palm Beach mother who was also a real estate agent described how she as a parent was able to deny potential family difficulties by diminishing the negative impact of her job: "Down deep I probably knew why there was so much loneliness and disappointment in my household . . . I wasn't there as much as my husband, and the kids wanted me there. But I was doing so well in my work that I just couldn't give it up or cut back even. I was making good money, meeting nice people, and besides, for the first time in a long time, I felt a sense of accomplishment. I certainly loved my children and my husband, but I just couldn't adjust my work schedule and goals to meet their needs. So I concentrated on my good feelings and all that I was able to buy for my family with the money I was making doing my real estate thing. I simply blocked out or discounted the potential damage of the tensions in our family which were obvious to everyone but me. I did this until it was almost too late."

Denial, then, is a defense mechanism which many parents may use for their own psychological well-being but by so doing may weaken the evaluation process because they are unable to objectively weigh the data. Suppose this Florida mother's lifestyle eventually led to a separation from her husband or to her children's turning to alcohol or drug abuse while unsupervised or as an alternative to the missing time and affection that they were not getting from their mother. Would her career still be worth the return that it was providing? The point is that she doesn't know and would most likely find herself in a crisis situation if any of these possibilities were to be realized. By denying the potential difficulties and concentrating solely on the benefits of her work, she is doing herself and her family a disservice. Wise parents look at *all* the potential consequences of their decisions and then make informed choices.

Avoidance

Some parents avoid the sources that are likely to provide discomforting or challenging information. By denying themselves access to these people, places, or things, they do not have to cope with the conflict between what *is* and any possible state of improvement. Some parents physically remove themselves from the source of information or remove the source from themselves: out of sight, out of mind. The parents who send their twelve-year-old son off to camp for the entire summer *may* be avoiding the difficulties of interacting with an adolescent. The father who gets overinvolved in work or community projects and is out four nights a week and three quarters of every weekend may be avoiding what he considers the "emotional drain" of dealing with preschoolers or teenagers. The mother who encourages her daughter to go off to college in another state may be avoiding her perceived inability to guide a young woman emotionally, morally, or socially: "What I don't know won't hurt me!"

Often parents avoid taking the initiative to seek information for fear of what they may discover. When suspecting health difficulties in their children, they may delay medical, dental, or psychological testing hoping the problem will simply go away. They may refrain from taking the initiative to visit their children's school and meet with the teachers for fear of learning something negative about their children's aptitude, attitude, or disposition. The possible pain of hearing that their children may be having difficulties immobilizes them. We have met many otherwise confident, self-assured, and intelligent parents who approach their children's physicians, teachers, and coaches with trepidation. Are they fearful of the people themselves? Usually not. What they fear is the information power held by them. These people know something that could make a difference in their lives: "What will I learn and what will that mean for my ego, my lifestyle, my past performance, and what I have to do in the future, not to mention what this means for my child, his emotions, his future, and his feelings toward me? I may learn that my son has a genetic health problem (such as high blood pressure or a proclivity for obesity), or that he is not at all adept in mathematics (my dream that he go to MIT is out now), or that he has difficulty fielding a baseball (perhaps I should spend more time teaching him how)." The avoidance that parents practice is no different psychologically than that used by patients relating to physicians or auto owners dealing with repair men: the information these people convey could have serious impact on physical, emotional, financial lives . . . it could affect longevity, mobility, and ultimately happiness.

Of course, as with personal health care and auto maintenance, problems that are not recognized early fester, become chronic, and are costly to solve, if they can be treated at all. Parents have the choice of viewing the initial pain as an enemy or an ally. If they choose to see it as an enemy, they will tend to deny their pain or attempt to squelch it in some way. If they accept it as an ally, then they will recognize it as a warning signal that something is wrong in the life of their family and correction is in order. Parents must remember that avoidance never resolves a genuine difficulty. An experienced elementary teacher in the Baltimore public schools had some advice for parents at a recent workshop: "If parents would only take the initiative to come in to see their children's teachers as soon as they suspect or recognize a problem, 50 percent of children's school difficulties could be drastically reduced. Denying that the problem exists or hoping that it will just go away will not work. I've seen too many mothers and fathers wake up when it was too late. Too much damage had already been done!"

Inability to Extract Critical Data

Sometimes parents are overwhelmed with information. Determining which data is important may be difficult. Unless a discriminating eye for what is important is developed, parents can waste their time collecting irrelevant information while missing the more meaningful. An essential part of all four phases of the evaluation process, but especially of the monitoring and completion operations, is the previous identification of just what it is that should happen to allow parents to determine whether or not the objectives have been achieved. This will make it possible to wade through the morass of information in any given household.

Many parents get lost in the mire of information or draw erroneous inferences from what they observe. They spend so much time sorting through nonessential information that they have little time left to analyze critically that which is important. For example, they may overhear a fourteen-year-old talking with friends and because of the slightly foul language overheard they may conclude that their son's behavior, when not in their presence, is just as foul. What they might not realize is that the language used may in no way be correlated with the boy's behavior: children often say things that they do not really understand, especially in the presence of peers. For a parent to assume in accusatory fashion behaviors or values or attitudes that are not present could lead to a breakdown in trust levels and sound relationships. It is important, then, for parents to be sure that their assumptions are well founded and that the observed behaviors are reflective of the presence or absence of the goals they have established for their families. Often children have school or health difficulties because of parents' marriage problems; mothers and fathers will look at every possible cause for this difficulty except their own relationship difficulties: they will blame teachers, textbooks, classmates, television . . . everyone but themselves.

At our workshops we often encounter fathers and mothers who have just experienced or are in the middle of nasty divorces and whose children are experiencing high incidences of social withdrawal as well as academic difficulties at school. To our amazement, rarely do parents initially see a causal connection between the two occurrences. A typical question by a parent might be: "My ten-year-old son has lost complete interest in school . . . he doesn't study and doesn't care about grades anymore. He also doesn't behave politely and is quickly becoming a discipline problem. What do you suppose could be wrong?" In the ensuing discussion we may discover that this mother eight months ago separated from her husband, who is now in court in an adultery trial, and that she is now dating another man who is growing fond of her children also. "Do you think that there is any connection between what is going on in your life and your son's poor school performance?" we might ask. The answer most often is: "Gee, I never really thought of the two as being related. Hmm, maybe there is."

Likewise, behavioral and sometimes mental health problems of children are causally connected to family policies and practices that may need modification. An ambitious, hard-driving father or mother may be creating a very tense environment by late hours, worrisome demeanor while at home, and encouragement of this competitive style in the children. The parent's need to maintain an emotional state of stability is put at odds with the need to have objective data for sound evaluation. Acquiring certain information may mean that the parent may have to make decisions, effect changes, or reassess opinions concerning the characteristics of sons or daughters or self. In even severe problem contexts like incest, the uninvolved parent (usually the mother and wife) will deny the reality of the situation which she instinctively knows is true . . . often until irreversible harm is done to the child. We have noticed a remarkable level of denial on the part of parents who are having marital problems. Very often they are unwilling to recognize the potential harm that their bickering, arguments, and even infidelity are having on their children.

"Family Think"

Occasionally families suffer from a tendency to foster conformity of thought to the point where family members are reluctant to raise objections to or ask questions about what the family is doing. We call this "family think," the phenomenon of developing one mind for the entire family. It is a plague of the closely knit family, not of a family that is disintegrating. It is the result of "overtogetherness" in thought, values, attitudes. Symptoms include family members' ability to fill in words or even sentences when other family members are pausing or at a loss while speaking. Another symptom is placing verbal and nonverbal pressure on certain family members to go along with the others: perhaps a comment ("We all can't wait to go to the picnic; it should be great! Don't you think so, Timmy?") or maybe a wince or frown or a raised eyebrow when a family member raises an issue that challenges a

particular family practice. Another characteristic of a family suffering
from "family think" is an insular spirit, a disassociation from the outside world accompanied by a tendency to discount external judgment
—a "bunker mentality."

Sara, a twenty-six-year-old nurse in San Francisco, grew up in a
household that practices "family think": "When I was a child and all
through my teens I remember feeling that loyalty to family, even as far
as ideas and opinions, was the most honorable virtue. Family values,
lifestyle, habits were just assumed by all of us to be the best. We were a
happy family, looking back, but we were also quite smug in our righteousness. Because of our internal family connectedness and strength,
we thought that we were invincible, immune from all the problems that
other people were supposedly exposed to. Our parents, who were and
still are wonderful people, led themselves to believe that we could
survive and prosper as a family by simply fostering internal togetherness and psychological, if not physical, isolation from the rest of the
world . . . I married a guy whom I truly found exciting because he
was the first person in years who allowed me to disagree and not feel
guilty. He was eighteen years older than me and the marriage was a
bust . . . lasted only eighteen months. My younger brother found his
freedom of expression through alcohol and pills, unfortunately . . .
Both of these 'failures' have sent shock waves through and splintered
my parents' master plan."

In so building a protective shield, parents guarantee the stability of
their family culture, but also screen out most objective analysis and
evaluation of what is going on in the family. Contrary to the perception
of the home as a safe harbor, it becomes a social and emotional ghetto
for family members, cutting them off from the flow of new life in the
environment and the chance to improve.

Parents who want close, stable families are the prime candidates for
"family think." They must be aware that this phenomenon develops
gradually and feeds on itself, each step of the way making it more and
more difficult for new light to shine in. It is a "fail-safe" system to ward
off incompatible ideas generated from within or from the outside. In so
doing, however, the family closes down the lifeline to the environment
through which it has the potential of getting much new energy.

SELECTIVE PERCEPTION

Having to reevaluate and change one's mind in light of new information can be stressful. Emotional pain often accompanies situations in

which fathers and mothers may have to relinquish some old ideas or review some past judgments; the pain is often obviated by the habit of seeing, hearing, or reading only that which supports the status quo and screening out that which challenges it: parents selectively perceive a reality that is compatible with their needs and desires.

Parents who use selective perception will likewise challenge the source of the information ("Who told you that?"), question credibility ("What do teachers know?"), imply persecution ("They're obviously out to get my son"), assert contradictory evidence ("I can find at least three pediatricians who will disagree!"), or explicitly banish the information from their presence ("Get that letter away from me. I don't even want to see it!"). The following scenario might take place between a father with a closed disbelief system and a good neighbor.

NEIGHBOR: Ted, I don't know how to put this . . . but I think I ought to let you know that I think your son Johnny is running with the wrong crowd of kids . . . and . . .

TED: What? I don't understand . . .

NEIGHBOR: Well . . . I don't want to accuse Johnny of anything, but I feel quite sure that they are involved in smoking marijuana and maybe even selling it.

TED: What are you talking about? Who do you think . . .

NEIGHBOR: Wait, Ted . . . Listen, I see them every Friday and Saturday night near my store . . . They go around the back of the shopping center near that new video parlor. Something's going on there . . . People know about it and I heard that the police are wise to it . . . They're going to clean 'em out soon . . . catch 'em red-handed! I don't want Johnny to ruin his whole life . . . you know, police record and all. He's a good kid! That's why I'm sticking my nose in and telling you . . . I've thought about this hard the past few days and decided I better talk to you.

TED: (while grinding his teeth with apparent anger) Well thanks . . . but I can assure you that Johnny wouldn't do such a thing. Besides, he has been home here for the past several Friday and Saturday evenings. You must have seen somebody who looked like him . . . You know these kids all dress the same. I appreciate your concern, but thought that you would have known better. After all, you know this family and have seen Johnny grow up. Do you think that he would do such a thing?

NEIGHBOR: But, Ted. I'm telling you it was Johnny . . . I know . . .

TED: (patting his neighbor firmly on the shoulder) Look, I have to run off to a meeting downtown tonight . . . I have to get going.

NEIGHBOR: (as he puts his head down and turns to leave) Ted, I hope you don't get the wrong impression . . . I was . . .

TED: Don't worry about it . . . See you around.

In this case Ted cannot bear the thought of what this information, if valid, would mean to the aspect of his belief system that relates to what he thinks of his son ("a marvelous, trustworthy boy with a great future") and what he thinks of himself as a father ("a dedicated, caring, hard-working dad with a close relationship with his children"). He is choosing not to perceive the information that is being presented and will most likely continue on his own course until his son's problem is so severe it cannot be ignored by him or others.

Parents with more open disbelief systems will allow themselves to take in information even if it does pose a threat to their mental and emotional certitude. In varying degrees they are willing to receive data and, if need be, adjust their belief dimension accordingly. Sometimes some fine-tuning is called for ("I guess Tommy doesn't have as much aptitude in science as we thought he had") and sometimes a major modification in the belief dimension is needed ("It is clear that Tommy has no intention of going on to college now or in the near future, even though we have been planning on it and saving for it by sacrificing for years"). The information that challenges parental belief systems can be infused gradually over a period of time ("It is becoming clearer and clearer to us that our son really lacks ambition") or quickly, even traumatically ("We found out today that our sixteen-year-old daughter is pregnant . . . She just walked in the kitchen this morning and told us . . . just like that . . . We're in a state of shock!"). Whatever the severity of the new information or the time duration for the transmission or its method, parents with open disbelief systems do not deny, discount, or immediately challenge the source of the information. They take it in, try to understand its meaning and validate it, and then begin to think about what it means for their own belief system: what changes have to be made, what new attitudes developed, what relationships evaluated, what priorities rearranged, what lifestyles modified.

The parent's belief-disbelief system, then, is a critical aspect of effective family evaluation. If the disbelief dimension is toward the closed end of the continuum, important information that could help the family modify itself and continuously grow will be smothered. Parents who build this type of belief-disbelief system usually surround themselves with a whole web of people, habits, customs, and family policies and practices that protect them from challenging information. Family members do not tell them certain things ("I would never tell my Mom this . . . she couldn't take it"); they themselves refrain from situations that might be sources of challenging news ("I'd just as soon not watch that TV special . . . I'm afraid to hear what it will have to say about teenage alcohol abuse"); and they will block out access to information that might bring about anxiety ("I don't even read the papers anymore . . . all you see is murders, robberies, car accidents . . . and they're all young kids involved. It gets me nervous just reading it").

Parents with open disbelief systems are more able to benefit from the feedback offered by the family's environment: they can often preclude problems or correct potential chronic difficulties by making modifications in a timely fashion. Ted had the choice of either examining the information that his neighbor presented to him or looking the other way. If he chose the former, his chances of intervening successfully would have increased tenfold, even though there would have been some initial emotional anguish. By choosing the latter approach he decided to flirt with disaster for his son as well as the rest of the family. Selective perception often is the tool that allows parents to choose between short-term and long-term pleasure and pain: real family problems do not go away no matter how hard fathers and mothers try not to see, hear, read about, or smell them.

Evaluation in the family can and must take place if progress is to occur and if parents are to receive the managerial and psychological feedback that they need for effective parentship. But evaluation is not something that comes at the end of one's life, or of one's parenting, or of an era or time period. Rather, it is best performed at the beginning, before all other family leadership behavior (situation analysis), during the course of family life (resource assessment), and at the conclusion of a leadership act (completion). It is a rod that runs through the core of parentship functions holding them together and keeping them connected. Traditionally, evaluation has been poorly done in families. Perhaps it is for this reason that the other parentship functions have only been implemented with partial success in the households of many. Evaluation, a term that may seem incongruous with family life, is the most neglected of all the aspects of parentship. For those parents who do it well, however, the returns are incomparable.

A critical aspect of evaluation in the family is the parent's ability to transmit the information garnered in the process to the appropriate family member in a way that is timely, intelligible, and conducive to

growth. Strong guidance attitudes and skills are most beneficial here
and will well service evaluation.

THE PARENT AS COUNSELOR IN THE EVALUATION PROCESS

An essential skill in effective evaluation in the family is the ability to
provide guidance and counseling for family members. This parentship
function is just as difficult as it is important. Very few parents have been
trained to perform the counseling task well. As a result, mothers and
fathers do it awkwardly and feel uncomfortable because they know that
they are not doing a very good job. While most parents counsel children without giving too much thought to the process, certain principles and practices of effective parent counseling will greatly enhance
success in this parentship skill. There are also some barriers that can
really block the success of parental counseling. These suggestions may
improve the performance of mothers and fathers:

1. The counseling setting should be a supportive environment where
    interruptions are minimized, if not eliminated. The child's room
    would be a good place, if privacy is guaranteed. Counseling should
    not be initiated in a "public" place where others are allowed to
    hear what is going on.
2. Assume that the child most likely is looking at the situation quite
    differently; he or she has a unique frame of reference, a personal
    perspective. If parents have empathy, they will be able to get in the
    shoes of the child and attempt to understand his or her point of
    view.
3. A good place to begin the counseling is to find out what the child
    really wants from the situation; what is his or her underlying
    agenda? What is causing the incorrect behavior? Usually it is not
    what initially meets the eye. A teenager may be shoplifting not
    because he wants the stolen items but because he wants to be
    accepted by his peers.
4. Assume that with good, active listening as well as guiding ques-
    tions, children are capable of eventually resolving problems for
    themselves. Externally imposed solutions are always second best.
    Solutions that come from the children themselves are always more
    meaningful and implementable.
5. Restrict value judgments or keep them to yourself. It is important
    that children be allowed to express themselves openly and freely

without risking premature judgment by their parents. This early judgment can be expressed verbally ("You don't really like him, do you?") or nonverbally (by frowns, raised eyebrows, silence, droopy eyes, silly grins, etc.).

6. Be warm, respectful, and supportive during counseling. This can be expressed through words, but more importantly, again, through nonverbal expressions, touching, hugging, etc.

7. Do not be afraid to disclose some things about yourself. Parents detract from their counseling role when they refrain from sharing any present frailties or past difficulties with their children. If children believe that their parents are somehow flawless, they will be reluctant to believe that the parents could truly understand what they are going through. Parents need not overwhelm their children by pointing out all of their shortcomings or by "outdoing" them: "You think that you have problems?" However, the knowledge that one's parents too have experienced some difficulties will be beneficial in cementing the relationship: "My dad must understand what I'm going through."

8. Do not fear confrontation. Parents may reach a point where they have to challenge their children in counseling them. Perhaps children are denying a factual situation or consistently misrepresenting information that they have. Parents may find themselves going around in circles and in need of directly confronting their children to make them face the truth, tell it like it is, or stop making excuses. The fewer the confrontations the better, but they certainly cannot be eliminated completely.

9. Give concrete direction to children. Boys and girls need to be listened to; they need an understanding, empathic parental ear, but they also need authoritative guidance. This is truly the *art* of counseling. Effective parent-counselors are able to accomplish both tasks. It is a delicate balance, but mothers and fathers get better at it with practice.

10. Do not push too hard. Readiness for change on the part of the child is a critical factor. If parents meet with a strong resistance from the children counseled, they ought to reassess their evaluation of where the child is in terms of recognition of the problem and willingness to make improvements. If parents recognize the process of counseling as integral to the evaluation function of

parentship and strive to improve their skills in this area through training, reading, and practice, they will make great strides in remaining connected to their families and thereby increase their capability to provide constructive evaluation.

14

The Stability of the Family: Will it Survive Without Me?

"I don't know what I would do if John were to die . . . I just couldn't go on," a mother recently pointed out at a parents' workshop in Minnesota. "I wouldn't even know where to begin. I know very little about the family's finances, nothing about home repairs, not to mention the difficulty of rearing our two young sons alone," she continued as many other parents shook their heads in sympathetic agreement. These kinds of feelings and comments are symptomatic of weakness in family stability. In short, if any member of the family is truly indispensable, the family as an organization needs strengthening. Indispensability is a sign of vulnerability. As the critical nature of the presence or involvement of any one family member increases, the stability of the family as a whole decreases.

Stable families, like other strong organizations, are not dependent on any one person for their strength, development, or survival. Prudent parent-executives make their families less and less dependent on them so that they can survive, function smoothly, and continue to grow even if they, by accident or choice, should not be around. If a whole family is only one paternal heartbeat away from total collapse, it is indeed too vulnerable. If the total internal operation of the household is a day away from chaos because mother is ill with the flu, again there is structural weakness in the family. If the bulk of the sense of parental lifelong accomplishment rests on young Kevin's becoming a brain surgeon or making the pros in football or any other goal, again the family is vulnerable. If any of these kinds of situations exist, parents need to determine why this is the case and make the necessary changes in attitudes, relationships, and family structures to strengthen the family as an organization. To do nothing is the greatest disservice parents could bestow on their families.

Often this obligation to build families that are not dependent on them can create a sense of ambivalence for parents. They want to feel needed—and what better way than through dependency? "Daddy, you are the best person in the world. I am so happy that I have *you* and not some other daddy. There is no daddy like you." What father can resist this kind of affection (and implied dependence)? Just as effective executives extricate their egos from the corporation ("The company is not *me!*"), so too must parents: "The family is not *me;* it is much more than me. And I will be an effective parent leader if I ensure its survival beyond and outside of me." It is sad and sometimes surprising to see families fall apart after the mother and father have died. We often hear children say, "It's not quite the same without Mom and Dad. I see my brothers and sisters occasionally, but we really are not that close." Usually and fortunately, this happens at a time when the children themselves are old enough to be less in need of the family stability and support. However, regardless of the need, a family has indeed died— gone out of business and, in a sense, become a discredit to the founders.

Many families, on the other hand, remain close even after Mom and Dad have passed on. They can serve as strong support systems to brothers and sisters even into old age. They continue to capitalize on the early investment made by the founders of the family and do them and each other an honor, tribute, and service. Like other solid organizations, strong families live on and become better as the years pass.

How strong is your family? Is it vulnerable to collapse or chaos? Are you or any other family member indispensable for the existence, growth, or success of the whole family? Complete the *Family Stability Index* and find out.

FAMILY STABILITY INDEX

Instructions: Answer "Yes" or "No" to the following questions. Think a few seconds before responding to each question.

_____ 1. Would your family have the same level of income if you were to die?

_____ 2. In your family do both husband and wife know the total financial picture (all debts, savings, insurance amounts, survivors' pension benefits, etc.)?

_____ 3. Does each spouse have adequate life insurance to allow the family to replace their services for a period of at least two years?

_____ 4. Do spouses (if two are at home) know enough about each other's household duties to be a replacement for a period of at least two years?

_____ 5. If you were absent from home for a week, would the family members meet with some serious logistical difficulties (e.g., transportation problems)?

_____ 6. If you were absent from home for a week, would the family members meet with some serious emotional difficulties (e.g., feeling unsafe at night)?

_____ 7. If a child does poorly in school does the whole family feel under pressure and stress?

_____ 8. Does the emotional state of the family depend on the mood of any one member?

_____ 9. Will the sudden illness or accident of any one family member severely upset family operations?

_____10. Would the course of family life be severely shaken if one of its members violated a social custom or legal code?

_____11. Would children vigorously continue to pursue academic, social, and personal growth goals if parental guidance were no longer present?

_____12. Does the family define its success by the accomplishments of its children?

_____13. If you were to die today, do you think that your family could make it reasonably well on its own?

_____14. If one of your children were to leave the family for some reason, do you think that the rest of the family could reasonably adjust and pursue a normal course within a two-year period?

Scoring: 1. Record the answer that you gave for each of the following items:

Column A	Column B
_____# 1	_____# 5
_____# 2	_____# 6
_____# 3	_____# 7
_____# 4	_____# 8
_____#11	_____# 9
_____#13	_____#10
_____#14	_____#12

Total "Yes"   Total "No"
answers in   answers in
Column A   _____.   Column B   _____.

2. Combine the totals in columns A and B:_____(Family Stability Index score).

3. Interpretation of this score:

      12–14: exceptionally stable family
       9–11: very stable family
       6– 8: moderate stability in the family
       3– 5: very unstable family
       0– 2: exceptionally unstable family

HOW TO INCREASE FAMILY STABILITY

In assessing and improving family stability parents have to first recognize a basic dilemma: their emotional needs will inevitably conflict with their managerial duties. The psychological high of realizing how much the family is dependent on them and their good works will have to be sacrificed for the sake of the structural strength of the family as an organization. Fathers and mothers will have to make their families parent-proof—a seeming contradiction, truly the paradox of the parent-leader's role. One of the most beneficial services parents can provide their families as a whole, as well as each individual member, is their independence from them, a spirit and practice of self-sufficiency that will ultimately cry out, "We don't *need* you anymore. We *want* you, but don't *have to* have you for our smooth functioning." The day that that happens the effective parent leader will be moved to the tears of rejection as well as the smiles of accomplishment, an inevitable mixture of emotions. The keenness to recognize the cause of this inner conflict and the ability to cope with it will be the major distinguishing mark between parents who can practice this aspect of parentship and those who cannot. Once the emotional difficulties of the task are understood, what can parents do to strengthen the stability of their families, if they need to? The strategies for building strength fall into two categories; (1) structure stability and (2) process stability.

Structure Stability

The organizational dimension of the family is critical to its smooth operation. As soon as families are born, they begin to develop a framework which includes chain of command (who's in charge of financial decisions?); distribution of responsibilities and duties (who will do the food shopping?); routine tasks (somebody always checks for the mail); sets of expectations (when the telephone rings, the nearest one to it answers it); and allocation of resources (money, space, time). This framework slowly but surely becomes the infrastructure of the family. For good or bad, it serves as the foundation for the family operations. It becomes ingrained in the family members' psyches and behaviors, a second nature that they count on. The structural underpinnings that created this second nature and made it dependable are often the result of family evolution. Each family was not created from scratch in a day, a week, a month, or even a year. It came into its present state over time. Gradually, sometimes unnoticeably, the component structures of each family come into being; there was a beginning for each of them, no doubt, but often it is difficult to determine the who, what, when, or why that initiated this particular aspect of the family's current design.

Often the structural components are integrally entwined with a certain family member: 30 percent of family's yard is devoted to flower gardens and shrubs because Dad loves to putter around; 20 percent of the family budget goes into family clothing because Mom feels that grooming and appearance are a top priority; a large amount of family money is allocated to private school tuition because a child is academically talented or needs special assistance for a learning disability. The family grows accustomed to these realities and designs and adapts itself accordingly. After a while, if the cause of this kind of substructure were to be extricated and removed, the whole family structure would reveal a gaping hole, something missing.

As with all excisions, preparation of the related components is critical in order to avoid trauma. For example, some parents go through a stressful period when children leave the home either to enter kindergarten for the first time, to go off to summer camp or college, to marry, or to move into their own apartment. Others are able to handle the absence of their children well and may even look forward to it. The difference usually is that one set of parents is not ready or prepared for the change, whereas the other one is. The stressed parents do not understand that a good part of their lives, activities, commitments, and even constraints are linked to their children's presence in the home. This lack of understanding and preparation bring about a family structural situation tantamount to having an organ ripped out of one's body. Parents who understand the potential for trauma prepare themselves and the family for the absence of the children and suffer less distress. Of course, the same principle holds for children and their understanding of and readiness for radical gaps in the family structure. Depending on their ages, children can and must be prepared for the eventuality of the absence of the parent. While this is indeed a touchy area and must be handled delicately, children with whom parents have discussed the possibility of their absence, and with it some of the basic structural components of the family, will have a much less difficult experience than children who have never considered the possibility; in any event, the total avoidance of trauma is unlikely, especially if the parental departure occurs with short notice.

It is critical, then, that parents first of all analyze exactly what is structurally contingent on each family member; in other words, what is likely to collapse or diminish with the absence or incapacitation of myself? my spouse? my son? my daughter? What will no longer be present or necessary? What will? The following kind of chart may prove helpful.

As a result of _____'s absence or incapacitation, the following things are likely to occur to the structure of the family:

1. _____

2. _____

3. _____

4. _____

5. _____

6. _____

The next step (if needed) is to then plan what could be done to preserve the family structure in the event that absence should occur. The family should have a "fall-back" position, a contingency plan that can go into operation as smoothly and quickly as possible: What has to be done? When? By whom? What are the implications for other family activities? (What will have to be given up in order to implement the contingency plan?)

In our parents' workshops and in our counseling we often encounter fathers and mothers who have expressed misgivings about this kind of exercise. Some have perceived it as a little far fetched and even morbid. As one Florida father put it, "I find this part of parentship depressing, somewhat depersonalizing, and pessimistic . . . I'm not going to dwell on such things. If an adjustment needs to be made in my family, I am sure that nature will take its course. Families have been surviving for years without this. I feel confident that mine will also." We basically agree. It is not pleasant to discuss the possibility of the loss of family members. To take the initiative in setting a time to think about such things and even writing down contingency plans may appear to border on the masochistic: "Who needs these imagined future disasters? We have enough real difficulties to deal with now!" We agree also that nature *will* take its course over the long haul; many families eventually do adjust. However, we do feel strongly that a systematic assessment of family stability and a well-designed set of contingencies will not only reduce the vulnerability of the family in time of crisis, but will also provide an inner comfort for parents now. To know that the "nurturing machine" that they have built will keep on running smoothly and continue to grow perpetually (from generation to generation) is its own reward. As in all strong organizations, family contingency plans are made with an eye to the strongest probability that they will be implemented, but with the deepest hope that they will never have to be used. It is only within such a management framework tempered by love that stable families can be built to be long-lasting.

The need for designing and building this kind of family stability is heightened by the increased odds favoring radical changes in family structure: marital separations and divorces are increasing at an exponential rate; remarriages are likewise increasing; more children are going through several rounds of moving out of their parents' homes and back in again between their late teens and early to mid-twenties. Of course, the rate of complete family abandonment by one or the other parent continues to rise, and the incidence of parent and child mortality or incapacitation (physical, mental, or emotional) has been holding steady. Both the greater and the immediate environment of most families are likewise less stable than even a few years ago. The institutions and agencies that families could once call on for help in time of crisis are having problems of their own: government agencies, social services, churches, and schools suffer from lack of money, personnel, and in some cases diminished interest in helping. The projected trend in this country is for less reliance on outside institutions and agencies and more self-dependence.*

In short, family contingency planning, while emotionally painful to address and while appearing to be an exotic or even morbid pastime, is absolutely essential for responsible parentship in the 1980s and beyond. To neglect this task would be to leave one's family a legacy of vulnerability and potential disintegration.

Process Stability

While the preservation of the functional structure of the family is necessary, it is not sufficient. It is only a framework. Family life also involves relationships and interactions among members that are in the process of formation. The family itself is in interaction with other families, friends, neighbors, and acquaintances. While these relationships and interactions are indeed dynamic, they do tend to follow a certain course through varying stages of maturity. The internal family relationships are usually integral to individual growth and/or sense of fulfillment (e.g., person-child bonding during infancy or father-son relationships during adolescence). Both parties' mutual involvement in the relationship makes each person's development/fulfillment sensitive and vulnerable to the destiny of a parent, spouse, son, or daughter. If for some reason (death, incapacitation, voluntary or involuntary separation) one person were to cease the relationship, it will affect the other family member with whom there was an interpersonal relationship. At certain periods in children's development, parental absence or separation would make them the most vulnerable to the effects of a severed relationship:

Age of Child	Possible Consequences of Severed Relationships
0–1	Absence of emotional bonding; sense of abandonment; lack of physical and psychological nurturing.
2	Lack of parental control; absence of appropriate discipline.
3–5	Absence of caring teaching of basic life skills (eating habits, rest, hygiene, etc.); lack of support for coping with emotions like fear or anger; absence of early skills instruction

* John Naisbitt, *Megatrends* (New York: Warner Books, 1982), Chap. 6.

	(drawing, cutting, knowing alphabet, etc.); absence of adult role model.
6–8	Lack of home instruction in social skills (how to get along with others), physical skills (e.g., how to play sports), and communication skills (reading, writing, etc.); absence of nurturing support for new adventures (school, travel, new friends). Absence of adult role model.
9–11	Absence of counseling and support when encountering first perceived difficulties (school, social, athletic, etc.); absence of help with school work and involvement in school activities.
12–14	Lack of parental counseling and support during physical, emotional, mental changes.
15–17	Lack of parental guidance, encouragement, and support (financial, moral, etc.) in preparation for college, world of work, marriage, adulthood.
18 and beyond	Absence of parental guidance, support, sharing of good times and bad. Lack of help with career choice.

Fathers and mothers ought to first analyze very carefully exactly what impact their relationship with their children has on the children's development. Next they should consider alternative ways of arranging for the benefits of these relationships to continue, if at all possible. This may indeed be very difficult, because either the parent or the child may be the key element in the relationship and may truly be irreplaceable, in which case parents need to plan for the next best situation. These kinds of issues must be addressed by parents, for instance, in writing their last will and testament. The elements of this document that address the issue of child care in the case of parental death are more important than the clauses relating to the material and financial aspects of the estate. For this reason more and more young parents with modest assets nevertheless have wills drawn up to assure proper care for their children in the event of their death. Most often the consideration of guardians has more to do with emotional and moral than financial support. Again, these kinds of contingency plans are made with the expectation that someday they may have to be used, but with the hope that they will never have to be. However, to let unharnessed hope cause the denial of the need to establish backup would be an irresponsible parentship act.

Families in their development and dynamics likewise interact with other families as well as individuals. These relationships are needed and serve several purposes—among them, social, economic, cultural, religious, recreational, or intellectual support. Often this outside family relationship has been initiated or is cemented by one family member: it could be a parent who leads the family in a relationship with the family of a co-worker, or a child who triggers a family friendship by playing with a neighborhood child or being on the same athletic team as a child in the other family. In time these friendships can become an integral part of each family's life and can be meaningful for the individual family member's growth and development. If the relationship between the families involved is dependent on any one or two family members' connection with individuals in the other family, the relationship could be very vulnerable to disintegration. Families of divorce often experience this difficulty. Two couples and their children may all be good friends; they visit, go on outings, travel together, share good times, comfort and support each other in times of trouble. Then it happens, sometimes suddenly: one of the families breaks apart. The four-part, mutually beneficial relationship between the two couples disintegrates as well, and often so does the friendship between the children. Usually the couple that is still together will initially attempt to remain close to both the divorcing friends, but often will eventually find itself choosing one over the other. The children may see each other much less frequently. Their friendship may even get caught in the crossfire as their respective parents begin to take opposite sides. The social and other benefits that reside in the families' friendship will most likely go out the window as well. A similar set of dynamics could result in the case of the death of one of the parents, possibly followed by remarriage, geographical relocation, and changes in social schedules, economic conditions, or interests.

Parents will serve their families well if they consider the family's outside relationships and how dependent the family is on them. A legitimate question is: What would happen to the family and to each individual member if this situation were to change? What would it mean? What can be done to preclude social stress in the event of such a breakdown?

FAMILY STABILITY EXERCISE

Once parents think about, determine, and analyze the particulars relating to family stability in light of their possible absence from the scene, they should mentally "act out" what they would in fact specifically do in the event of loss of a family member, particularly a spouse. These mental dry runs allow parents to "test" out the system that they may have vaguely developed and stored in the recesses of their psyches. After several possible dry runs and once they have their family survival contingency plans in the best possible shape, they ought to write them down in step-by-step fashion, especially those decisions and tasks that would be necessary immediately after the death or departure of a spouse. While not all the possibilities can be imagined nor all the emotional factors be included in preplanning, use of foresight in this exercise will decrease the probability of serious trauma to the family and often diminish the severity of the blow. It is a matter of degrees of pain. While this exercise will in no way eliminate the anguish that comes with loss, it will prevent the further unnecessary suffering that results from a state of low certitude and high confusion. The exercise may appear to be cold and even calculating; but if fathers and mothers really were to think about the importance of family stability, they would see the exercise as a necessary aspect of responsible parentship.

Stable families, then, are those which are characterized by a paradox: they are founded and managed by strong, loving parents who are integrally involved in family life, but who at the same time lead their families to a state of independence from them. The ultimate sign of stability becomes the dispensability of the family leader. This symptom of successful family building plays havoc with the emotional core of the parent's *raison d'être:* by tolerating this "personal emotion/family management conflict" and thriving within its framework, they will set their families on the road to longevity. Parents must remember that the psychological high of feeling indispensable is also a managerial low.

15
Parentship Resources

A critical skill for successful parentship is the ability to recognize and utilize resources that are or could be available. Creativity in the identification of potential resources and their use will be an important factor. Like their counterparts in other management roles, parent leaders often have to make the choice between acting alone ("doing it myself") and getting outside help in the form of service, advice, or consultation. The criteria for making that determination will often include such factors as parental know-how, financial and emotional costs and benefits, family relationships, energy, and time. Guiding questions like the following will also help parents decide whether outside help is required: Do I have the knowledge or capability to perform this task? Do I want to do it? How much will it cost to do the task? Am I temperamentally fit to perform it? Will my doing the task myself bring us all closer together or drive us apart? Will my child be better trained if I teach him or if an outsider does?

While parents doubtless need to perform family tasks, it is often necessary to call on individuals, organizations, and agencies to assist. Who and what these resources are will vary from household to household. Such factors as geographical setting, socioeconomic levels, cultural traditions, family income, and parental health will have an impact. Of course, there are some outside consultants over whom parents have little choice: health care, legal, and educational services are generally provided by others routinely. The discretionary areas are more sensitive to sound leadership practices. These areas include financial advice, housecleaning services, and landscaping, as well as tutoring children and teaching them other skills like music or sports. For example, is it better for a father who could earn one hundred and fifty dollars each Saturday to spend that day coaching his nine-year-old son in the fine art of throwing curveballs, or is it better to have the boy coached by someone who knows more about baseball, at a cost of fifty dollars for the day, for a net gain of one hundred dollars? The answer to this will depend on the purpose of the coaching. If it is to bring or keep father and son together in a close relationship, the next question is: How much is this worth? Not ultimately, of course, but right now, for that Saturday? Would the answer be the same if the father was earning five hundred dollars per Saturday? If the purpose of the coaching is to train the boy to be a better pitcher and maybe shoot for the big leagues, then it may well be that private coaching *is* the better route, and the father could best serve the whole family by going to work those days.

In order to determine when it is cost-effective to call in outside help, parents must do several things: (1) know their own real specific talents and lack thereof; (2) know their real likes and dislikes (a mother who has no patience for her daughter's errors while trying to teach her how to swim is better off having her learn at the YWCA: it will be better for everybody!); (3) determine their actual financial worth per hour (if they were going to do an hour's work in their current job, what would they make?); (4) identify those family activities and responsibilities that are enjoyable, energizing, and uplifting; and (5) identify those family activities and responsibilities that are not enjoyable and that drain their energy.

With a knowledge of these factors parents will be able to make better decisions concerning the use of outside help. There are so many resources available to the American family today—all kinds of services ranging from people who will plan and organize your child's next birthday party (magician included!) to computer camps which combine Apple or Atari wizardry and hiking skills right in the middle of the Catskills of New York or the Cascades of Northern California. Every family will be invaded by direct and more subtle marketing approaches by those offering these services: brochures, phone calls, television and radio ads, word-of-mouth campaigns, junk mail, etc. The key skill for the family leader is to control the resources and not be controlled by them. The fundamental question that every responsible parent must ask is: What is the return on investment for our family? It is critical to consider *all* costs and *all* returns.

If parents are to use outside resources wisely, it is important for them to be able to consider as many resources as possible and as many uses for the identified resources as possible. The ability to identify resources varies widely among parents. Some fathers and mothers are myopic and miss all but the very obvious sources of help. Others are much more creative and are able to recognize the many people, materials, and organizations that can be of assistance.

These are some of the more common resources that can be of use to mothers and fathers in their family leadership role.

RESOURCES FOR PARENTS

The following resources, which include people as well as private and public sources, could be useful for parents in the establishment of their resource file. Their potential use will vary from parent to parent, depending on needs and circumstances. Fathers and mothers will do well to familiarize themselves with these kinds of potential resources.

1. *Educational agencies and institutions.* Public and private elementary and secondary schools, as well as institutions of higher education, provide abundant resources for parents. In addition to providing forums for meeting other parents and discussing common interests and problems (PTAs, Home and School Associations, etc.), school staffs are often trained in skills and knowledge that could be useful for mothers and fathers—for example, in the areas of communication, child development, motivation, or discipline. In addition, parents can often locate needed materials through schools (books, tapes, filmstrips) that can be helpful in developing parenting skills. An appointment with a local educator at one's child's school will often bring rewarding knowledge and insights on how best to improve parentship skills. During the past several years, educational systems have increasingly recognized the essential relationship between the home and the school in the learning process. As a result, more and more programs and services have been provided to help parents, including workshops, lectures, support groups, and counseling sessions. There is no doubt that school will become an even greater resource to parents in the years ahead.

Colleges and universities likewise can be a valuable resource for fathers and mothers. In addition to offering many courses, workshops, and seminars in parenting or in key management skills which can be applied to the art and science of parentship, they often offer extension services for household management. For example, university or community college personnel will provide free or low-cost advice on such diverse topics as landscaping problems, poison control, or how to eradicate insects. Some will inspect homes for energy loss, fire safety, or interior space utilization. In addition, members of the counseling, legal, medical, and other professional staff may be willing to provide occasional advice or answer questions at little or no cost. Most higher education institutions will provide speakers at a nominal cost, if any. Parents who get together for meetings or who take the initiative to form support groups will have a valuable resource here.

College and university libraries are another useful resource. Many allow community members to use the books and periodicals that are part of their holdings. Likewise, the reference librarians can help parents locate other useful sources of information. Other services that are increasingly being offered by colleges and universities include summer academic and cultural enrichment programs for children (e.g., "College for Kids" programs, offering courses in computers, French, mathematics, science, etc.); athletic camps and sports clinics; and recreation programs which allow, for example, the use of swimming pools or ball fields.

In short, the education establishment should be viewed by parents as a major potential resource for the entire family.

The following education-related national organizations can be useful, in addition to the local ones, in providing resources for parents:

National Committee for Citizens in Education
Wild Lake Village Green, Suite 410
Columbia, MD 21044
• Promotes parent participation in education matters. Distributes information to parents. Parents who need legal advice and information on education and related issues can call the national number: 800-NET-WORK. Publishes materials including newsletter.

Home and School Institute
1201 16th Street, N.W.
Washington, DC 20036
• Researches practical ways for parents to make the home become a learning environment. Sponsors special projects, workshops, and training programs for parents and those helping parents.

National Association for the Education of Young Children
1834 Connecticut Avenue, N.W.
Washington, DC 20009
• Provides help for parents and teachers of preschool children.
  Publishes books, brochures, posters, etc.

2. *Churches and synagogues.* In addition to providing spiritual and moral
   guidance, these institutions can be a valuable resource for fathers
   and mothers by providing low-cost, quality counseling services.
   Some have taken the initiative to offer general parenting programs, film series, or sessions focusing on specific dimensions of
   the role. Some large denominations through the past several years
   have established whole bureaus and agencies devoted primarily to
   family life.

   Church personnel (ministers, rabbis, priests, deacons, etc.) can
   be most helpful as counselors and advisors for many parents.
   Many are being trained as pastoral counselors and are skilled in
   providing effective short-term and long-term therapy. There is
   now a greater recognition of the difficulties of the parenting role
   and more emphasis on treatment that is as much temporal as
   spiritual. Of course, prayer can be helpful for some in the parenting role. Churches and synagogues can provide the major forum
   for the public expression of a call for help from one's God.

   The following religion-oriented education organizations can be
   valuable resources for parents:

United Parent-Teacher Association of Jewish Schools
426 West 58th Street
New York, NY 10019
• Builds a partnership between the Jewish home and the Jewish
  school. Provides reading material on topics such as Jewish holidays, education, and social questions.

National Forum of Catholic Parent Organizations
c/o National Catholic Educational Association
1077 13th Street, N.W.
Washington, DC 20007
• Supports the concept of the parent as the primary educator of
  the child. Provides information and advice on religious training
  as well as school-home partnerships. Publishes materials and
  maintains resource file.

National Lutheran Parent-Teacher League
3558 South Jefferson Avenue
St. Louis, MO 63118
 • Provides help to parents in Christian child training and promotes closer relationships between the home and the church's
educational agencies.

3. *Hospitals and medical centers.* In addition to providing treatment for
the ill, hospitals can be good resources for helping parents practice preventive medicine—physically, mentally, and managerially.
More and more hospitals are providing direct training for parents
through workshops and lectures as well as indirect help through
"wellness" programs. Parents can avail themselves of the many
programs that have been developed to teach all family members
about nutrition, exercise, rest, weight control, stress management,
fitness, etc. Parents would do well to remember the following
axiom: "In order to put the love that I have for my children into
action, I have to take care of myself." This is a major premise of
our book *Parent Burnout* (Garden City, N.Y.: Doubleday, 1983).
Hospitals can be valuable partners in teaching parents how to do
this.

Community health agencies, as well as private hospitals, are also
offering more and more prevention and wellness programs. Lectures, forums, films, and workshops focusing on the various physical and mental health issues are offered in most communities at
little or no cost to participants. Some lend out video- and audio-
casettes on health issues which parents can take home and view in
privacy or for use as a focal point in family discussion. There is
even an entire cable television channel devoted exclusively to
health issues. Many of the programs offer useful advice on topics
that are relevant to all family members, such as hygiene, eating
habits, early warning signs for disease, and beneficial dental practices.

In addition to health care agencies, physicians in private practice
can be most helpful resources. Pediatricians and family physicians
are getting much more skilled in counseling techniques and are
more interested in and sensitive to the difficulties of parenting and
the debilitating effect that the role can have on physical and mental
health. They can be excellent resources for immediate help or for
referral to others who can assist. Psychologists can be another
worthwhile resource for parents. Some provide individual coun-

seling for parents while others tend to work with whole families or groups of parents.

A good way to locate a family physician, pediatrician, or psychologist is through referral by a trusted professional (e.g., a clergyman or a teacher), the state or local professional association, or a local hospital or university.

Health care associations and organizations can also be good sources of information for parentship. Many of the following provide useful information or programs, and most have state and local affiliates:

American Academy of Pediatrics
P.O. Box 1034
1801 Hinman Avenue
Evanston, IL 60204
• Promotes increased attention to health care for children; provides materials for parents on preventive care.

American Academy of Family Physicians
1740 West 92nd Street
Kansas City, MO 64114
• Good initial referral service for information on family health care.

National Institute of Mental Health
5600 Fishers Lane
Rockville, MD 20852
• Provides information on resources available for help with mental illness in children, as well as information on depression, child abuse, and other areas. Write for publication list.

National Association for Mental Health
1800 North Kent Avenue
Rosslyn, VA 22209
• Provides information to help parents recognize the early symptoms of mental illness in children. Can direct parents to counseling services. Materials available.

National Association of Children's Hospitals and Related Institutions
1601 Concord Pike; Suite 34
Wilmington, DE 19803

- Promotes child health care through research and education program. Publishes newsletter.

American Dental Association
211 East Chicago Avenue
Chicago, IL 60611
- Professional society of dentists. Good initial resource for information on dental care for the family. Dental care information available.

4. *Social service agencies.* At the federal, state, and local levels there are many public and private agencies that can be very useful for parents themselves and/or for children. The white pages of the telephone directory will contain the name, address, and telephone number of the appropriate office. More and more of these are providing services to mothers and fathers. For example, at the federal level the Department of Health and Human Services offers information and provides answers to questions on topics relating to the welfare, safety, and health of the entire family. The Internal Revenue Service will provide tax-paying parents with assistance in tax preparation and planning. In many locales, departments at the state level can provide services which could be helpful for some fathers and mothers: the department of agriculture might provide advice on vegetable gardening; the department of health and mental hygiene could provide varying types of care for parents, children, or adolescents; the department of human resources could provide job or career training opportunities for family members.

Local social services agencies can likewise be very useful for parents: the local health department often provides useful preventive advice; the consumer affairs office can support parents or children who experience difficulties with local businesses; the housing authority may assist with tenant/landlord difficulties.

Most social service agencies have social workers available who are trained to help parents deal with many and diverse family problems stemming from the environment. Through their training and experience these social workers are able to help parents use available services that they might not otherwise be aware of. Parents must remember that their hard-earned tax dollars support these federal, state, and local agencies; they should feel comfortable using any service provided and should encourage the provision of additional services that they may deem necessary.

5. *Legal community.* Parents often need legal advice and assistance either for routine family tasks or for family difficulties. We highly recommend that all parents have a family lawyer and consult with him or her on such issues as real estate transactions, estate planning, trusts, and business decisions. Above all, the family attorney should prepare wills for both parents. Parents, in turn, should prepare specific instructions for contacting the attorney in the event of their death. While private legal advice can be costly, not securing counsel before questionable decisions (e.g., real estate contracts) can be even more expensive. If funds are not available for private attorney consultation, parents can contact one of the many low-cost legal clinics that are now available in almost every location. The yellow pages of the phone directory will contain names, addresses, and telephone numbers. Another good low-cost source for legal advice (usually simple one-time counseling) is the law school of a local public or private university. Often these schools will have legal clinics of their own, or professors might be willing to give *pro bono* (free) counsel as a community service. In addition, government legal agencies (attorney general, state's attorney, public defender, consumer affairs division, etc.) can be resourceful in assisting parents in legal matters.

Every parent, insofar as possible, ought to anticipate emergencies or problems that may require legal services, such as auto accidents, liability suits, and claims for damages. All family members who are old enough to understand should be taught the procedures to follow for contacting the family attorney or the alternative source of legal counsel.

Litigation, as well as legal planning and protection, is very much a part of American family life in the 1980s. An important part of parentship is the establishment of a smooth mechanism for obtaining quality legal advice and representation when it is needed. Anticipation and prearrangement are the key factors that enhance parentship in this area. When in serious doubt about where to turn for legal counsel, begin by contacting the state or local bar association for initial answers to questions.

6. *Financial planning and advice.* With the variety, complexity, and individual nature of each family's financial status and goals, parents will sometimes decide that outside counsel is needed. While this is available in many forms and places, the field of financial planning and advice is unregulated and filled with people of various backgrounds. Many are more interested in selling something (insur-

ance, money funds, real estate, etc.) than in counseling clients, so parents must be on guard and select sources of assistance wisely.

Parents may use several financial advisors, including the attorney who prepared their wills, an insurance agent, a banker, a broker, an accountant, or a tax preparer. Sometimes it is beneficial for the family to rely on the advice of members of this team, but each is likely to see only one part of the picture. A better source of advice could be someone who is qualified to assess the overall financial situation, find the weak spots, and make suggestions for improvements. This financial planner would not replace any of the other advisors, but would recommend when they are needed. While there are many professional and legitimate financial advisors and planners, there are also poorly trained and dishonest people calling themselves experts in this field. Parents should ask for recommendations from the family lawyer or accountant or from a friend or relative whose judgment they trust. They should then interview several financial advisors and planners, asking questions such as "How many families do you advise? Can you supply references? Are you registered to sell securities? Insurance? Real estate? How are fees determined? How long have you been in the financial planning business?" Fees, services, and personalities differ widely. Parents should interview several planners and compare answers and impressions. Knowing their own financial goals will help them decide who can serve them best.

Parents should not be ashamed to seek financial advice in their roles as family executives. This in no way implies a deficiency on their part. The financial environment is becoming more and more complex in terms of legal factors, investment opportunities, and security. It is difficult for almost any parent, regardless of the amount of assets, to be able to keep up to date. Most parents, no matter what their socioeconomic level, can benefit from financial advice. Some may learn how to make more money; others may gain insights on how to manage what they have. Of course, in addition to outside advice, parents can and should do some independent study in the area of financial planning management. The more is done in this area, the better for the family ultimately. The following are some good resources for parents' self-instruction:

MAGAZINES:

(1) *Money;* (2) *Changing Times;* (3) *Forbes;* (4) *Fortune;* (5) *Business Week;* (6) Financial advice columns of weekly magazines.

NEWSPAPERS:

(1) *The Wall Street Journal;* (2) *Barron's;* (3) Financial sections of local newspapers.

7. *Businesses.* The business community can be a valuable resource for parents. In addition to providing commodities for a price, it also offers services that can cost parents very little, if anything. For example, many supermarkets, especially the large chains, make available literature on family nutrition and such services as free measurement of blood pressure. More and more department stores offer community lectures and demonstrations relating to interior decorating, fashions, personal development, and parenting. The private business sector has recently increased its interest in parenting problems because of their impact on worker productivity. They are offering more help not only to their employees but also to the community at large.

In addition to availing themselves of these low-cost or free services, parents should be aware of and consider utilizing the increasing number of services designed to assist the homemaker and homeowner, including birthday party planners, house cleaners, yard caretakers, and shopping services. In our service-oriented society, parents literally have a whole array of possibilities available to them. If they select among them judiciously and with an eye to the value of their own time as compared to the cost of the service offered, they can utilize the offerings of the many businesses in their environment.

The effective leader of any organization, including the family, is the one who utilizes his or her time, energy, interest, money, and other resources where they will have the greatest return. He or she is sensitive to the value of all these precious resources. For a mother to spend four hours driving all over town to save twenty dollars on the purchase of a new sofa may not be a very good return on her time (isn't she worth more than five dollars an hour?) or energy (she now is exhausted from going in and out of stores). For a father to spend an hour driving to a store to buy oil for his automobile and changing it himself to save eight dollars may likewise be far below the return he could have received if he had used that hour for something else (including chatting with his children).

8. *Libraries.* The public library system continues to be one of the major potential resources for parents, if they choose to use it. In addition to providing reading material, the library is an incredible storehouse of information relevant to the quality of family life. The

books, films, directories, reference books, almanacs, microfilm, etc., included in libraries can enrich the lives of all family members. Reference librarians are skilled in guiding users' search for information by asking questions that help crystallize their problems. They hold one of the most resourceful roles in the local community: they know how to obtain the needed information needed in a timely fashion. Many libraries now are linked, through computers and modems, to an array of data bases that can provide instantaneous information on anything from train schedules to stock quotations. Some libraries lend out not only reading material but also records, video- and audiotapes, and framed pictures and artifacts for household use. Some now provide personal computers for patron use. Libraries are truly becoming the information nerve centers of local communities. They collect and store information, and they also take the initiative to disseminate it through public lectures, workshops, and discussion sessions on various subjects, including parenting skills.

Fathers and mothers will do themselves a great service if they view and utilize their local library as a major resource for their parenting role. They ought to take full advantage of what it has to offer and encourage the library administration to offer more direct help to parents through training lectures and workshops.

9. *Political leaders.* An integral part of effective parentship is the ability to control the family's destiny by influencing the environment. A major part of that environment is the political structure at the local, state, and federal levels. Elected officials can be effective sources of information as well as advocates for issues, problems, or causes affecting parents. At the macro-level, parents should lobby their political representatives (congressmen, state senators, councilmen, etc.) to introduce and support legislation that will be in the best interest of families (e.g., education bills, environmental protection, or drug and alcohol laws). At the micro-level, elected officials should be called upon as the need arises to assist parents in getting responses and appropriate services from the various government bureaus and agencies (traffic control near schools, police patrolling at playgrounds, etc.).

Parents who are familiar with the political process and know how to contact and influence their elected representatives as well as the executive branches of government do a service to all the members of their families. Their proactive approach increases the probability of controlling their own family's destiny. Those parents who do not understand or interact with the political establishment allow their families to become reactive and controlled by the "system."

10. *Police and fire departments.* Because parents are managers of the interior and exterior of the home, they often can be assisted by the police and fire departments. These agencies are resourceful in times of emergency, when they are needed for protection, rescue services, fire control, and other help. They can also be most useful in preventing difficulties and problems. For example, police departments in most locations will inspect homes for their vulnerability to burglary; they will recommend better ways to safeguard property and allow alarm systems to be connected to the police station so that they will be notified if a break-in is attempted. They will also check homes regularly if the family is out of town on vacation or visiting friends or relatives. In addition, the police department can help teach children how to protect themselves and take preventive action to avoid becoming the victims of crime. School PTA groups as well as neighborhood associations would serve their parent members well by arranging such sessions for children and parents alike. With the steady increase in the number of "latchkey children" (boys and girls who are home alone after school each day before their parents return from work), this kind of training will be most useful.

The fire department can be equally helpful. In addition to providing emergency services, they will often be available to inspect homes for fire safety, appropriate escape routes, and the possibility of fire hazards. Like their police counterparts, firemen can often be recruited to demonstrate fire safety principles and practices for children who might be spending time at home alone.

Wise parent leaders will utilize the talent, training, and equipment of these two vital forces in the community. They will likewise have their telephone numbers posted conspicuously next to every telephone in the home.

11. *Parenting associations and special interest groups.* The past several years have seen an increase in the number of associations and groups formed for the specific purpose of helping fathers and mothers in their parenting role. They provide training, materials, and advice, and they may even hold conferences and meetings for parents. Much interest, time, money, and effort has gone into the formation and maintenance of these organizations. They provide opportunities to meet other parents and/or to read or hear the advice of experts in particular aspects of parenting. Listed below are organi-

zations that may provide beneficial resources for mothers and fathers.

American Association for Marriage and Family Therapy
1000 Connecticut Avenue, N.W.; Suite 407
Washington, DC 20036
· Has nationwide marriage and family therapy referral.

American Family Therapy Association
2550 M Street, N.W.; Suite 275
Washington, DC 20037
· Promotes understanding of family as a complete system.

The American National Red Cross
(contact the local Red Cross chapter in your own geographical area)
· Provides parenting programs and courses. Has recommended readings and other services of help for parents.

Center for the Study of Parent Involvement
5237 College Avenue
Oakland, CA 94618
· Collects and provides information on parent involvement; offers training for mothers and fathers and professionals on parenting. Newsletter and other materials available.

National Association of Extension Home Economists
315 North 6th Street
De Kalb, IL 60115
· Helps parents find solutions to problems concerning family life, such as child care, nutrition, budgeting, and family recreation.

National Institute of Family Relations
6116 Rolling Road; Suite 316
Springfield, VA 22152
· Provides training in family relationships and assists family in coping with and working through problems. Conducts workshops and seminars.

National Parent-Teacher Association
700 North Rush Street
Chicago, IL 60611
· Publishes materials on parent education and on relationships between parents, teachers, and school administrators.

Parents Choice Foundation
P.O. Box 185
Waban, MA 02168
• Provides parents with information concerning games, books, records, television programs, and movies for children.

Princeton Center for Infancy
306 Alexander Street
Princeton, NJ 08540
• Does research and develops materials for parents and professionals. Collects research results on parenting techniques. Developed the *Parent's Yellow Pages,* a comprehensive resource book for parents.

Profession of Parenting Institute
1609 Poplar Street
Philadelphia, PA 19130
• Conducts workshops on methods to "professionalize" parenting. Some materials available.

To receive additional information, write directly to the organization.

12. *Magazines.* Parents can often turn to reading materials, which are amply available. Articles in the following magazines can be useful for parents who want to develop parenting skills or who have particular needs or problems.

American Baby Magazine
575 Lexington Avenue
New York, NY 10022
• Focuses on the "how to" of parenting. There is a special emphasis on medical information. Personal parental experiences are recounted and interviews with specialists included.

Exceptional Parent
296 Boylston Street
Boston, MA 02116
• This magazine includes information for parents who have the responsibility of taking care of children with physical, emotional, or learning problems.

Mother's Manual Magazine
441 Lexington Avenue
New York, NY 10017

• This includes well-researched "how to" articles focusing on the parenting of young children as well as pregnancy.

Parents' Magazine
52 Vanderbilt Avenue
New York, NY 10017
• Includes good practical suggestions on parenting duties and responsibilities, with a focus on preschool, school-age, and adolescent children.

Practical Parenting
15235 Minnetonka Boulevard
Minnetonka, MN 55343
• In addition to advice from experts, this serves as an exchange forum for parenting ideas, problems, and suggestions.

Today's Child
School Lane
Roosevelt, NJ 08555
• This is a digest of important articles on parents. It also includes a column on children's books.

Women Who Work
Family Circle
488 Madison Avenue
New York, NY 10022
• Features articles that include practical suggestions for the working mother.

Working Mother
McCall Publishing Company
230 Park Avenue
New York, NY 10169
• Serves as a clearinghouse for information of interest to working mothers. It includes articles on conflicts between career and parenting.

Working Woman
600 Madison Avenue
New York, NY 10022
• Focuses on the dilemmas of working and raising a family; mothers and career success; and work/home conflicts.

13. *Books.* Parenting books can be most useful for fathers and mothers. Books have the advantage of being available when needed and

being portable; they can be conveniently read on trips, at the beach, or in bed. Parents should continuously read books that may help them in their parenting skills. The following bibliography may be helpful as a starting point for mothers and fathers.

Ashery, Rebecca Sager, and Michele Marolin Basen. *The Parents with Careers Workbook.* Washington, D.C.: Acropolis Books, 1983.
Practical tips on how to balance the full-time roles of parent and worker.

Auerbach, Steveanne. *The Whole Child: A Sourcebook.* New York: G. P. Putnam's Sons, 1980.
A valuable compendium of child care and child-rearing information: includes book reviews, lists helpful organizations, recommends sources of fun for the family, etc.

Bayard, Robert T., and Jean Bayard. *How to Deal with Your Acting-Up Teenager.* New York: M. Evans, 1983.
Includes concrete recommendations for parenting teenagers; especially helpful for mothers and fathers with children who are behavior and/or discipline problems.

Behrstock, Barry, M.D., with Richard Trubo. *The Parent's When-Not-To-Worry Book.* New York: Harper & Row, 1981.
Examines and refutes some commonly held myths relating to child care and child-rearing practices.

Berends, Polly Berrien. *Whole Child, Whole Parent.* New York: Harper & Row, 1983.
A spiritual, philosophical, and uplifting view of the parenting role; especially useful for those who feel they have lost sight of the light at the end of the tunnel.

Bramnick, Lea S., and Anita Simon. *The Parents' Solution Book.* New York: Franklin Watts, 1983.
A practical handbook with useful tips, activities, and sample dialogue for everyday family situations; the material is designed to teach parents how to foster growth in their children.

Brooks, Jane B. *The Process of Parenting.* Palo Alto, Cal.: Mayfield Publishing, 1981.
Focuses on the importance of the parent's active participation in the development of children.

Canter, Lee. *Assertive Discipline for Parents.* Santa Monica, Cal.: Canter and Associates, 1982.

A clearly presented set of directions to guide children's behavior; parents learn when and how to lay down the law as well as methods for providing positive support.

Carton, Lonnie. *Raise Your Kids Right.* New York: G. P. Putnam's Sons, 1980.

Explains how to discipline children in a consistent, caring, and loving way.

Curran, Dolores. *Traits of a Healthy Family.* Minneapolis: Winston Press, 1983.

Presents a group of fifteen characteristics, as selected by parents as well as experts on family life, which are found in the most successful and effective families.

Dinkmeyer, Don C., and Gary D. McKay. *The Parent's Handbook: Systematic Training for Effective Parenting (STEP).* Circle Pines, Minn.: American Guidance Service, 1982.

Offers parents a practical and comprehensive approach to raising children today; it is built on a democratic philosophy of parenting.

Dodson, Fitzhugh. *How to Parent.* New York: Signet/New American Library, 1970.

A classic "how to" book for parents who want to understand their children better so that they can be more successful as fathers and mothers.

Dodson, Fitzhugh. *How to Discipline with Love.* New York: Signet/ New American Library, 1978.

Teaches parents when and how to discipline; distinguishes between discipline and punishment.

Dreikurs, Rudolph, Shirley Gould, and Raymond J. Corsini. *Family Council.* Chicago: Henry Regnery Co./Contemporary Books, 1974.

A step-by-step method for establishing a system of decision making and conflict resolution in the family: the family council.

Eden, Alvin N. *Positive Parenting: How to Raise a Healthier and Happier Child.* New York: New American Library, 1982.

Explains what to expect of children up to age three, emotionally and physically; especially useful for first-time parents.

Elkind, David. *The Hurried Child.* Reading, Mass.: Addison-Wesley, 1981.

Focuses on the stress on children who are either forced or encouraged to grow up and develop too fast; offers suggestions to parents on how they can slow the process.

Galinsky, Ellen. *Between Generations: The Six Stages of Parenthood.* New York: Times Books, 1981.

Describes the significant effects that children have on parents; good insights on what it means to be a parent.

Gibson, Janice T. *Discipline Is Not a Dirty Word: A Positive Learning Approach.* Lexington, Mass.: Lewis Publishing, 1983.

Focuses on discipline as a learning process and teaches parents how to present themselves as models for their children.

Ginott, Haim G. *Between Parent and Child: New Solutions to Old Problems.* New York: Avon Books, 1977.

A classic on communication in the family; parents are taught how to listen to their children.

Gordon, Thomas. *P.E.T.: Parent Effectiveness Training.* New York: Peter H. Wyden, 1970.

A comprehensive training program for parents that focuses on assertiveness; it is based on a very successful series of workshops.

Gottesman, David M. *The Powerful Parent.* Norwalk, Conn.: Appleton-Century-Crofts, 1982.

A useful guide, including strategies and checklists, for parents to use in selecting professionals and public services to help their children.

Kiley, Dan. *Keeping Parents Out of Trouble.* New York: Warner Books, 1982.

A no-nonsense guide to effective parenting; the issues of authority, willpower, and parent/child responsibilities are emphasized.

Lickona, Thomas. *Raising Good Children.* New York: Bantam Books, 1983.

With many practical examples parents are shown how to teach such basic values as honesty, courtesy, respect for others, and helpfulness.

McCullough, Bonnie Runyan, and Susan Walker Monson. *401 Ways to Get Your Kids to Work at Home.* New York: St. Martin's Press, 1981.

A practical guide for getting children to participate in housework and develop basic living skills which will help them in adulthood.

Pizzo, Peggy Daly. *Parent to Parent: Working Together for Ourselves and Our Children.* Boston: Beacon Press, 1983.

A guide to existing child advocacy groups and a description of how parents join together to form them.

Plutzik, Roberta, and Maria Laghi. *The Private Life of Parents.* New York: Everest House, 1983.

A "survival guide" of practical recommendations for parents which focuses on taking care of oneself while raising happy children.

Procaccini, Joseph, and Mark W. Kiefaber. *Parent Burnout.* Garden City, N.Y.: Doubleday, 1983.

Explains the causes of parent burnout, decribes the symptoms, and recommends treatment and prevention plans.

Salk, Lee. *The Complete Dr. Salk: An A-to-Z Guide to Raising Your Child.* New York: New American Library, 1983.

Arranged as an encyclopedia and filled with anecdotes, the book covers topics that are of interest to most parents: anger, allowances, responsibilities, etc.

Schaefer, Charles E. *How to Influence Children* (2nd ed.). New York: Van Nostrand Reinhold, 1982.

A presentation of practical child-rearing skills; clear description of the behavior modification technique.

Sears, William, M.D. *Creative Parenting.* New York: Everest House, 1982.

A comprehensive, practical child care book that focuses on the use of the continuum concept for raising children from birth to adolescence.

Tower, Kathleen. *Parent Tricks of the Trade.* Washington, D.C.: Acropolis Books, 1981.

A compendium of money- and time-saving solutions to common problems facing most busy parents.

Winship, Elizabeth C. *Reaching Your Teenager*. Boston: Houghton Mifflin, 1983.

Assists parents in dealing with the typical problems of teenagers; does a good job of addressing the tough issues—drugs, sex, cars, etc.

14. *Service clubs*. Most communities have an array of clubs that serve a social function for members, but that also provide services to the community. Parents should get to know these organizations and become aware of what they have to offer. Most of the clubs listed below have local clubs and/or chapters:

Unites States Jaycees
P.O. Box 7
4 West 21st Street
Tulsa, OK 74121
• Sponsors programs for youth development as well as community-oriented social activities for families.

Kiwanis Club
3636 Woodview Trace
Indianapolis, IN 46268
• Sponsors many youth activities and offers career guidance for youngsters. Sponsors community service clubs for junior high, high school, and college students.

Lions Club
300 22nd Street
Oak Brook, IL 60570
• Provides education, health, and social services for the community. Also has a few clubs for young adults.

Optimist Clubs
4494 Lindell Boulevard
St. Louis, MO 63108
• Sponsors a wide range of community programs and services: children's sports programs; bike safety; public speaking projects for young men and women; youth appreciation week. Octagon Clubs for boys and girls in junior and senior high school.

Big Brothers/Big Sisters
117 South 17th Street; Suite 1200
Philadelphia, PA 19103
• Assists boys and girls between ages six and eighteen who are

from single-parent families. Children are assigned to an adult volunteer who provides guidance and friendship.

Every parent has at his or her disposal literally hundreds of sources of assistance in parentship: people, organizations, reading materials, etc. The key skills are being able to recognize the resources and knowing how to gain access to them. The resources included here are only a beginning. There are many more in each community. If you cannot find what you need or if you have special problems or interests and do not know where to turn, we may be able to refer you to the appropriate resource. Feel free to contact us at Loyola College, 4501 North Charles Street, Baltimore, MD 21210.

APPENDIX I*

The Computerized Family: Present and Future

"I don't believe this. You mean that I can store all my financial records right here and press these buttons, and everything will be retrieved instantaneously? Incredible!" exclaimed a young father as his ten-year-old son simply shrugged his shoulders and said, "Of course, Dad." Both were browsing in one of the growing number of family computer centers. The ascendancy of the computer as a family management tool during the past two or three years has been meteoric. What was once out of the financial reach of most American households is now getting to be more and more affordable. The basic computer model is within the price range of a portable television set. The prediction is that within a short period of time more sophisticated computers will be within the budget capability of many American households. And what computers can do and will be able to do is mind-boggling.

Generally children have been more accepting of computers than their parents. As with most technological innovations, adults have to put aside old habits, ways of operating that have become ingrained.

* This Appendix is designed for the growing number of families who either currently utilize some form of computer technology in the management of their family or are contemplating doing so. Parents who already have a computer can use these suggestions and recommendations for improved utilization. Those trying to decide whether or not to obtain one can find guidance for making the correct decision.

"While keeping all the family bills and other records in the old shoe box is awkward and even borders on the irresponsible, I like it this way because I know where everything is. I must admit I do spend a lot of time sifting through all the papers and looking for things. And if I should become incapacitated or, God forbid, die, I don't know who could make heads or tails out of this mess," a Nashville father told us recently.

The effective use of personal computers is now very much a part of our culture, and it will take on more importance as we move on toward the year 2000. But what do they have to do with parenting? Is a personal computer—as the advertisers would have us believe—a genuine, all-purpose tool that can enrich parents' lives and smooth out the functioning of families? Maybe. But first, consider this: Americans have always loved technological gadgets. And we have demonstrated our affection since the beginning of the technological revolution by laying out millions of dollars for ever newer/bigger/better technology. Many of these gadgets turned out to be mere gimmicks, here today and gone tomorrow. Some, like unloved toys or unused woks and pasta makers, gather dust in forgotten corners of homes. Others, which promised to relieve us of life's tedious tasks, often created more problems than they solved.

Judging from recent sales figures, the personal computer is the newest "high-tech gadget" to romance the American family. As one father in Sacramento put it, "Conversations in the donut shop in the morning, in the lunchroom at work, and at cocktail parties are spiced with references to printers, disk drives, monitors, and modems. It is like a whole new language thrust upon us overnight."

Several parents have noted that even ads for furniture and other household goods often include a computer in the setting. Likewise, television and magazine advertising by computer companies carries a very clear message to mothers and fathers: good parenting requires getting a computer for your children. One ad is quite explicit: *"Spend* for your children; do not only save for them." Converging on the home from four different directions—business, industry, arcades, and schools—the personal computer is offering seemingly unlimited services to families as a manager, communicator, playmate, and teacher. The following are common sales pitches:

"As a playmate, your personal computer ("PC") can entertain your family with more than 400 different electronic games, from simple video games to poker and chess, to sophisticated games of logic and deduction."

"As a manager, your computer can do the family budget, balance the checkbook, set up cross-referenced files of books, records, and recipes, figure out and save money on your taxes, and design complicated financial investment plans."

"As a telecommunicator, your computer can do your banking, shopping, and letter writing. In the future, it may even replace your telephone."

"As a word processor, your computer can help you write almost as fast as you can think. It can correct your errors and rearrange paragraphs automatically, and . . . with the aid of a printer . . . it can type out letter-perfect documents."

"As a teacher, your computer can help your kids with the basic '3 R's' or it can enrich your entire family's education by teaching you art, music, typing, languages, or just about any topic you can think of."

The advertisers admit that there are limits—financial if not practical ones—to what a PC can do. But they say that the only limit that really counts is the extent of your ability or willingness to put it to its maximum use. Industry claims aside, most experts predict that by the twenty-first century personal computers will be as commonplace in the American home as the telephone. And if their predictions prove to be true, then the question parents must ask themselves is this: *How is the personal computer going to affect my job as a parent and family leader?*

Several use trends for the home computer have developed. Phyllis, a mother of six, said, "I had to buy a computer to keep my husband and kids at home. They were spending all their time playing with the neighbor's computer! I was becoming a computer widow!" Other parents—like Don, a Cleveland father of three daughters—viewed buying a personal computer as "an investment in the future—both ours and our kids'." Whenever we talk to parents about personal computers, or skim through ads and journals about what PCs are and what they can do, the analogy that keeps popping up is that "a personal computer is like an automobile for your mind." The analogy seems apt. America's current love affair with personal computers certainly seems to rival its past love affair with cars. In families across America, the universal cry of "Mom, may I borrow the car tonight?" is being replaced by "Mom, may I use the computer tonight?" And families are using them for a multitude of purposes. These are some examples of uses of computers by parents and children we have encountered in our interviews, counseling, and workshops:

- Beatrice, thirty-five-year-old mother of three, keeps track of the family's finances with a "money manager" and writes personal correspondence.
- Glen, a college professor, keeps his course outlines, bibliographies, and notes stored and can modify them easily.
- Jason, age thirteen, with a friend designed a fifteen-step fantasy game.
- Jeff, age eleven, designs colorful space war games.
- Sean, age four, is learning basic concepts of "up, down, above, and below" using a preprogrammed package.
- Neil, forty-two-year-old father of two teenagers, uses his PC to manage his assets of stock and bond holdings and rental property.
- Katie, age five, "draws" houses, people, and animals.
- Sandy, age twelve, keeps track of her Girl Scout troop's income.
- Bill, a thirty-three-year-old husband and father of an infant, uses a PC to record household items for insurance purposes.

Additional uses mentioned by parents include home budget maintenance; balancing the checkbook; investment decisions; mailing lists for greeting cards, invitations, etc.; and inventories of food and other household supplies.

From our interviews and research, we found that of all the applications of the personal computer, the most far-reaching may be in the area of education, although, at present, this is a hotly debated topic. Some educators say that the personal computer is "just another flashy medium for presenting the same old ideas." Others insist that "it's the most revolutionary education tool since the advent of chalk." Cheryl, the mother of a learning-disabled child, zeroed in on the educational benefits for children such as hers. She pointed out that "time and again, tests show that today's children are more attuned to audiovisual teaching techniques than traditional paper-and-pencil lessons . . . *particularly* children with learning disabilities." "For years, I spent money on tutors for Cara," Cheryl explained. "But it didn't really work. Cara was still self-conscious about her disability, and she was embarrassed about making mistakes in front of her tutors." That's when Cheryl decided to buy a personal computer. "The money I would have spent on tutors, I spent on the computer," she said. "And the results have been fantastic. Cara loves the computer because it's fun, it gives immediate feedback, it's never critical or impatient. Knowing she can't fail gives her the courage to try more things, take more risks."

On the other side of the fence are the experts who fear that relying on technology will lead to an even further decline in students' reading and writing abilities. These critics blame "modern teaching techniques" for the startling statistics reported recently by the U.S. Department of Education and the National Science Foundation. In short, the report stated that "for the first time in American history the generation moving into adulthood is less skilled than its parents." Computer critics claim that the personal computer doesn't really teach: "It's nothing more than a drillmaster." Computer proponents, on the other hand, insist that "computer programs today teach kids not just *what* to think, but *how* to think. They make abstract concepts concrete—even for small children."

While educators may disagree as to whether or not computers help children learn the "3 R's," almost all agree that a new "basic" in education must now be mastered by all students: "computer literacy." What is computer literacy and why is it so important? One school principal put it this way: "Youngsters who don't know how to use computers will be at a serious disadvantage when they enter the job market." Some educators estimate that 75 percent of all jobs in 1990 will involve computers in some way. "But knowing how to use a computer isn't as awesome as it sounds. It simply means that a worker is able to insert user-friendly software and will be familiar with a basic programming language," another school administrator pointed out.

A computer is a tool, nothing more and nothing less. And, as one New Orleans elementary school teacher explained, "the purpose of any tool is to help human beings become more human. What the personal computer can do for us is to help us cope with a society that is becoming more and more complex every day." Educators are not the only ones debating the impact of the computer on kids. Many parents feel ambivalent, even threatened by computer-assisted instruction.

"I was never trained in using computers. How will I be able to help with homework assignments?" asked one worried father in Seattle. The concern is a legitimate one. To someone who has not grown up with a computer, it can seem mysterious—even magical or supernatural. "Some people are actually terrified of computers, to the point of being phobic," explained an industrial psychologist of our acquaintance. The cure for "computer phobia" is like the cure for any phobia: "You have to get to know the beast so you can stop being afraid of it," he continued.

Learning to use a personal computer is a lot like learning to drive a car: you can study the book all you want, but you can only learn to drive by driving. And you can only learn to compute by computing. Fortunately, computing—like driving—is a lot easier than it looks. It probably takes less time than learning to drive, and most people find it less stressful.

Said many parents who own home computers: "Just having a computer in the house is good. Even if you only play games with it, you learn to be comfortable with the machine. And that's half the battle." On the other hand, one mother whom we spoke to didn't want to buy a personal computer for her kids because, she said, "Then I'll have to learn to use the blasted thing!"

Where computer literacy is concerned, one expert made this suggestion: "It's okay if parents don't want to learn computing. But if they're serious about their children learning—'Do as I do' is a lot more effective than 'Do as I say.' " As any parent knows, modeling behavior is the most powerful way to teach kids. Another strong argument we heard from parents in favor of personal computers is that "schools have a much more limited role in our children's education than we used to believe." Cheryl, the mother of the learning-disabled child, commented: "There's too much to learn, and schools can't do it all." As the home becomes more and more involved in supplementing the role of the school in the child's education, as no doubt it will,† the computer will have an even more prominent place in family life.

CHANGING FAMILY DYNAMICS

"Adding a computer to your home is like adopting a new family member," several parents said. There is no question that a PC changes the dynamics of family life.

How so? A computer in the home can make life easier in some ways, and harder in others.

First, let us look at the plus side:

- As a management tool, the PC can improve the quality of home life by taking care of the "humdrum" and leaving time for learning and playing. It can be used to store the vital and medical records of the family members, telephone numbers and addresses, tax information, recipes, etc., and as a cross-reference file.
- As an educational tool, the PC can do the work of a team of tutors. A child can often learn twice as much in half the time. It is helpful for

† See John Naisbitt, *Megatrends* (New York: Warner Books, 1982).

drilling, review, testing, exercises, composition, college board exam preparation, self-tutoring, etc.

- As a telecommunicator, the PC can improve the timeliness and accuracy of communications, both incoming and outgoing.
- As a source of entertainment, the PC can be an individual as well as a family sport. Kids can entertain themselves, or parents and kids can team up to "beat the computer." Games range from the simple to the complex, from games of pure fun to games of logic.
- With the use of a telephone modem, the family can quickly obtain vast amounts of information (e.g., airline schedules, daily news, or up-to-the hour stock and bond quotations); order items through catalogs; play games with others who have a computer and modem; do work at home and have it stored, printed, and retrieved at work; do electronic banking; use electronic encyclopedias, etc.
- Children with computers in the home will learn to feel comfortable with computers in their future experiences in education and work.
- As a stress reducer, the computer may serve an indirect purpose: when parents or children are absorbed in a task that requires a high degree of attention, they are less self-aware and more relaxed.
- As a social instrument, it extends neighborhood and community for children: through the use of certain devices they are able to play games, "chat," and work on joint projects with other children who live miles away.

Having a computer in the home can make parenting easier in many ways. But it can also make parenting harder.

Why harder? "It requires more *creative* parenting," offered Phyllis, mother of six, who said that keeping her kids from becoming "completely wired to the computer" was a full-time job.

As we wrote in our previous book,‡ the impact of technology on children is irrefutable. Video games are reinforcing television as the "universal pacifier." So what are parents to do? One possibility is to compensate for the technology by spending more time with nature— drawing your children away from video games to take them fishing, bicycling, camping, or to the seashore.

‡ *Parent Burnout* (Garden City, N.Y.: Doubleday, 1983), p. 77.

GETTING TO KNOW THE PERSONAL COMPUTER

A personal computer is simply a tool to be used for personal solutions—just as an automobile is a tool for taking you from one place to another. The difference between a computer and an automobile is that the automobile takes *you* to the *world,* while the personal computer brings the *world* to *you.* The automobile has been around so long that most of us know, more or less, how it works. But the computer is still so new that parents are not even quite sure what it is, let alone how it works.

The answer to the question "How does a computer work?" is actually a paradox: it works like a human brain—only it's different. Like the brain, the computer can do arithmetic, make comparisons, and "remember" what it has done. And it does these things at blinding speed, faster than any human brain. But a computer has no "mind." It can only do what it has been told to do and remember how it has been told to do it. "This is where the human being comes in: a computer is your tool, not your master," one computer expert assured us.

So, a computer system is not as complex as parents often think. The basic system consists of only four components: hardware, input devices, output devices, and software.

Hardware. As its name suggests, hardware is the machinery of a computer system—the electronics, the wires, the plastic, the glass, and the metal.

Input/output. While the hardware is the heart of the computer, without input and output devices the computer is essentially deaf, dumb, and blind.

"Input" is how one talks to a computer—either by typing on a keyboard or by inserting cassette tapes or little disks that look like small 45-RPM records. Some of the disks are soft and are thus called "floppy" disks.

"Output," on the other hand, is how the computer talks to the user. It can "read" whatever information is requested (such as words, numbers, or pictures) and display it instantly on a video-monitor. Or it can "write" the information on a disk by means of a disk drive. A disk drive is both an input and an output device. Like a record player, it can "play" the disks fed into it; and like a recorder, it can "play back" and "record" information for permanent storage. But unlike a record player or tape recorder, the disk drive operates at lightning speeds.

As mentioned earlier, the computer has a "memory"—that is, it can "remember" what it is told. It can store a certain amount of information for a period of time within the machine itself, or it can transfer the information to disks or tapes. How much or how long a computer can "remember" will vary depending on the type of computer. Usually, the greater the memory, the greater the cost of the computer.

Another term often heard in regard to computer hardware is "peripherals." These are all the extras that turn the home computer into a fully functioning system. For example, one could add a modem, a device that allows the user to talk to any computer in the world by means of a telephone hookup; a printer, to produce "hard" copy of information from the computer itself or from any other source the computer is connected to; and a voice synthesizer that allows the computer to "talk" in the user's language.

Software. "Hardware, input, output, disk drives, modems, printers, and voice synthesizers." It all sounds very impressive, doesn't it? But parents must remember this: without software, a computer is just a hunk of machinery. Software is the set of written instructions—either from the user through the keyboard or from a preprogrammed package—that tells the computer what to do. Software is what makes the computer "go"—like gas in a car. But more than that, software provides the road map for the computer to travel on. For example, one can load the computer with a program that will sort, categorize, code, and store information to be used for household records, financial statements, and projections. There are all kinds of software for family use: educational, recreational, financial, record keeping, etc. The software is often designed to be compatible with certain brands of hardware (e.g., Apple, IBM, Coleco). These are some good sources for learning about available software:

Courseware Report Card
150 West Carob Street
Compton, CA 90220

Electronic Learning
730 Broadway
New York, NY 10003

EPIE Micro-Courseware PRO/FILES
EPIE Institute
P.O. Box 839
Water Mill, NY 11976

Teaching and Computers
730 Broadway
New York, NY 10003

Datapro Directory of Microcomputer Software
Datapro Research Corporation
1805 Underwood Boulevard
Delran, NJ 08075

Educational Software Directory
Idea Consortium
P.O. Box 4202
Chevy Chase, MD 20815

Educational Software Directory
Library Unlimited, Inc.
P.O. Box 263
Littleton, CO 80160

SHOULD I BUY A PERSONAL COMPUTER?

Today, there are hundreds of ready-made programs available to perform a multitude of functions. And computer systems needed to run these programs are now the fastest-growing category of electronic products on the market today.

But according to several studies, Americans are spending billions for the machines, companion equipment, and software without even knowing just how they intend to use them. Many plan to use their computers primarily for education, family accounting, and telecommunications, but find that they are using them most often for games and other forms of entertainment, as well as for their novelty value—for example, demonstrating what the computer can do to friends and neighbors who do not have one. We know of several families whose computers are linked to an information data base through a modem and whose young children run up all kinds of telephone bills by searching for information that is either esoteric or useless for them. One Chicago father told how his twelve-year-old son conducts computer inquiries for such frivolous information as skiing in Austria, transatlantic airline schedules, and soybean prices! We highly advise that parents be realistic about how they plan to use their personal computer. The computer is not magic. If a parent has never so much as organized a

simple card file without a computer, owning a computer probably will
not inspire him or her to organize a computer file.

MAKING THE DECISION

"Deciding whether or not to buy a home computer can feel like
trying to merge onto the Los Angeles freeway," is how one West Coast
parent described it. "You can't be too cautious or you'll never make the
move. But you can't just rush in without looking." How can parents
decide whether or not they should purchase one? The following checklist will help decide whether they could seriously benefit from a personal home computer.

Parent Computer Index

Instructions: Answer "Yes" or "No" to the following questions.

_____ 1. Do I keep good records?

_____ 2. Do I have children who are school age?

_____ 3. Would I like to improve my household management in one
or more of the following areas: filing, correspondence, tax
records, budgeting?

_____ 4. Am I willing to spend an initial 25–40 hours learning how to
use the hardware and software?

_____ 5. Am I willing to spend at least $2,000 for the hardware and
software in the first year?

_____ 6. Do I have 8 hours of free time to devote to the computer
each week?

_____ 7. Do I complete at least 6 hours of paperwork at home each
week?

_____ 8. Do my family and I enjoy engaging in recreation activities in
our home?

_____ 9. Do I encourage my children to engage in self-instructional
activities?

_____10. Am I willing to spend at least 5 hours a month putting data
into the computer?

Scoring:

8–10 "Yes" answers: You would be served well by a home computer;
strongly consider buying one.

| 5–7: | You might benefit from a home computer, but look at alternatives carefully before buying one. |
| 0–4: | You are not ready for a home computer yet. |

HOW MUCH SHOULD WE SPEND?

Depending on need and pocketbook, parents can buy a Chevy of a personal computer or a Cadillac—or, as one advertiser boasts, "A Maserati for your mind." The same is true for software. Parents can buy expensive general-purpose software that requires more skill from the user. Or they can buy specific-purpose software that may not be so versatile but is inexpensive and easy to use.

The following set of questions will help parents determine whether they should buy general-purpose or specific-purpose programs.

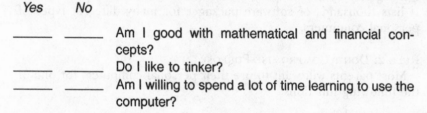

Yes	No	
_____	_____	Am I good with mathematical and financial concepts?
_____	_____	Do I like to tinker?
_____	_____	Am I willing to spend a lot of time learning to use the computer?

If you answered "Yes" to all these questions, then you may prefer to buy more *general* programs that are harder to master. If you answered "No" to any of them, then you should buy *specific* programs that are somewhat limited but easy to use.

When it comes to cost, a good rule of thumb is to spend as little as possible to get programs that can do what is needed by family members. However, it is important that present and *future* needs of *all* family members be considered. Being shortsighted can cost more in the long run.

HOW TO CHOOSE THE RIGHT SYSTEM

The rule of thumb for selecting the right system is summed up in four three-word aphorisms:
1. Software dictates hardware.
2. Don't compromise purpose.
3. Test drive it.
4. Do your homework.

RULE 1: SOFTWARE DICTATES HARDWARE

In some ways, buying a computer system is as tricky as shopping for a used car. Let the buyer beware! There is no substitute for careful shopping. But in a significant way, buying a computer system is *not* like buying a car. How so? Imagine buying a car and discovering that it only runs on a certain type of gas—a gas that has a "secret code," so to speak, that will allow it to work only in certain vehicles. Well, that is the bad news about the computer industry: each computer is purposely rigged to accept only certain software. In computer jargon, this is what is known as "compatibility." Therefore, it is critical that parents first decide what software they want before deciding on hardware. If they do not, they may find themselves locked out of many possible uses for their computer. An excellent resource for selecting software is *The PC Clearinghouse Software Directory,* available in most retail computer stores. It lists thousands of software packages for many different types of personal computers.

RULE 2: DON'T COMPROMISE PURPOSE

Most parents will want to use their personal computers for one of the following functions:

- personal finance
- education
- entertainment
- data management
- communications
- word processing

Most experts say, "Pick the ONE primary function you intend to use your computer for most often and make sure it does that one thing well." Others advise: "Don't underestimate the versatility of a computer. Try the integrated approach to selecting a computer system. Pick three primary applications or purposes and integrate them—such as tying in budget, record keeping of expenses, and tax management." Another way of putting it is to select software in matched sets.

RULE 3: TEST DRIVE IT

Would a wise buyer purchase a car without taking it for a test drive? Of course not. Nor should parents buy a computer without making sure they and the children can use it. How do you "test drive" a computer? You can go to a computer store and tell the salesperson that you want to look at some programs (following Rule 1: "software dictates hardware"). You must be specific and explain what kind of work you want to do in what categories. The salesperson should provide two or three programs in each category for you to try out.

You should try to load the computer yourself after the salesperson has shown you how, while asking the question: "Is it easy to load?" This is especially important if children will be using the computer. Next, you should skim through the software instruction manuals: can they be understood? If they sound like jibberish, you should not purchase them but should select another program with instructions that can be understood. After all, the best program is no good if parents and children cannot understand how to use it. The computer is supposed to *solve* problems, not *create* them! Parents should be aware that many computer salespeople will coax unwary customers into buying machines but provide little guidance in how to use them. They make money by selling, not by giving guidance. Therefore, you have to take it upon yourself to examine some key factors before making purchasing decisions. If you cannot answer "Yes" to all of the following questions, you should look at other possible computers and not stop looking until you can respond affirmatively:

_____Can this dealer service my computer?

_____Are the instructions complete, clearly written, and sufficiently detailed?

_____Will the selection of compatible software meet *my* family's needs?

RULE 4: DO YOUR HOMEWORK

After visiting one or more computer stores, and developing a feel for what the machines can do, you will have developed an idea of what it is you want the computer to do for you. Now you should read books, magazines, and buyer guides on personal computers, many of which are available in newsstands, computer stores, and libraries. There are at present about seventy-five computer magazines in the field. Some provide general information, others cater to the special features of a particular computer. Printed materials can help you get a realistic idea of the capabilities of a personal computer; they can familiarize you with the jargon so you can communicate effectively with salespeople; and the advertisements can give a good idea of price ranges. Some caution, however, is recommended. These are some of the more common complaints of parents who have had some experience with home computers: "Advertising is misleading. They entice you by telling you the hundreds of things a certain computer can do, but they don't tell you that you need a lot of expensive peripheral equipment to do it." "With my system, it might take the computer four to six minutes to look up a recipe. I can do it myself faster than that. You need to have the entire system in order to store everything on disks instead of casette tapes so you can retrieve information rapidly. That can run from five hundred to a thousand dollars!" "Computer companies make a lot of promises they may not keep. They may advertise a product that isn't developed yet." "Some salespeople are more interested in impressing the customers with computer jargon than communicating with them—by saying 'terminal emulator II' when what they mean is 'telephone hookup.' "

Another word of caution is in order: while it can be helpful to seek advice from friends, neighbors, and colleagues at work who already have computers, beware—most people who buy a computer think that the one they have is the *best* one to have. They *have to* think that to justify their investment. Some even become advocates and zealots: every time somebody else purchases a similar computer, their own earlier decision to buy one is reaffirmed. Take their advice with a grain of salt and ask yourself: "Do they use it the way I want to use it?"

Lastly, it is important for parents to have reasonable expectations for computer use. Other factors should be considered. Do you really want a computer in the kitchen, where cooking grease and crumbs could destroy it? A file box is faster and more convenient.

A computer does very repetitive things a lot faster than a human can do them. There are, however, many things that a human can do more efficiently. It is also unreasonable to assume that one computer can do everything perfectly. For example, computers that give the best graphics for games may not have the best attributes for word processing and other adult kinds of functions. Just like a person, a computer may do a *few* things *very* well, or it may do *many* things *fairly* well.

A FINAL WORD OF CAUTION

Parents who are in the market for a computer ought to keep the following recommendations in mind to avoid the typical evaluation and selection pitfalls:

• *Select the type of software you want (and make sure it's available) before going out and buying an expensive computer.* If you are looking for games, you don't want to buy the "best" computer only to find out no one is making games for it.

- *Make sure the hardware you buy is compatible with your software.* There are horror stories about people spending hundreds of dollars on incompatible hardware and software.
- *Select a system that is compatible with other systems.* You will get more mileage for your money.
- *Compare prices.* From store to store, you will find price differences of several hundred dollars on the same piece of equipment, and an average difference of ten to thirty dollars on software.
- *Select a hardware and software company with a solid reputation.* The computer industry is a highly competitive field and a lot of companies go out of business. You will also want to be assured of reliable and efficient service.
- *Select a system that will "grow" with you.* First of all, be certain that the system you buy can do what you want it to do *now*. Companies may tell you that a capability will be available in six months, but don't count on it. At the same time, you want to buy a system that will "age" well so that you can upgrade it as your needs change.
- *Find a user's group.* Your computer dealer can put you in touch with "computer-philes" all over the country. User's groups are an excellent source of information, ideas, and assistance both before and after you purchase your personal computer.

The personal computer can be a valuable tool in the parentship process. Like all technology, it is a means to an end: form must follow function. If parents understand the uses and abuses of the computer, select hardware and software wisely, and have realistic expectations for its capabilities, the "computerization" of their home will increase their effectiveness and efficiency.

APPENDIX II

P.L.U.S. Parenting Workshops

Schools, social agencies, hospitals, churches, and parent organizations may wish to sponsor or offer P.L.U.S. Parenting workshops. During the past several years we have witnessed many such groups implement workshops with wonderful results. Some have been remedial in nature and were triggered by expressed needs because of widespread parenting difficulties. For example, several affluent suburban areas found the program useful because mothers and fathers found it more and more difficult to manage their families in an age of quickly changing values. A serious drug and alcohol problem among teenagers triggered their interest. Others found the workshops most helpful in building planning and financial management skills in an age of inflation and increased family needs and wants. Parents whose children were discipline problems for them likewise found the presentations and discussions most useful.

A good number of other organizations have offered the workshops in a preventive fashion. These parents felt that the more they learned about leadership in the family, the more successful they would be and the fewer difficulties they would encounter. Still other parents have used the workshops to move an already well-functioning family to higher levels of development.

Whatever the reason, other small groups of mothers and fathers may wish to take the initiative to organize and implement workshops in their neighborhoods or communities. The parentship material included in this book will serve as the major content of such workshops. We offer several model workshop formats that can be followed depending on particular needs, time available, schedule, level of interest, etc. These have worked well for others. Workshop planners should feel free to make slight modifications in the recommended workshop models as they see fit. There are three workshop designs: (a) a three-hour program, which includes a basic overview of parentship and the presentation and discussion of selected leadership/management skills; (b) a one-day (six-hour) program, which includes everything in the three-hour program but allows more time for discussion and sharing among participants; and (c) a series of two-hour sessions, held once a week, over the course of eight weeks, during which participants spend even more time discussing parentship skills and attempt to put them into practice between sessions.

Three-Hour Workshop

MATERIALS NEEDED
- Chalkboard and chalk or easel pad and markers
- Copy of *P.L.U.S. Parenting* for each participant
- Name tags
- Ashtrays (possibly a smoking and nonsmoking section if the room is big enough)
- Coffee, tea, juice, or other refreshments, cups, etc.
- Tables for five or six participants each—arranged so everybody is able to see everybody else with minimum effort

ROOM ARRANGEMENT

It is always a challenge to promote an atmosphere of trust and intimacy with a group that is larger than ten to twelve people. If the participant group is that size or smaller, there is no need to make special arrangements other than those mentioned above. If the group is larger, however, the goal must be to break it up in such a way that each person within a subgroup gets a chance to speak and ask questions, and at the same time everyone is able to know what is going on in the group as a whole, and a sense of commonality and togetherness is maintained. We recommend that groups of over ten or twelve people be divided into subgroups of approximately six people who will sit around tables (round, if possible) and participate in the workshop as a small group. At times indicated later in the outlines, each small group will choose one of its members to give a short report (one or two

minutes) to the larger group. This arrangement, which we have used
with some large groups, accomplishes the dual goal of promoting
intimacy while maintaining a sense of wholeness within the larger
group.

WORKSHOP PROCESS

Registration:
Sign in participants, hand out name tags, etc.

*Leader Introduction(s)** (15 minutes)
Brief introduction of leader(s) followed by outline of the workshop schedule.

Primitive Principles of Parentship (45 minutes)
Briefly present the twelve principles (Chapter 1) and encourage
discussion within the small groups. Ask each table to appoint someone to present a short (two-minute) summary of the group's discussion.

Parent and Child Styles (30 minutes)
Have the parents complete both the *Parentship Style Inventory* and
the *Children's Followership Inventory* (Chapter 2). Have them score the
inventories and discuss the implications of a match in styles, a difference in styles, and/or different children within a family needing
different types of parental leadership.

Communication (45 minutes)
Have each parent respond to the *Parental Communication Inventory*
(Chapter 4). If both spouses are present, have them check each
other's responses. If there are many single parents in the group,
encourage them to discuss their responses in their small groups.
Again, have a spokesperson for each small group give a brief summary of what was discussed. Stress the importance of communication in the family, and then focus on listening as the most critical
communication skill. Administer the *Parental Listening-Response Index*
(Chapter 5). Use the same procedure as with the communication
inventories to check the responses and discuss the implications of
being "stuck" in any of the response styles.

* This is designed as a self-help workshop. Leadership by a professional is not necessary. The most effective leader is a parent who excels in a leadership role at home, at
work, or at both. Some ability in group process is clearly necessary. For help in developing these skills, contact the behavioral science, psychology, or education departments of
a local college or university or your local school system.

Delegating (30 minutes)

Stress the importance of delegating tasks to children as a means of helping children become more responsible, helping them develop their own management skills, and giving parents more time to carry out the family management tasks which require their levels of sophistication and life experience. Present the seven steps used in successful delegation. Follow that by having the parents each choose a task which they currently perform and have them go through the steps as practice for delegating the task to their children.

Discipline (30 minutes)

Make it very clear that the purpose of discipline is to instill *self-discipline* in children. Encourage some discussion on this point. Present the four-step discipline process and any other material from the chapter which seems appropriate for the group and which time allows. End with the *Discipline Skills Inventory* (Chapter 10). Encourage the parents to choose two or three skills which they will make efforts to improve.

Conclusion (15 minutes)

Have each group spend five minutes discussing what benefits they have received or insights they have realized from this workshop. In the remaining ten minutes have each small group report to all the participants. If any of the participants request more time later or a follow-up workshop, use either the six-hour or the eight-week outline as a guide.

Six-Hour Workshop

MATERIALS NEEDED
- Same as in previous format.

ROOM ARRANGEMENT
- Same as in previous format.

WORKSHOP PROCESS

Registration
- Same as in previous format.

Leader Introduction(s) (15 minutes)

Brief introduction of leader(s) followed by outline of the workshop schedule.

Parent Leadership Index (60 minutes)

Direct each participant to complete the *Parent Leadership Index* (Prologue). Then have participants total their scores for each of the ten sub-areas. Present a brief definition for each of the ten parentship areas. Encourage each of the small groups to discuss any insights they may have gained from the exercise. Have a spokesperson for each small group give a brief (two-minute) synopsis of what their group discussed so that all participants can share insights.

Primitive Principles of Parentship (45 minutes)

Briefly present the twelve principles (Chapter 1) and encourage discussion within the small groups. Ask each table to appoint someone to present a short (two-minute) summary of the group's discussion.

Break (15 minutes)

Parent and Child Styles (45 minutes)

Have the parents complete both the *Parentship Style Inventory* and the *Children's Followership Inventory* (Chapter 2). Have them score the inventories and discuss the implications of a match in styles, a difference in styles, and/or different children within a family needing different types of parental leadership. Direct the groups to choose a spokesperson to present a summary of their group's insights and conclusions to all the participants.

Lunch (60 minutes)

Communication (45 minutes)

Have each parent respond to the *Parental Communication Inventory* (Chapter 4). If both spouses are present, have them check each other's responses. If there are many single parents in the group, encourage them to discuss their responses in their small groups. Again, have a spokesperson for each small group give a brief summary of what was discussed. Stress the importance of communication in the family, and then move on to focus on listening as the most critical communication skill. Administer the *Parental Listening-Response Index* (Chapter 5). Use the same procedure as with the communication inventories to check the responses and discuss the implications of being "stuck" in any of the response styles.

Delegating (45 minutes)

Stress the importance of delegating tasks to children as a means of helping children become more responsible, helping them develop their own management skills, and giving parents more time to carry out the family management tasks which require their levels of sophistication and life experience. Present the seven steps used in successful delegation. Follow that by having the parents each choose a task which they currently perform and have them go through the steps as practice for delegating the task over to their children. Direct groups to share their plans to delegate and describe how they will do it.

Break (15 minutes)

Discipline (45 minutes)

Make it very clear that the purpose of the discipline is to instill *self-discipline* in children. Encourage some discussion on this point. Present the four-step discipline process and any other material from Chapter 10 which seems appropriate for the group and which time allows. End with the *Discipline Skills Inventory*. Encourage the parents to choose two or three skills which they will make efforts to improve. Direct the groups to share the skills that they will try to improve and to discuss how they will do it. A brief discussion can follow.

Conclusion (30 minutes)

Have each group spend fifteen minutes discussing what benefits they have received or insights they have realized from this workshop. In the remaining fifteen minutes have each group report to all the participants. If any of the participants request more time later or a follow-up workshop, use the eight-week outline as a guide.

Eight-Week Workshop

Session 1 (120 minutes)

Registration is the same as in the three-hour and one-day workshops. Each leader (if there are more than one) is introduced to the group, and each participant is asked to give his or her name and a brief description of the family. The eight-week schedule is then put on the board or flip chart. The *Parent Leadership Index* (Prologue) is administered, scored, and interpreted. After that, each parent should be encouraged to express what he or she expects to get out of the workshop. This is particularly important. Fathers and mothers are attending the workshop for a reason. Usually parents are experiencing a specific issue or difficulty that served as a catalyst for their decision to attend. This information can be useful in planning later workshop presentations and discussions. The thrust of the presentation and discussion in this session is to focus on the whole concept of parentship, showing that parents, in fact, are leaders of the world's oldest organization. They must think of themselves as such and prepare for the role in terms of knowledge, skills, and emotionality.

The session should end with the leaders telling about their own experiences in leading their families and inviting the participants to join in sharing their own successes and difficulties.

Homework for Participants (optional)

The participants are to discuss the results of the *Parent Leadership Index* with the rest of the family and see if their children's are similar to the parents'.

Session 2 (120 minutes)

Begin this session by having the participants discuss in small groups the reactions of their families to their scores on the *Parent Leadership Index*. Ask a group spokesperson to give brief synopses of the group discussions. Then present the twelve primitive principles of parentship (Chapter 1) and encourage discussion of these within the small groups. After sufficient discussion (fifteen to twenty minutes) ask each group's spokesperson to report the key points of his or her group's findings to all of the workshop participants. Allow several minutes for questions, comments, and reactions from participating parents.

Homework for Participants (optional)

Each participant is to make a list of all the "shoulds" or "should nots" that he or she can think of regarding family life—for example: What should mothers and fathers do? How should children behave? How involved should parents be in school, children's recreational activities, friendships? What role should grandparents have?

Session 3 (120 minutes)

Begin this session by encouraging discussion of the homework assignment or, if none was assigned, discuss the issue of "shoulds" in this session. After this discussion (fifteen to twenty minutes) spend the bulk of this session presenting and discussing family climate. Have participants complete and score the *Family Climate Scale* (Chapter 3). Present and discuss the strengths and weaknesses of the eight climate types.

Homework for Session 3 (optional)

Participants should study the ten key factors determining family climate and design a plan to modify their family's climate through these factors if they see fit to do so.

Session 4 (120 minutes)

This session will focus on parentship styles (sixty minutes) and communication (sixty minutes). Presentations and discussions of the material included in Chapters 2 and 4 respectively will serve as the content of the session. Variations in format (lecture, small group discussion, etc.) are at the discretion of the leaders.

Homework for Session 4 (optional)

Participants should complete and score the following: *Parentship Style Inventory, Children's Followership Inventory,* and *Family Task Inventory* (Chapter 2). At least an hour should be spent considering and/or discussing (e.g., with spouse) the results of these self-assessments.

Sessions 5–7 (120 minutes each)

During each of these sessions, *two* of the following topics should be covered, depending on the experience, interests, and needs of the participants; planning (Chapter 6); decision making (Chapter 7); financial management and budgeting (Chapter 8); delegating (Chapter 9); discipline (Chapter 10); motivating the family (Chapter 11); family information control (Chapter 12); evaluation in the family (Chapter 13); family stability (Chapter 14); and computers in the family (Appendix I).

These sessions should include a presentation and/or discussion of the key concepts relating to each of the topics as presented in the designated chapters. We have found that it is most beneficial to allow and encourage participants to relate and share experiences, seek advice from each other, or ask questions of fellow participants. Whenever appropriate, participants can be encouraged to role-play or simulate various family situations, parent-child relations, etc. On occasion, we have witnessed groups using videotaping equipment to allow participants to view and critique their own behavior in these exercises; however, to incorporate this experiential dimension into the sessions it is necessary to have leadership skilled in this type of activity.

This phase of the workshop will be most beneficial if it is planned and designed within a climate of trust and if it stimulates a high degree of exchange among participants. Likewise, it will be effective if it leads parents to concrete action that they can use in their daily lives almost immediately.

Homework for Sessions 5–7 (optional)

Participants can be directed to complete, score, think about, and/ or discuss results of the several self-assessment instruments relating to the topics selected.

Session 8 (approximately 120 minutes)

It is likely that the participants and leaders of this workshop will have grown very attached to each other during the eight-week period. A good, solid thirty-minute presentation summing up the essence of parentship should be included, as well as closing statements by the groups' spokespersons and/or individual participants.

Some kind of ceremony to celebrate the completion of the workshop is in order as well. We suggest a social occasion as the concluding activity, such as a presentation of certificates to be followed by coffee and cake, or a whole meal if desired. This will put the final wrapping on the feelings of support and mutual experience that the participants will be sharing.

CONCLUDING NOTE

One of the most rewarding experiences that we have witnessed in our professional as well as our personal lives has been the observation of mothers and fathers participating in the P.L.U.S. workshops. The immediate link between the parents present, brought about by the common bond of their love for their children, becomes evident at once and is emotionally moving. All other parental characteristics which can sometimes be divisive (age, socioeconomic status, occupation, race, color, religion, etc.) melt away to their true level of unimportance as parents coalesce into a closely knit group.

To witness this atmosphere and to see the marked development of parentship skills is enough to keep us interested and committed to researching, counseling, and writing for parents for a long time. We hope that you too will have the opportunity to engage in this rewarding growth experience as a participant or organizer.

Index